Be
The Change

Be
The Change

Action and reflection from people transforming our world

Interviews by Trenna Cormack

Love Books

Love Books

Published 2007 by Love Books, 35 King Street, Bristol BS1 4DZ

Designed by Rick Lawrence, Samskara Design
www.samskara-design.com
email: *rick@samskara-design.com*

Printed by Beacon Press, Bellbrook Park, Uckfield, East Sussex TN22 1PL

Printed using their *pure*print® environmental print technology. All the electricity used
in the production of this book was generated from renewable sources and vegetable-based
inks were used throughout. The laminate used is biodegradable, and 95% of any
solvents and 90% of all dry waste used in the process have been recycled.
Beacon Press is a CarbonNeutral® company and accredited with
Environmental Management System, ISO 14001 and registered to EMAS,
the Eco Management and Audit Scheme. The paper is FSC certified: the text and
cover are Revive 100 uncoated comprising 100% post-consumer waste.

Recycled
Supporting responsible use
of forest resources
www.fsc.org Cert no. SGS-COC-0620
© 1996 Forest Stewardship Council
FSC

100%

A catalogue record for this book is available from the British Library

ISBN 978 0 9555213 0 0

To all the imaginal cells, wherever you may be.

Contents

Acknowledgements

My first thanks must go to the team who created the *Be The Change* conference that inspired this book, and who then gave me their goodwill and support to help make it happen: Lawrence Bloom, Ursula Capell, Christopher Cooke, Hetty Einzig, Tatiana Glad, Susie Kershaw, Tim Macartney, Colin Morley, Helen-Jane Nelson, Pippa Vine, John Whitmore and especially Nick Hart-Williams, who gave many useful tips and much encouragement.

And then, of course, this book would not have been possible without the magnificent people who gave their stories. I am deeply grateful to all of them for their generosity, their trust, their openness and their willingness to share their experiences.

Many people have been helpful and supportive along the way, and I appreciate it enormously. Hamish Cormack, Clare Dakin, Andrew Davis, Jemima Kenchington, Ollie Kenchington, Virginia Harrison, Rachel Maund, Julia Smith, Katherine Vine, Mike Zeidler and everyone at The Hub — I salute you. Special thanks go to Elisabet Sahtouris who so kindly provided the afterword.

And finally, there are four people whose assistance has been absolutely invaluable. The deeply talented and extremely patient Rick Lawrence took 100,000 words of text and turned them into this vision of loveliness. Gill Wilkinson was a typing dynamo and all-round force for good. Pippa Vine provided eagle eyes, professional guidance and bags of moral support, often working late into the night. And Denny Dakin offered infinite wisdom, energy, reassurance and love. Thank you all so much for holding this vision with me, for going beyond the call of duty, for putting your love and care into this book alongside mine. It's all the better for it, and you've made this project a delight.

Preface

This book was inspired by my attendance at the Be The Change conference in London in May, 2005. A newcomer to the event — the first one was held in 2004 — I found myself in a hall full of people who cared passionately about creating a better world.

During an extraordinary three days we heard from many speakers engaged in wonderful activities — cleaning dirty businesses, regenerating polluted land, applying integrated health care, reinventing financial systems... I thought to myself, 'This is brilliant! There should be a book about this.' And then the question was turned to the audience, 'This isn't just about sages on stages. What are *you* going to do to be the change you wish to see? What's yours to do?'

That's when I gulped and realised that this book was mine to do. And so the adventure began. I wanted to offer a flavour of Be The Change in book form, to provide inspiration through the first-hand accounts of individuals creating positive change. All these wonderful people gave me — or rather us — their time and their stories. The more usual way to present them would have been with a chapter on each person, written by me in the third person, about them. However, these aren't essays or articles, they're interviews. I wanted to make it more direct, and kept each piece in the first person, so that the words come straight from the horse's mouth (so to speak). I took out my questions to let the narrative flow more freely, avoiding the backwards and forwards ping-pong effect of Q&A. Sometimes, though, it helps to signal a progression or a change in direction, so I introduced the headings for this purpose.

Enjoy!

Trenna Cormack

hafsat abiola-costello

Women are standing up to make a change...
We help them to envision a bigger life for themselves.

hafsat abiola-costello is the founder of KIND, the Kudirat Initiative for Democracy, named after her mother. KIND's work now focuses on the empowerment of women, promoting their leadership and advancement in Nigerian society, and campaigning against the ingrained culture of domestic violence. However, KIND had originally been established to participate in the push for democracy in Nigeria, a movement in which abiola-costello's parents played key roles. Her father won the democratic presidential election in 1993, but was jailed by the military who wanted to remain in power. Her mother became an activist, to try and secure his release, but was assassinated in 1996. At this time, abiola-costello was in her final year at Harvard University. She continued to campaign for her father's freedom, but he died in prison on the eve of his release, supposedly of a heart attack.

I want to see people connecting with themselves and with each other at a very deep level. Connecting in a way that says they recognise that we're part of one human family, instead of connecting with all the barriers as we normally do — language, religion, economic circumstances, all kinds of barriers that we impose. We have the ability to see that we're part of one human family, and I'd like us to choose to remove our barriers and actually connect at a deeper level.

My own work is about women. It's promoting women's leadership, women's ability to participate in creating a better world. I find that when I talk to a lot of women, they say, 'Oh well, we just want to take care of our kids, so we want to be in the background and let other people take care of it.' If we actually were connected at the deeper level, we'd understand that we all have a responsibility to make the world better, and we'd all want to participate in doing that. I think we have these illusions about what our responsibilities are, so it allows us to think that it's an honourable thing to just stay at home and take care of your kids. When I think about that, I think about all the children who are dying needlessly, because of things that we could resolve in the world. Then I think of all the mothers of those children, who probably were hoping for somebody to reach out and help them, while the rest of us who can help are choosing to live in a smaller way.

KIND

KIND was born when my mum was assassinated. She was killed in the course of trying to bring about political change in Nigeria. We had had decades of military rule, and my father, through a democratic election that the military ruler held, won the presidential election. But the military ruler decided that he wanted to continue to rule the country, and started to try to negotiate with my dad, and that didn't go very far. They said he had committed treason because he kept insisting on his democratic mandate to be president of Nigeria. So they put him in prison, and my mum became an activist.

She began to organise demonstrations, she worked with the different pro-democracy organisations, and she gave interviews to national and international media. As her profile increased and the movement got stronger, the military decided that this pro-democracy issue was a problem that wasn't going away, and that putting its leaders in jail wasn't resolving the issue. So instead of putting my mum in jail like they'd done with my dad, they assassinated her.

I was a senior in university at the time that this happened, and I decided to create an organisation that would continue to build on that work, to participate in the movement for democracy in Nigeria. When we created KIND — the Kudirat Initiative for Democracy — the vision was an Africa where women and youth were equal participants in shaping the continent's economic, social and political development, and our mission was to strengthen organisations and create initiatives that advanced women. At first though, our focus was really on building the pro-democracy movement and restoring democracy to Nigeria. That happened in 1999, and we then decided that within that remit, women's participation is critical to a well-functioning democracy, so we should work to help build women leaders in Nigeria, by offering training, support and mentoring opportunities to help women be involved in rebuilding the country. That's what KIND has been doing since.

We have a leadership programme, our key programme, that we offer to about 1,300 young women each year in universities across Nigeria, and we often work with partners on projects in other parts of Africa. For example in January, with one of our partners, we held a meeting of 300 women from 30 African countries, looking at the challenges the continent faces and how we as women can contribute to resolving them. We do those kinds of projects all the time. Also we have a campaign called '30 by 11', which is to get 30 per cent of women's representation in government by 2011. And the third thing we do is a Make Women Safe campaign, because we find violence against women is institutionalised in our culture.

A man beating his wife is seen as acceptable by many Nigerians so long as he doesn't harm her physically. We think that this is one of the reasons why women are not taking part in the public affairs of our country, because they are afraid that if they step beyond the boundaries that have been determined for them by this society, they will face some form of violence. We're trying to reduce the society's tolerance of that. We put on plays about it that have been very popular within Lagos and Abuja, seen by thousands of people, and we give the money we make from the plays to a project that helps victims of domestic violence.

Leadership programme

The initial findings that we're getting from our leadership programme are quite exciting. Our graduates are running for positions within their student governments, positions beyond those that are usually considered acceptable for

*We're part of one human family.
I'd like us to choose to remove our barriers
and connect at a deeper level.*

---

women. Women often run for the office of treasurer, because people think women are honest. We're encouraging them to run for positions of president, vice-president, press secretary. We want women to be participating at par with their male counterparts — 50 per cent. They are beginning to do that.

One of the areas that is affecting young women on the university campuses is sexual harassment by professors, and it's becoming endemic. Professors will terrorise students and tell them that if they don't please them by having sex with them, the young women won't get good grades for their class, even if they do the work and they do well. Unfortunately, when the young women have gone to other professors or to the school council, they have not been believed. Some students have been repeating exams for a year, two years, three years, and can't graduate because the teachers are harassing them for sex and will not pass them.

Women have been traumatised by things like this for many years in Nigeria, but have not done anything about it, so through our leadership programme, we're beginning a campaign on this with the students. After we left one university in the delta, a young woman came to the school president and reported that one of the professors had been harassing her for over a year. She came with her father and the school began an investigation. We see several things like this happening, where women are standing up to make a change that might affect them personally or others in their community; our programme is supporting their ability to do that.

I think the programme is helping young women build their sense of confidence, a sense of their rights. From the time they're born, they're socialised to think that they're second-class citizens and that that's acceptable; that they should submit and step back, so the men in their lives can step forward. Many of them go to university hoping to get qualifications because they think that would make them more marketable, more attractive to men so they can get married. Their whole life's ambition is to be married and have children. In our programme we look at the culture and the religion. We show them how, within the religion, whether it's Christianity or Islam, women have played a key role to advance their faith and to contribute to their society. We show them how women still are able to play a key role. They don't just have to stay in the kitchen, and cook and care for the house; they are active in the community, also on the national stage and on the international stage. We help them to envision a bigger life for themselves.

Then we also teach them about their rights, which is important, because if they don't know them, then it's easier for others to violate them. So the women start to learn that they have a right to education, that they have a right to say no if their professor wants to be intimate with them. Then they can take better care of themselves and greater responsibility for their own situation. They start to think of creating a small business; even if they're getting married, they should also have their own source of income. We are seeing a lot of the young women setting up their own small-scale business and doing other things to engage in their communities. By the end of the programme, the women start to talk about who they would like to be in the future. Some of them will name prominent lawyers in Nigeria; many of them think of people like Ellen Johnson-Sirleaf, the president of Liberia, and they think, 'If she can do it, if we focus, we can do it as well. We can also lead our own country.'

One of our graduates now represents the Nigerian government at the International Labour Organisation in Switzerland. Also, she organises projects for young people to learn how to set up their own businesses. She's doing all of this, from coming out of our leadership programme. There are many other stories as well. There's a part of Nigeria where the poverty's so dire that the young people get taken from their villages to other places to farm, and they're paid so little that you can just as well think of them as slaves. Another graduate of our programme has been working with the young people to help them to develop new options for securing their livelihood without becoming slaves. Another graduate had gotten pregnant when she was at university, and she'd become stigmatised. She now teaches thousands of young girls and boys in Lagos about safe sex. What we teach the students in our leadership programme is that they have a responsibility to serve, and Nigeria's the perfect place to serve because there are so many problems.

I think the impact on Nigerian society is going to be seen in the medium to long term, but even in the short term we should see their impact on issues like

*Change doesn't happen just by itself —
people have to initiate action, they
have to sustain pressure.*

---

sexual harassment. Now women are taking it on and starting to work to resolve it within the university campuses. Change happens because people decide that they have had enough of a certain situation. It doesn't happen just by itself — people have to initiate action, they have to sustain pressure to force the situation to change. If the graduates of our programme succeed in tackling the issues that concern them directly, they will begin to understand how change happens within a society. I hope that knowledge spurs them to begin to tackle the larger problems in Nigerian society — the issues of corruption, poor governance, the excessive allocation of resources by our government to armaments and defence and lack of investment in education and health care. Whatever the issues are that affect us, we're not leaving it to other people to discuss and hoping that they'll come up with the right answers; we are directly engaged in those discussions. That's my long-term vision.

Lessons

The most important thing I've learned is that process is as important as the end goal, and I'm beginning to see that more and more. I've worked for many years with certain groups of people, on different projects. Now, I've always wanted to do much bigger things that have much bigger impacts. For example, our campaign about violence against women has reached over a million people already, and I'd like to have even more impacts soon. I'm working now with some of the people that I started working with in the earlier years, where we did smaller things. We're now doing bigger things together, and I think that wouldn't be the case had I been so committed to the end result that I didn't manage those relationships carefully.

Sometimes in the course of our work we're so committed to the result, we don't realise that more important than that are the relationships we're building. Relationships are the assets that can allow us to really confront issues at the level at which they are occurring. We must keep expanding the relationships, expanding the communities of people who are aligned with what we are trying to accomplish. Process helps us do that because when you work with people with a good process, you build trust. You trust each other, you have a sense of each other's integrity and what each group is bringing to the table, and that kind of relationship expands. A community that focuses on good process draws in more people. People are attracted to work with such a community because it's not dysfunctional, and the community grows bigger; then as the communities that are involved grow, the things that we can do together expand. In this way, the impact we can have expands also.

The way I see it, we have the possibility to contribute significantly. And yet we all have weaknesses. Maybe I procrastinate, or maybe because of my patriarchal background, I've had this sense that as a woman I shouldn't be troublesome, I shouldn't be persistent. I often find that when I'm trying to push for certain things in society, sometimes I don't push as much as I could, because I feel that would be bad manners — 'What would people say about you? They'll think you're pushy.' And yet you've got to push. If you're going to have change, you've got to push, you've got to make yourself a nuisance, you've got to bring the issue to people's faces all the time so that they can't avoid it, so that they have to address it. You have to make yourself a nuisance and you're trying to be so well-mannered.

Of course it's not a bad thing to be well-mannered, but in trying to have an impact, it's a weakness. So I'm working on building my reserves so that I can be more of a nuisance with certain people, especially around the issue of women's representation in government. I want a certain percentage of women represented in government and so far we've been asking nicely. We have to start thinking of how to make a nuisance of ourselves so that we cannot be avoided until we get what we want. I think all over the world we need to do it, not just in Africa. Even in Europe, the average representation of women in government is about 17 per cent and that's ridiculous. It's not like the men have done such a great job that we should be intimidated by their performance.

Patriarchy was entrenched in my own family to an extent. When I wanted to study to be a diplomat, my father said 'What kind of husband are you going to marry, gallivanting around the world?' He felt that there were certain professions that were not appropriate for women, and he actually was quite patriarchal; he

*If you're going to have change, you've got to push,
you've got to make yourself a nuisance… So I'm working on
building my reserves so that I can be more of a nuisance…*

had very traditional ideas about the role of men and women. But when he was thrown into jail, I became involved with some activists to get him out. I had to travel all over the United States and then later to Canada and through Europe, lobbying other governments and organisations to put pressure on the Nigerian government to release him. So I ended up gallivanting around the world anyway. It wasn't with his blessing, although I'm sure if he had come out of jail alive he would have been happy that I did that. It wasn't something that he had actually set before me as a possibility; it was just something that I started to do because I wanted to contribute to resolving the problem.

Opportunity

I wanted to do something and then I had the opportunity. One day I was working in my dorm room at university after one of my classes. A group of young people had a table and were petitioning students for signatures. I thought they were petitioning for something ridiculous, like the right to walk barefoot on campus. This was at the time when my father was in jail and my mother was an activist in danger, and I felt like I had bigger issues to deal with than signing up for the right to walk barefoot around campus. So I was looking to avoid them, and I was actually trying to walk around the table in a way that would not bring me in directly in front of them. But two of them were quite insistent, and they walked around the table and stopped me. They said to me, 'Please, we're gathering signatures. There's an elected president in jail in Nigeria, and we're gathering signatures to help him, to send to the military dictator to demand that he be released.'

I felt so moved and I said to them, 'Do you know you're speaking about my father?' They hadn't known that. They were part of a group called Amnesty International; they'd gotten information about the situation in Nigeria and they were now getting signatures to help with that. They said, 'Actually, we don't know a lot about Nigeria. Could you come and talk to us about it?' So I went home and prepared my presentation to them. I talked to my mum about what parts of the story were important to communicate, and then I went and talked to them. We started raising awareness within the university and we started working with the primary schools and high schools in the neighbourhood, because we decided that we wanted the city of Cambridge, Massachusetts to pass a resolution supporting democracy in Nigeria.

I don't even know where those two people are today. What's funny about them is that one of them had very, very long hair, which in the US always makes me think of flower children in the 1960s; and then the other one had the sides of his head shaven, and the hair in the middle was spiked and purple. You have to remember that I'm from a conservative Muslim family — they were the last people that I generally would have talked to on campus. Yet, they had something magical to say to me. Since that time I've always looked out for people who don't conform. Sometimes they have something special to offer.

That's really how I got started. I think a lot of people hear about problems, whatever they are, anywhere in the world, or even in their own community, and they may be interested in helping; but I think there needs to be a link between people's desire to make a difference, and an opportunity to do something that is credible, that they think could actually have an impact. I think we need to develop more initiatives that help connect people, so that they can have an impact. So for me, just having that opportunity really made the difference. I have many siblings and we all wanted to help, but not all of us met people who gave us an opening where we could do something.

Being the change

Challenging any aspect of culture is hard because it's swimming against the current. It takes energy and you get isolated because it involves risks. Like my parents, you could be attacked, you could be jailed, you could be imprisoned, you could be killed, but you could just lose your place. First of all you lose your old communities, because those friends don't understand you any more, and they just think you're a loose cannon now, even if what you're saying is right. They may agree that it's right, but they don't understand why you must be the one to do something about it. They think that there's risk involved, and they think that the risk could be contagious, so they kind of isolate you. What I've found in taking that stand is that all of a sudden you connect to other, new communities. So first you lose the community that you knew, but the good thing is you now find new friends who are like you, oftentimes people who have taken the kind of decisions you've taken, so they understand the perspective that you have. So you lose your standing in your society, and you find a different one. I don't know that either is better or worse, they're just different. It can be troubling because you lose your mooring. You know what you're doing, but you don't know if it's going to make a difference, so you don't know if you've paid that price for nothing. All of those things make it very difficult to try to be involved in making change.

I draw my strength from a commitment to the vision that I have, which is that things should be better, and things should be fair. And then I really believe in the understanding of *noblesse oblige* — from those to whom much is given, much is expected. I feel that being born into an affluent family in Nigeria has given me so many advantages, so I should be able to give back, I should be able to help other people out. I shouldn't just say, 'Oh well, it doesn't have to be my problem, I can just ignore it.' I think that's not an appropriate thing to say; I think we all must work for things to be better. I'm crystal clear about that. I've a very strong sense of my conscience, and my conscience wouldn't allow me not to take the steps I take and not to do the things that I do.

Inspirations

In Africa, we have a different understanding from the monotheistic religions about the hereafter. For us, our ancestors are already in the hereafter and when we cross over, we'll be reunited. One of the things that inspires me is I want to have wonderful stories to tell them. When I meet up with them again I want to be able to sit down with them and they'll say, 'So, what were you thinking at this point?' And I'll have really interesting stories. I worry that if the stories are boring, they won't even have time to sit and listen and talk to me! For me, connecting with my ancestors and with the future spirits and sitting in community with them, all of us rejoicing in what we were able to contribute on earth — that would be Paradise. That's priceless, and so you are willing to do pretty much anything so that you can keep pushing the boundaries and seeing what gives, seeing what could change and seeing what news and stories and jokes and experiences you will have to share later.

But I'm not waiting for the hereafter, really. I have a son now and I can't wait for him to be talking, I can't wait for him to be old enough for me to engage with him in conversation. And when he asks what I was doing at this time or that time, I want to have something credible to tell him.

I'm very proud of my parents. I think they did well, and if there's any sense of sadness it's because I can't say to them, 'You did well.' I did tell them, but I would have wanted to keep telling them every day. But even if they're absent, they're very present in Nigerian society; people still respect and honour them in many ways. And they're very present in the lives of their children. Since they've died we've had many children that would be their grandchildren, and they will all hear many stories of their grandparents, so they'll have a very strong sense of who they were.

You can't live forever, but show up, let people know who you are. Whether you live to the age of 33 as I'm told Jesus Christ did or you live for many, many decades, let people know who was here, leave very clear footprints in the sand. It could inspire other people to live their lives in a bold way, to make an important contribution to the world. I think that my parents did that and we have a very clear understanding of who our parents were, even though my mum died at 44 years old and my dad at 62. Even now when we confront challenges, we have a good sense of what they would say if they were around to say it. My siblings and I make jokes about that. I think, just leave a clear sense of who you are; don't be afraid to show up. Show up. You might inspire people, or even if you don't, at least you inspire yourself and you earn your own self-respect.

www.kind.org

Katie Alcott

I realised that you couldn't lift people out of poverty until they had access to clean water.

Katie Alcott founded Frank Water as a social enterprise in 2005, and runs it with the support of her husband Tom, one part-time employee and a team of 15 volunteers. Frank Water is bottled at a spring in Devon and distributed to conscientious consumers throughout the UK via a network of ethical retailers. In June 2006, the 4,000 villagers and neighbours of Kothapeta village in Andhra Pradesh, India, were the first beneficiaries of Frank's policy of donating all profits to fund clean water projects in developing countries. A year later, 20,000 people in four communities in India are drinking clean water thanks to Frank. In 2008, the company plans to provide clean water facilities in eight more communities in India and Ghana. Every litre of Frank Water sold in the UK provides 200 litres of clean water overseas.

The story of Frank really began when I was 18 and I worked for a community school in India. The thing that hit me was the amount of effort that the family I stayed with had to go to, to get clean water, and then the incredible effort they put in to make sure the water was clean enough for me, to make sure I didn't get ill. The last thing they wanted was for me to get ill while I was living with them. So they would filter it three times, and boil it twice for half an hour, and they made sure that I only ever took water from their house, that was as clean as they could make it with the technology that they had.

My first meal out was with one of the teachers from the school, and it was really spicy. I'm not great with spicy food, but because it was offered, I felt obliged to keep eating it. I was suffering quite a lot from the heat of it, and I'd finished all the water that I took with me from my family. I asked the people I was with whether it was OK to drink the water that they had, and they said yes. I don't think they understood that what I was actually asking was, was it safe to drink, was it clean, and I think that because they drink it, they automatically thought it would be OK for me. They'd built up resistance and I obviously was still very weak in that respect. So I had this water, and the next day I came down with dysentery.

It didn't put me off travelling, but I found a real interest in water. I did a lot of research into water issues. Travelling to different continents, South America and Africa, and seeing the same issues in every place, I realised that actually, in Europe and most of North America we're really lucky. Every time I went away, quite often I was ill, but I always knew I could come home to England and everything would be fine. We've got good doctors, we've got clean food and we've got clean water. I knew I'd be better within a week, and realised how much we take everything for granted. I really wanted to do something about it. Also I did some journalism in Bolivia, where there's an issue with the privatisation of water. I realised there were so many issues surrounding water and how important it was, that you couldn't really lift people out of poverty until they had access to clean water. That was where the idea initially came from, and obviously I looked at a few different ways before I came to Frank.

Frank in business

I thought about how we can use business to create something much more sustainable long term, that would make a much bigger difference and also would

With social enterprise… people love what you're doing and you love what they're doing, and automatically you find a brilliant allegiance.

---

include and involve many more people than just myself. At the time, the bottled water industry in the UK was taking off. There were lots of articles in the newspapers about it, and there just happened to be lots of articles about world water issues as well. These two things came together — water for water. So many people were drinking bottled water, it just seemed like a perfect option. All the water companies at the time were run by big companies who notoriously have bad reputations for things that they do in developing countries, so it seemed like a perfect opportunity to offer people who do drink bottled water the opportunity to buy something that was actually giving something back. And it was a small thing, a small consumer item that wasn't asking them to dig deep into their pockets. We didn't really want to encourage the drinking of bottled water, just give people who were already drinking bottled water an opportunity to buy something different.

We contract bottle, which means we subcontract our bottling to a spring in Devon. Our initial expenses are quite a lot higher, but it also means that we have a lot less risk than if we owned our own spring. It took about a year for us to really understand the profit margins that we could make, so in our first year we waited till our year-end and donated our profit. Since then we've been able to clarify a lot more the way the business runs, which part of the money goes where, and we have a fixed price for each bottle we sell to the wholesalers and retailers, which is very unusual. Most companies tend to have different prices for different customers. We needed to keep the price fixed so that 20p for every litre of Frank sold in the UK can go to the projects.

Frank in India

The way it works is that we support a specific village. We work with our NGO partner in India to find a village that doesn't have access to clean water. They work with the villagers to identify whether they want a facility or not, where that facility would go, and do all the pre-education. Then we pay £7,000 for the installation of the project itself — the construction of the facility and the technology inside it, which cleans the water. To be sustainable, the villagers have to own the project, so through discussions with the *panchayat*, who's the chief of the village, and the elders, an amount of money is agreed upon that the villagers are willing to contribute to the cost of the facility. They have to be part of it, so our projects employ three people from the village to operate the facility, deal with customer service, change the filters and repair anything that's damaged. Therefore, our projects are community-owned and community-run. £7,000 pays for the facility to go in and then the villagers pay one rupee for every 15 litres of water. That's the price set by Naandi, the local NGO, who have stated that this is a fair price, the villagers can all afford it. It works out as equivalent to 70p per person per year.

That one rupee is then split three ways. The first third goes to the operators to pay for their salaries, the second third goes into a pot which is used for repairs and new filters for the machinery (all the parts can be replaced within India), and then the last third builds a pot of money which the villagers put back into the community in some way, as they choose. The *panchayat* helps coordinate the project. Kothapeta are using that money to buy desks and books for their local school. The whole idea is that it's a sustainable project in many ways, not just in the way that it runs itself, but in the way that it involves villagers, it creates jobs, and it creates spin-off benefits for the community. The villagers are creating their own businesses. They found that there was demand from further afield. Some of the locals who have access to a vehicle are filling up cans and doing a delivery service for an extra quarter of a rupee to nearby villages, so more people have access to the clean water.

In our first year we donated our full profit of £4,000. That's a percentage of a clean water facility in Kothapeta village in Andhra Pradesh. In 2007 we'll have put in another three facilities. And then in 2008, things kick off in a different way, because we're also hoping that the water will only provide a percentage of the funds that we raise, so it will only be part of the business. We're hoping to create other ways of raising money for the projects, to become more of a charity.

Not just bottled water

We've found that Frank is a very strong brand. And because we do lots of festivals, we come into direct contact with a lot of our customers. A lot of people, because they like the brand, ask things like, do we have T-shirts, do we have

*It's nice to be involved in something
that's bigger than you as a person, something
that makes a difference on such a big scale.*

badges etc? So we've started to create merchandise. Organic fair trade t-shirts are a new thing that we've started selling on our website, and we're looking into doing reusable bags as well, as we get asked a lot for those kinds of things. Also we work with a water cooler company who are partnering with us as a charity rather than us as Frank Water Ltd, and for every water cooler they sell, they're donating a percentage of their profits. Instead of that coming to Frank Water Ltd, the business, it's going into our company limited by guarantee, which we're hoping to get charitable status with. It's like Oxfam in the company set-up, they can't trade directly from a charity. You have to have a separate trading arm. So we started Frank Water Ltd, trading, and then we have a policy that all profits made from that company go into Frank Water Projects which is the company limited by guarantee, awaiting charitable status. And then we also plan to do general fundraising in other ways.

The ultimate vision of Frank Water as a bottled water company really is to put ourselves out of business because everybody's been given access to clean water. Or to influence other businesses to do something similar. I mean, if Coca-Cola just put 1p on every can they sold, they would rid us of the whole issue in the first place. So if we could just encourage a few other water or drinks companies to contribute in some way, that would make a massive difference. So, more than anything, it's about hopefully influencing other businesses to do something similar that will help other people in other ways. To inspire others. We're certainly on the radar of a lot of the big companies, I know they're watching. Hopefully they're inspired and they're learning. Hopefully they will do something themselves.

Ethical business dilemmas

Distribution is probably our biggest issue. And it's costly as well. Every new distributor you involve is another bit of money going out. Although we were passionate about it, not everyone was going to be as passionate as we were about it. Just because we thought it was a good idea, not everybody was going to be willing to cut down on their profits to enable it to work. Our initial idea was the idea of equity, in that the retail price of each bottle should be split into thirds — a third on manufacture and distribution, a second third to the retailer as their margin, and the last third to the Frank projects. That was our idea about it, but the fact is that shops and cafes have very different margins. So for example, if we sell through a shop, they might only put 20 per cent, maybe 30 per cent, on that bottle. Their overheads are less because they're selling so many products. Whereas if we sell through a cafe or a restaurant, their overheads are so much higher, they want to put on 100 per cent, if not more. So we couldn't really go into all these different sales streams with a fixed retail price, saying, 'You can only make 20p on this bottle because we're only making 20p on this bottle for the projects.' That didn't work, whereas initially we thought that was a great idea and that everybody would be up for it. That was showing our naivety in business, really.

So gradually we've learned, but at the same time I think what's hardest is sticking to your values. We always wanted to be as equitable as possible, and we always wanted a flat rate pricing policy. That's how we chose to show our equity, and it allows us to have that direct link to how much we can provide at the projects as well. Our retailers accept it, but we do have problems. We haven't gone towards supermarket sales. They would want us to compromise a lot of our values, and yes, that would mean we'd get more volume and that would ultimately mean that we'd probably put in more projects, but what's more important — putting in the projects, or putting in the projects using the most ethical values and ways of doing things that we could in the UK? It was getting that balance right, really.

We're trying not to encourage the buying of bottled water. We're the only bottled water company who have on all our bottles, 'reduce, reuse, recycle'. We're trying to encourage people to think more about the impact that they're having by drinking bottled water, and if you have the option to use tap water, then use it. Part of the issue about supermarket sales is that their largest market is the take-home market, and we really don't believe people should be going into a supermarket and buying packs of bottled water to drink at home when you've got tap water or you can use filters to make your tap water better if you don't like it.

A small percentage of people feel that bottled water is not an industry that should be encouraged, which is, to be honest, very much where we come from.

I haven't waited for other people or relied on other people for things. If I believe in something, I go and do it.

Water for water, just the simplicity of the idea seemed perfect. We weren't creating a new market. We were creating a new category in a market that already existed and was growing at some speed. We felt it was more important to enter a market with a new product, and a new concept, to inspire others to do something similar, than to not enter that market at all. Every business has its foibles, its areas that aren't 100 per cent perfect, that you can improve on, and certainly packaging is one area that we are aware of and working on.

Frank's delights

One of the best things about Frank is going over to India and seeing the results, going to Kothapeta and meeting the villagers. We've seen that we've helped them have clean water and the effect that that has. It's incredible. Last year, we had the most amazing welcome from the villagers. It was an incredible situation, going back. I saw someone I'd taken photos of the year before, which we had on our website and our postcard. He saw himself on our postcard, carrying this massive bowl of water on his head that he'd just carried from the desert. He looked so much healthier this time. It was an amazing feeling. Also, I was doing interviews with the operators and they said how, before they had this job operating the facility, they worked in a town ten kilometres away. They don't have their own transport, they either walked there or they tried to hitch with a lorry or whatever to get to work. I remember the guy's face when he said, 'It's amazing to be able to contribute to the health of my own family and my own village, and to be doing something for my own people rather than working for a big company ten kilometres away from my home. Here I can see the effects of the work that I do.'

I was talking to the villagers as they came and collected water. They were already seeing other benefits, like the fact that it makes the most amazing dhal, and they were so overjoyed about that. Of course, they have dhal for every meal, and it boils so much quicker, so it saves on the amount of fuel and it saves time cooking. It's to do with the hardness of the water, and it makes it much fluffier. That's one of the amazing things, going to the projects and seeing the end product.

In the UK, we've had amazing support and met amazing people through doing Frank. With the kind of business that it is, a social enterprise, you meet so many people who are on the same wavelength as you, doing similar things. You find so much support through that. When I worked for Tom's business, whenever we used to go to an event, everyone was just trying to sell to you, it was always sell, sell, sell. Everyone was so concerned with profit for personal gain. The majority of the people we've met through Frank, who are all doing similar things, have so much of a wider view and vision. Yes, of course they're concerned about themselves, and living a good life for themselves, but they also care about other people and the environment. You meet them and you don't sell to each other. It's not about selling to each other, it's about raising awareness of the issues that you're aware of, and through that people just love what you're doing and you love what they're doing, and automatically you find a brilliant allegiance with them. You're not sold to or bought from, it's just that the idea itself propels your relationship and you tell other people about it, and it spreads like that through goodness rather than people thinking about personal gain.

Frank relies a lot on volunteers. Having volunteers involved in your business is a challenge, but what's more amazing is the passion that you get from them, and the other things that they bring as well. Other ideas, other ways of expanding your business, other people that they know — it automatically increases your network. It's lovely to have volunteers involved, whether they are the core of the business or on the periphery. You get something so much more powerful than something that's just driven out of money. They feel that they can get involved because it's not profiting shareholders. There are no shareholders. Pete, our designer, created a really strong brand because he was so passionate about it. He's a volunteer. And because all the people that were involved in Frank in the start-up phases were so passionate about it, we created something that much more powerful, and that was crucial.

Frank's roots

My father and mother were both involved in farming, which is a very community-led business. Everybody helps everybody out quite a lot, so a lot of farmers have cooperatives where you share machinery and come together to do jobs and things, which is really nice. Working off the land, working with what you've

We're certainly on the radar of a lot of the big companies, I know they're watching. Hopefully they're inspired and they're learning.

already got, the self-sufficiency to a certain extent influenced me. They worked for themselves, so I've been brought up with that sort of working for yourself mentality. And my degree in fine art was very creative, and you had to be self-motivated in order to do it. I've always gone out and done stuff, I haven't waited for other people or relied on other people for things. If I believe in something, I go and do it.

If I started again there's nothing specific that I would do differently. We created a business very much based around a core of ethical values, and we've been strong enough to stick with that. Yes, it means that we haven't got as much distribution, we're not supplying the supermarkets etc, but ultimately, that's a decision we've made with informed reasoning, so I don't think there's anything I would have done differently.

Being the change

I would say, do it, be the change. So many people think about it. I think a lot of people don't do it because they're concerned about the finance, about where they'd get the funding from, or whether it would actually run in profit at all, how they could actually make it work as a business. I think you just have to be brave. Get all the advice you can possibly get. There are so many people out there who want to help and advise with social businesses. Just don't be afraid. Do it. Make sure you're in a positive position and you've got the support behind you before you do it. There is so much out there, you would find support without a problem. Through moving in the ethical/social business area, you do meet a lot of people who are being the change. I've met loads of people on a smaller scale, people who are out there, volunteering, working on projects just because they want to be part of the change in their own way.

What gives me hope is that since starting Frank, there have been other entrants to the ethical water market. The more of us there are, the more it will influence the bigger companies to do something; they really can make an even bigger difference than we're making. The ethical market as a whole is growing phenomenally, and conscious consumerism is going mainstream. So many more people are aware of it. People are encouraged to think more about their impact on the environment and on other people, and we're encouraged to do what we can where we can. It's really positive, and that gives me a lot of hope.

www.frankwater.com

Boo Armstrong

What we're promoting is integrated health care, where you get the best of all different kinds of medical systems so that patients get better, and aren't dependent on drugs forever.

Boo Armstrong was struck by the following statistics: that 20 per cent of people in the UK use complementary medicine; that 90 per cent of them pay for it privately; and that 75 per cent of UK citizens would like to see it provided for free on the NHS. Her work running London's most eco-friendly community health centre showed her that complementary therapies worked. So, motivated by a passion for fairness and justice, she set about the task of integrating complementary health care into the NHS and enabling greater access to it for all people, regardless of their ability to pay. In 2004, she created the social enterprise Get Well UK to do just that, and has developed and run three successful programmes providing complementary health care through GP surgeries.

I guess I've been socially motivated since I was really young. I was the local ARK green campaigning group area coordinator when I was 11, doing paper recycling on a Saturday morning, then selling the paper and planting trees. Then I got into animal rights and ecological rights and kind of cared a lot. Probably what prepared me on a very practical level was not going to university but the university of life, and having opportunities through volunteering to get really involved in how organisations run. By the time I was 18 I was a director of a company which had over 200 volunteers, and I learned quite quickly about the responsibility of taking on work. If you take it on and you do it, then you can keep your responsibilities.

Integrated health care for all

There was a big unfairness in health care, which is that rich people can choose a kind of medicine which is really prevalent, but poor people typically can't because it's really expensive. And even though we have a National Health Service in this country that we've all paid for with our taxes (which last year cost £76 billion), loads of people can't get the most effective medicine, a kind of medicine which typically doesn't cause bad side effects, often gets you better, often increases your well-being in ways beyond just helping your disease. We're disenfranchising people, so the change I wanted to see was specifically about making complementary medicine available on the NHS. What we're promoting is integrated health care, where you get the best of all different kinds of medical systems so that patients get better, and aren't dependent on drugs forever.

I made a number of observations that led to the idea. I used to run a community health centre in Camden and I noticed three things. One is that complementary medicine works. A piece of research had been published saying that in the UK, people who use complementary medicine typically have higher education, they're more likely to be white, and so on. I thought, hang on a minute, why is this? My experience was that complementary medicine actually works for everybody. We were working with refugees, single mothers, older women, people on really low incomes, and it seemed to work across the board. Therefore, it was only about who was accessing it, and it was because there was this financial barrier. So I noticed, complementary medicine works.

The second thing I noticed was that for lots of practitioners, it's really hard to be able to share your skills in your community. Your career path is to set up a pri-

In the UK, there are 60,000 alternative therapists and 40,000 GPs. So who's the alternative?

vate business, typically. You can do really well and help people get better. But the people you see walking up and down the street, who you know would benefit, you can't see them because the doctors won't refer them. So there was a frustration I had that people want to work to make their communities better. Within our communities we have amazing resources. There are more complementary therapists in the UK than there are GPs. And we know we've got a shortage of health staff. We've got all these people, so why don't we just create a system which integrates into the NHS? That was my second observation, that it's a bit of a rubbish system.

Part of my job was to make this community health centre financially viable, so I started selling contracts to the local social services and the health authority, and during these negotiations discovered that the commissioners were quite keen to commission complementary medicine. Some of them used it themselves, they knew that their patients wanted it, but they didn't know how. They didn't know about the quality standards or what it cost or any of that stuff, and it was at that point I realised the third thing. There was a gap in the market — for a kind of brokering agency, someone to bring together the people with the money, the practitioners and the patients. There was a piece of the puzzle missing — how would we manage it?

In November 2000, the House of Lords published an enquiry they had conducted into complementary medicine. They had spent 15 months interviewing the great and the good, scientists and all kinds of people. They made three main recommendations: that we need more research to find out if it works; we need better regulation to ensure patient safety; and crucially, for me, that we should make complementary medicine available through the NHS with GPs acting as the gatekeepers. This was the final piece in the puzzle. If we bring GPs into the picture, and ensure that a GP refers a patient, then not only will we give increasing confidence to patients who don't necessarily know what these strange therapies are, but also we'll have a way to manage the demand. So that was the big idea, that was when the light came on, and it took me quite a long time of saying to other people, I've got this great idea, do you want it? And trying to give it away to entrepreneurial types that I know. Then one day I just woke up and thought, this is mine, and I'd better just get on with it.

From ideas to action

I worked for three years in a very focused way, running some pilot projects to find out if my theory works. Because I tell everyone I've got this great idea to get the GPs to refer the patients, but is it true? I was very fortunate that someone who knew my work in Camden had just got a job running a health project in Haringey, and what they were looking for was some complementary health provision in a GP surgery, integrated into the NHS. They were looking for a provider of that service. Get Well UK began delivering services there in May of last year. Later in the year, we got another contract in Islington.

We worked with GPs locally to find out what complementary therapies they would feel confident referring their patients to, and what conditions they were struggling with where they thought there was enough evidence to show complementary medicine could work. Then we went out and recruited practitioners of those disciplines to work with us, based in the GP surgery. One of the things we had to do was to share information between the different groups of people, because neither of them had enough time to understand each other. So with the GPs we spent a long time explaining what the therapies are, how they work, who's insured, what training they've had, what the evidence is and all of that. And with the practitioners, we recruited the very best ones, and we trained them to understand more about the modern NHS and the conditions that they'd be working in and the needs and so on of the GPs and the patients they would see. Then of course we had to provide information for the patients before setting this whole thing up. So the pilot itself was making it possible for GPs to refer their patients to a quality-assured practitioner.

So we worked with quite a few hundred patients, mainly with musculo-skeletal conditions, like back pain and arthritis, and quite a lot of mental health problems as well. And so they would come and have a very different experience of the NHS. It was the same in that they walked through the same door and saw the

If you're in service to something bigger than yourself,
you have to trust.

same receptionist, but then they would have a totally different kind of treatment. And for many of them it was the first time they could try a treatment like that, because normally they're so expensive.

Proof

The two different projects were audited by different professors, and they showed very similar results — people got significantly better, they were much less worried, they took less medication, and they went to the doctor less often. My favourite number is that 81 per cent of GPs said the treatment was beneficial for their patients, and 80 per cent of patients reported improvement in general health. These audits seem to replicate what other grassroots projects have shown across the UK, so we can be increasingly confident that this stuff definitely works. And the patients who were generally referred to us were very ill. Many of them had had their condition for a long time, and many of them had been signed off work for a long time, unable to work because of pain and disability. A number of people ended up going back to work. So I think for some of our patients we changed their lives significantly, and for others we changed it a bit by helping them to live with less pain or increased mobility.

So I'd run some pilot projects and had them audited independently. The plan was — prove it works, prove you can save money, and then sell it to the NHS who will welcome you with open arms. I was very focused on that. Then we contacted every one of the 302 Primary Care Trusts in England, and had 302 'go-aways'.

I think the main challenge is that complementary medicine isn't often recognised politically. And that the Department of Health views health care in Britain as the NHS and insurance. Even though one in five people use complementary medicine, it's somehow still invisible. Across all sorts of public policy documents, there's very occasionally a mention of it, but never in a way that says you should buy it, or it's a thing to be encouraged. For example, in the NHS, one of the main thrusts at the moment is about patient choice. But this is choice of who provides the hospital care you get, not choice over what kind of care you get, even though loads of people would want complementary medicine. So we commissioned some research into public policy and where it fits, and it fits in so many places.

The government's main thrust at each of the three elections it's been successful in winning since 1997 has been about inequalities and ending inequalities. Complementary medicine is an issue about inequalities. Rich people in the UK buy it — loads of them, they vote with their feet. And it must be because it works. It's not just because they want to throw their money away because actually it's quite expensive. So that political hurdle is the main one, and even though lots of things have been decentralised at the moment, that's quite challenging. We did have 302 commissioners to convince, but now there are 40,000 GPs. So somehow our marketing has to shift and we have to compete against the pharmaceuticals, who have 8,000 drug reps operating in the UK at the moment. And we've got two full-time staff. So in terms of competition, we've got things against us.

A timely breakthrough

All these Primary Care Trusts were saying no, and we had a few dark months when it was quite difficult. We were due to run out of money within a few weeks, so I don't know what we would have done. But then a wonderful thing happened. On 5th October 2006 Paul Goggins, the Health Minister for Northern Ireland, made an announcement that he wanted to make complementary medicine available to everybody in Northern Ireland, and that he was trying to set up a fund and run a pilot scheme to find out how to do it. His department knew nothing about this, and didn't know very much about complementary medicine. They approached me because I had spoken at a conference over there and they'd met me. They said, 'How would you go about it and could you set it up for us for January?'

On 13th December we got the go-ahead to run this contract for them, and it's a pilot. If we can demonstrate that people's health improves and we save them money, then their commitment is to roll it out to everyone in Northern Ireland. The study will be big enough and solid enough that it will influence Scotland, Wales and England. It's really funny that I'd been chasing all these people in England particularly and getting nowhere, just tons of rejections. I hadn't even thought about Northern Ireland, and then from the first contact that I had with them, it only took two months to have this contract.

*You need a health service that responds to
all the different parts of you.*

We're working in two specific areas, Belfast and Derry, treating 700 patients in the course of the year. We're working on two different areas, musculo-skeletal problems and anxiety/stress, which is pretty true for everybody in Northern Ireland — the consequences of a war. A lot of the trauma is that loads of people feel that. One of the doctors that I met was saying, 'I don't want to be medicating people. The medication is really effective but the more often you use it the less effective it becomes. So if there was something else that would work, where people would feel supported and valued and their self-esteem would improve and all of that as well…' They're interested in that.

Integration

The main problem I think is a lack of information on both sides, on all sides actually — the GPs don't know enough about these therapies and how to refer to them, and how they work, and if they work. And the practitioners don't know how the NHS works and what GPs can offer. They don't know how to communicate with each other. I think the ones we work with are fantastic and doing a great job, but the big picture of change in the health service will depend on information-sharing and overcoming some prejudices on all sides — there's arrogance, fear, chips on shoulders — and if we're to really help people and patients get better, then we've got to get over some of that stuff.

We've got different auditors working there, but we haven't got their findings yet. The main things we've learned are that people are really ill, and have been living with their illnesses for a long time, and the NHS, although it can offer a lot, hasn't been able to offer solutions. I think the GPs and the patients are really happy that this has come along. I'm really confident that we are delivering a successful service, that people are getting better and we are saving money, and if so, like I said, the government's committed to rolling it out across Northern Ireland. That's going to be really interesting. It's not my job to work out how to do that, but I'd love to play a part in it. There aren't enough practitioners, there's not enough infrastructure — all kinds of things are lacking, but we can now work towards creating a sector.

It would to take a long-term commitment from the government to train people up and integrate them into the NHS. It used to be just people who could afford to go off and invest money to train, and there'd be people volunteering in hospices and so on, and that's not an industry, is it? But now young people are leaving school and going off to study acupuncture, and we need to create career paths for them. I think Northern Ireland is going to be the place where that happens. That's about creating a new world, where there are local health services that don't harm people, that aren't about profiteering, that are actually about making people well and recognising the complexity of what it's like to be a human in modern Britain. And actually, that you need a health service that responds to all the different parts of you. It feels like that's happening, so it's fantastically exciting.

Being the change

It's very surprising to one day wake up and realise that actually, I'm an administrator. My personal joy is about storytelling. Because of the way this has been set up, I have the opportunity to meet lots of different people in lots of different spheres of life, and often to take somebody's story and tell it to someone else who wouldn't otherwise get to hear it. That's my favourite thing. So, occasionally having a tea party for our patients for example, and finding out actually what it's like for them, and then when I'm meeting a commissioner saying, 'It's amazing, you know, because there are people who couldn't carry their shopping home, or they couldn't afford treatment, and now they can.' Understanding more about how people's lives change. It seems absolutely precious to be told that stuff and know that it's going on, and then also to have the opportunity to rave on about it.

Lots and lots of things support me — good food, great relationship, brilliant colleagues, knowing that we're making a difference, knowing that patients' health is improving, seeing a therapist once a week, looking after my own health. Having a great board of directors, particularly our chair, who is totally solid, committed, really experienced. He's double my age, so he's got tons and tons of useful experience to draw on, amazing contacts and he's utterly supportive and a brilliant teacher in a not-heavy-handed way. That's been great. Generally having a whole network of people from all kinds of different places who teach me stuff. I'm quite sponge-like and like learning something from the financial markets sector, which suddenly applies to the IT system, and so on. My aspiration is to create a fantastic health system that's healthy in and of itself, so it's thrilling to me to look at what best practice is in all these different areas and try and bring it together in this new thing.

What's been crucial has been access to people who've been really helpful. Someone who goes 'Yes, of course I'll give you an hour, because it's good, what you're doing.' I think it's surprising sometimes, actually, how many people are on the side of wanting the world to be better. Even people who you might criticise because of the job that they're in, they really care too. And perhaps their day is a touch less boring than it might otherwise have been. It's nice to help an enthusiastic person. I've got a mentor in the City and I've got support from UnLtd, which is an organisation that helps social entrepreneurs with finance and developing skills. For me it's really important. I'm all too aware that people get stressed and burnt out, and this is a big project. If we really are going to revolutionise health care, I need to be supported. I think it's awful that so many doctors are really unwell. And through how they manage their stress, alcoholism, drug use, suicide, and a whole range of other things are rife. I would want my health care professional to be a role model to me. I think the Gandhian concept that the only way to teach is by example is really true. If your doctor's really unwell, it's not very good. So, to me it's really important to practise what you preach. Roughly. You know, with a little bit of fun. Fun's important.

www.getwelluk.com

Maude Barlow

This issue of water is probably the most important issue in the third world now, more than AIDS, more than hunger. More people are dying of dirty water than those two put together.

Maude Barlow is the National Chairperson of the Council of Canadians, Canada's largest public advocacy organisation. This reflects her passionate belief in the power and importance of collective citizen activism. She has spent her whole life engaged in different areas of social justice, especially with regard to trade and economic globalisation. She is particularly interested in the growing issue of water — protecting it from pollution, ensuring clean water for all, and enshrining it as a fundamental human right, as it is becoming increasingly commodified and access to it more limited. She co-founded the Blue Planet Project, and is a leader in a worldwide network of water activists.

I wish to see the human species form a new relationship to water. I call it a covenant. I say that we need a blue covenant from the human species to nature, in regard to water. We need to stop seeing ourselves as somehow above nature, and water as merely a commodity that serves our lifestyle. Rather, we must understand that water is the life-blood of our planet and just as if you make the blood in your body sick, you make yourself sick, as we make the water-blood of the planet sick, we are killing ourselves as well. So I want us to have a new relationship, one to the other, and a covenant with the earth to protect the earth's dwindling and very precious water supplies.

Water issues

Less than 0.5 per cent of all the water on earth is available fresh water. The rest is sea water, or is frozen in polar ice. Fresh water is only renewable by rainfall. We were all taught in school that there is a closed hydrological cycle, that water goes through this cycle and it cannot possibly go anywhere else and it will be there forever. But in fact that's not so. It turns out that the human species has been capable of polluting and diverting and actually destroying freshwater sources to the point where we are actually running out of fresh water on the planet.

We have polluted surface water massively. Then we have turned to groundwater (fresh water underneath the ground), to pump up and replace the surface water because we can't access or use that any more. We are mining groundwater as if it were gold — removing water from aquifers and watersheds. The water is taken from the land or from aquifers and moved into cities and then flushed into the ocean and not replaced back into the system. So what we're doing is we're actually taking water and moving it from where it was put by nature. There may technically be the same amount of water on earth but more of it is now inaccessible to us. The result is that about two billion people now live in areas of the world that are considered water-stressed. Over a billion of them have no access to clean water at all at this moment and all of the predictions are that this is going to get much worse quite quickly.

One more part of the problem is that there is a huge dispute in our world around who is going to control water. As it becomes what I have called 'blue gold', it is becoming more contested. All of a sudden, there's a huge global contest about who's going to control water, who's going to make the decisions about it.

One of the big disputes is around the role of the private sector. There are those who think the answer is that water should be made a marketable commodity like Coca-Cola or running shoes, put on the open market for sale to the highest bidder — basically, just commodified. We have a number of ways in which water is being commodified. We put over two hundred billion litres of water in plastic bottles last year across the world and it's growing at about 20 per cent a year. There are the big utility service providers, most of them from France, who come into developing countries (and now, of course, want to move into the developed world as well), who are backed by the World Bank to provide water on a for-profit basis and deny it to people who cannot pay. You've also got the water re-use technology, which is the fastest growing area of the corporate takeover of water. That includes desalination plants, nanotechnology, atmospheric water generation, even cloud-seeding — ways to find water, control it and sell it back at a profit. That's one side. There's a huge power struggle going on around that.

Protecting water and the right to water

On the other side are those of us who believe that water is part of the global commons, it's part of the collective heritage of both the earth and all humans and future generations; that no one should be able to appropriate it from the earth or from others to make a personal profit; and that it should be considered that no one owns water, that it belongs to the earth and all future generations and other species; and that we need strict laws in place to protect it. One of those ways that we're seeking to protect it is to have a human rights covenant or convention at the United Nations, which would declare water a public good, a common heritage and a human right. We are making advances at the UN on that.

To me, the answer lies in first having this common understanding that water isn't like running shoes. I don't mean to say that there aren't other areas where people have fundamental rights to clothing and housing and that kind of thing, but you'll die without water. So the first step, to me, would be that common agreement that we have to see water as a collective heritage and that everyone has a right to adequate water for life, as does nature.

The second step would be massive ecological protection, this covenant with the earth. There are many ways to go about this. We need to stop polluting. Until about 50 or 60 years ago, the vast majority of the world's population used local

*It's a powerful thing to watch people wake up
and get excited about the fact that they can change the world.*

water sources — rivers, lakes, and wells — and now many of them are contaminated. So the most important thing to do is to stop doing what's creating the problem in the first place. One of the reasons that I'm so concerned about the high-tech answer to water, these water re-use technologies, is that I think the millions and billions of dollars being put into it is a disincentive to stop pollution. There's money to be made from cleaning up dirty water — 'Let that water keep getting dirty and we'll clean it up and we'll sell it back to you.'

We also have to look at agriculture and agricultural practices. The leading cause of water destruction in the world is our poor farming practices — industrial farming, intensive livestock operations, the use of chemical pesticides and fertilisers, not allowing the land to regenerate, monoculture crops — these are all part of a mechanical way of producing food that is destroying water. There's also something called 'virtual' water trade, where a country or community uses its water to produce something that needs water to produce, like beef or rice or roses for instance, and then they ship that product to a part of the world that doesn't want to use its water for that. For instance, most of the roses that you see in Europe come from Lake Naivasha in Nairobi, where *Out of Africa* was made. This lake is going to be, in the words of one scientist, a 'putrid puddle' in five years, because it's being destroyed to produce the roses for Europe. So we have a huge volume of water transported out of watersheds every day in this virtual water trade that should be staying there, to keep ecological sustainability in communities.

We know the answers. We actually know the answers to the global water crisis ecologically; we just don't have the collective political will to make it happen. Yet. It's happening.

Coalition of water activists

We have a number of countries that have finally come around to promoting the notion of the right to water, including some countries that were not supportive previously, so this is very good. Water was not included in the original Universal Declaration of Human Rights back in 1948 because back then nobody could conceive of a world without water, so it wasn't an issue. It wasn't left out deliberately; it simply wasn't considered something that one would think of when one thought of human rights. We want to rectify that omission. You can't re-open that Universal Declaration, it's a sealed document, but we think a covenant would be a step forward in defining water as a human right, much like other covenants or conventions, for example on landmines, and the rights of women and children. That would mean that governments do have the responsibility to provide clean water to their people and not just to those who can afford to buy it. It would be the beginning of an understanding that governments are going to work together collectively to change the situation and to reverse the destruction of the world's fresh water.

We started working with grassroots groups 15 years ago. My personal interest in water started with the first free trade agreement in the world, which was the Canada-US Free Trade Agreement. It was signed in 1989 and became the prototype for NAFTA, the North America Free Trade Agreement, which in turn became the prototype for the World Trade Organisation. Way back in the mid-1980s, I was concerned, with a number of other people in Canada, about the fact that water was included as a tradeable good in these agreements, and in fact as an investment. These trade agreements are actually protecting the rights of these corporate water investors. That was my first interest in it and it grew from there to realising that globalisation was allowing corporations to go into every part of the world and lay claim to people's water, in some cases physically. 'We bought this whole watershed, we own it and we'll deny it to those we don't want to have access to it.' It's as extreme as that in some cases.

We started working with grassroots movements who were beginning to fight back against corporate control of water. We've been working with groups in the developing world for 15 years now, to put together a pretty formidable global water justice movement to bring back the notion of local control, local rights over local water, local responsibility for local water sources, and to wrest water back from these transnational corporations who seem to think that just because they can, it's OK for them to come in and lay claim to people's local water resources.

It consists of organisations like my own in the so-called first world who are working in solidarity to bring resources and support and solidarity to local groups. The vast majority of the groups are local grassroots organisations —

*I've met the bravest, smartest, loveliest people in the world
in this movement. We've formed a kind of global family,
and we really, truly care for each other.*

peasants, farmers, indigenous groups, women's groups and so on in the third world, who have been fighting on their own, and who really needed the support that some of our groups were able to provide to help make this a global movement, through computers and the internet and through getting together. We get together in the annual World Social Forums and also at the World Water Forum, which is held by the World Bank and the big water companies every three years. After many years of working with the individual groups in South Africa, Namibia, Ethiopia and so on, suddenly we're bringing people together and we're forming a new movement. The internet has really been a godsend to our groups because you don't have to have a computer in every home. All you need is somebody with a computer in a local community who can then spread the word. We've really been able to pull together a movement and have an impact on each other's worlds.

One example is when the first water war happened in Cochabamba, Bolivia, in 1997. This was when the World Bank brought in the Bechtel corporation to provide private water services. Their subsidiary immediately tripled the price of water, and people couldn't afford it and took to the streets. There was literally a civil war, the army was brought in and people were shot. But Bechtel was forced to leave, and it was a huge victory. We were there physically on the streets with the people, and also we got the story told in the global north. We got thousands of letters to the President of Bolivia and to the World Bank so that they would know that the international community was watching this. That's the kind of thing we've been able to do as a community. It's fraught with difficulties, and we never have enough money, but we really are building an enormously powerful movement. We're really fighting back and saying we need to maintain public control of this water. We have won this argument in many important ways. It's a wonderful David and Goliath story, which I'm very proud of. It's not the people in the first world being do-gooders but rather being there in truth and solidarity and support with the people fighting in their communities in Asia or Africa or Latin America. It's the most wonderful process to be involved in.

Reasons to act

My father was a wonderful man involved in social justice. He led the fight against capital punishment in Canada and was instrumental in getting capital and corporal punishment ended in my country. So maybe it came with my morning oatmeal — I was raised to believe that you had to give something back. I've always had a clear sense of social justice and when I get upset about things, I stew if I don't do something about them. I have bad dreams. The only way that I can sleep well is if I do something in my own small way to make the world different.

Why this issue of water? It just spoke to me at every level. I'm a deep environmentalist in the sense that I love nature; nature is my cathedral. It's where I'm most at peace. I so value the natural world and so want to protect it. The issue of water for me was absolutely central to that vision of preserving this beautiful world of ours. At the same time, I have a very strong sense of social justice and this issue of water is also probably the most important issue in the third world now, more than AIDS, more than hunger. More people are dying of dirty water than those two put together. It's really time we understood that this is not inevitable, that we actually can make a difference. This does not have to be.

The issue of water called to me because it spoke to me at both of those levels, it was one of those issues that hit every part of who I am. And I love the people I work with. I've met the bravest, smartest, loveliest people in the world in this movement. We've formed a kind of a global family and we care for each other — really, truly care for each other. And so we get great sustenance back, we have a ball. We actually like getting tear-gassed together and telling the stories later and being there in solidarity with each other. It's a very rich life. I can't imagine just getting up and going off to a job to make money for no reason, I can't think what that would be like, honestly. I don't mean to judge anybody, it's just if you get up in the morning and what you're doing that day is about something other than yourself, I think you'll live a better life. I feel very humbled to be allowed to be a part of this fabulous movement.

Intentional citizens

My organisation in Canada is called the Council of Canadians. We're a citizens' movement, with close to 100,000 members. We effect change by getting those people and others to send in petitions to politicians, write letters to the newspapers, hold panel discussions, inform their neighbours, become what I call intentional citizens. Informed, intentional citizens, who form the backbone of social change. It's a powerful thing to watch people wake up and become involved and get excited about the fact that they can change the world. Pretty well every single important movement — women's emancipation, the emancipation of slavery — mostly did not come from politicians from the top; they came from the fight from below. Things like violence, family violence, violence against children — there was a time when that was a taboo subject. It took long, hard work by individuals. Drinking and driving, smoking in public, homophobia. These are all fights that have taken place socially, and now the environmental movement has come along and it's the voices of the people who are living with the polluted water or the dirty air, or the lake that doesn't have fish in it any more, who are leading the fight. These are the most important voices in our world and we must build political systems where these are recognised by the politicians as being more important than the corporate interests that now are so tightly involved with them.

We do it the old-fashioned way, through hard work, becoming organised, coming together around a common cause, understanding that there are people out there doing similar work in other places. When you're doing your part, you may feel it's small, but if you know that you're part of something that's much larger, you actually can get there. There's lots that people can do if they're interested: from looking at their own waterways and how much water they waste; or looking towards fighting privatisation of their local water sources; seeking out the groups in their own communities that are doing this work; to becoming part of this global water movement.

There's not going to be any way around the destruction of the planet if we don't reverse course, which means reversing the dominant economic system of our time. We must question the system that says that there is no limit to what we can have and buy and consume and produce, and it doesn't matter where it comes from, or who it hurts, or what natural systems it destroys. This system's got to be questioned and not just because suddenly we're hearing that the toys from China are poisoned, but because we shouldn't have destroyed China. Collectively, China shouldn't be destroyed for this economic system. We have to start living sustainably again and take responsibility for others and for future generations. We have to go back to a much more responsible relationship — I call it a covenant — with the earth.

I put my energy into building civil society movements that then I hope will translate into political transformations. I'm not saying there is nothing to be done in politics. In fact, we need our politicians obviously in the end to enact the laws, but I learned a long time ago that they're not going to do it on their own. The only way that they are going to effect change, or we are going to effect change, is if there are enough of us telling those politicians that they will not be voted for the next time. These corporations don't vote for them, they may back them and they may pay the bills, but in the end it's individual citizens who do or do not vote for them, and we have to have a politicised, radicalised, informed citizenry. The worry that I have is how much people turn away from the information that they need to have, to be these informed citizens. They'd rather be consumers, they'd rather sit and watch TV, they'd rather buy stuff and not engage their minds and their souls in the journey that takes them to the place where they are informed voters and citizens. And that, to me, is the most important work that we can do.

The answer lies in social transformation. We have all witnessed real societal changes around race, the role of women, and so on. We have watched major changes in our lifetime. It can happen, and so too can a real challenge against this economic system. I don't think it's going to come from the traditional left. I think it's going to come from those of us concerned about the environment, from the recognition that this system is not sustainable. The more we can work for social change, and the greater number of people sharing this vision, the more likely we will be to have politicians that we can vote for in good conscience. Meanwhile, we have to hold the ones we have to account. We have to work and work and work towards the social conditions to make that change.

Inspirations

Always, it's been this notion of justice, but in the last five years I've been blessed with four little grandkids and now, it's them. What kind of a world are they growing up in? These kids are so young and so innocent and so eager to join our world, and so malleable. We must put the right thoughts in their minds; give them a sense of the beauty of the world and their place in keeping that beauty, and the honour of being alive, and what they can do to give back that gift. I look at these kids and they touch my heart. That's a good enough reason to keep going, to get up in the morning and give those babies whatever I can, to go over and grab them and hug them and work for the next generation. They deserve a clean world and they deserve a just world. It's our responsibility to make that happen.

I would really give tribute to the grassroots people that I work with, particularly the poorest people on earth who, in spite of being threatened with violence and sometimes being victims of violence, in some cases being killed, who are poor, who are disenfranchised, nevertheless stand up and speak their truth to the power that oppresses them, and who are funny, and wise, and brave, and who meet life with joy. These are the people who inspire me. These are the people who are walking the walk. They are the change that they seek in the world. They will not adopt the model that they reject and they live in a different model. They live much more simply, obviously, than anybody can in the so-called first world and they are filled with courage. I have great faith in the Bible. I'm not a religious person but I remember some lovely things in the Bible and one is that the meek shall inherit the earth. I do deeply believe that the people who are fighting for justice at this level in the most deprived communities in the world are our leaders.

All over the world there are these wonderful people who have a vision of what life could be. We come together at the World Social Forums every year. In Porto Alegre, Brazil, there were 150,000 people there, coming together to share a vision of being the change. Showing by your own being, the food you choose, the people you are with, the way you treat your family and your friends. You're living what you dream the world will be like and there are 150,000 of you together talking, sharing, dancing, struggling through this thing. I keep using the word 'humbling', but it is. It's amazing when this energy comes together.

www.canadians.org

Blue Covenant: The global water crisis and the coming battle for the right to water, Maude Barlow, New Press, 2008

Blue Gold, Maude Barlow, New Press, 2005

Taddy Blecher

We wanted to create the first free university in sub-Saharan Africa. Everybody thought we were absolutely crazy.

Taddy Blecher was about to emigrate from South Africa, when he realised that if everybody did that, the country could never develop. He stayed and joined CIDA, a Community and Individual Development Association that was teaching children in townships to meditate. The startling successes of this programme left brilliant young adults with nowhere to go on to after schooling. They weren't qualified for any jobs, and higher education was financially out of reach. So Blecher and his four colleagues from CIDA created a virtually free university, from scratch, for them and others like them from all over the country, providing an excellent business degree and vocational programmes. The individual students can now get good jobs and lift their families out of poverty, and the country has a larger, more highly qualified workforce for its greater economic transformation.

We started CIDA City Campus in Johannesburg in South Africa in 2000, as the first free university in sub-Saharan Africa. We wanted to prove that you could take somebody who at 12 had been sniffing glue on the streets, and that individual could become a chartered accountant, a merchant banker, a stockbroker, something enormously aspirational in society. But over and above that, that they could be a happy, well-adjusted human being, who's passionate about life and really has a contribution to give.

CIDA is the first free university in sub-Saharan Africa, or virtually free. We charge about £25 for the first year, which includes tuition, books and materials. In years two, three and four we charge about £10 per month. In South Africa, a good education is enormously expensive, so we've tried to make higher education accessible to the poorest of the poor.

We've been going for seven years, and about 3,500 graduates have come through our degree and vocational programs. Those students between them are now earning R154 million in annual salaries, about £11 million, and those were kids off the streets. If you take the net present value of those earnings over a 40 year period — I'm an actuary so I'm always working out numbers — it's about R4.5 billion, £370 million, that will go into the hands of the poor over the next 40 years. So it's very exciting.

Vision

Of course, everybody thought we were absolutely crazy. We wanted to create this boat that would take people across the unemployment river. On this side of the river, it's dark and gloomy. Everything's dead and there's no opportunity. On that side of the river, there's dignity, food, security and a life. That was the idea — how could we move people across this river?

We wrote a letter to 350 schools in three provinces and asked them to send us their brightest top three kids, from very poor families, who could never afford to go to university, and we would give them a world-class business degree, for £25 for the year. At that stage, we didn't even have a phone number that people could phone through to, other than our cellphones. My old company, Monitor, is a big strategy firm and they've supported us right throughout. We gave Monitor's fax number. We didn't ask them for permission, I didn't think it would be a problem. I thought we'd just get a couple of faxes.

For two weeks we heard nothing. Then we got the first fax, the first five students wanting to come to this imaginary university that didn't exist. It was very, very exciting. We drew a picture on the wall, which I have never erased. It was a picture of how we were going to create Africa's first free university for the poor. It had a picture of the infinity symbol and we said, 'This is about giving people infinity in their lives — the dignity of what life is, and the number of students we are going to reach, and the number of lives we hope to affect in the right direction.'

Beginnings

Over five months, we ended up getting 3,500 applications through Monitor's one and only fax machine, so they got over 30,000 pieces of paper. I had put Monitor's logo on the letter that we sent out, saying, 'This is our first donor.' People were queuing up outside Monitor, begging us to take their children, and security was trying to shoo them away, saying, 'This is a consulting firm, not a university.' A friend of mine has a telemarketing company and they agreed to be the face of the university. People would phone into this call centre and say, 'Where must we take our children, where is this university? Did you leave the address off the brochure you sent us?' Of course, we had no address, and then the call centre staff would say, 'Phone in a week and we will tell you which of our many buildings in the city of Johannesburg to bring your child to for registration.'

We didn't have a building. I used to drive around and look at pieces of grass and think, 'Could we erect a tent, and have the first tented university?' Two weeks before we were about to start, we got the use of a building in downtown Johannesburg. It was dark and dank and it stank. It had broken beer bottles and urine outside, but we had two weeks to clean up just the fifth floor of this building. Magically, we found 400 plastic chairs on the fifth floor. We had no money. It was like a sign from God. There is a beautiful German proverb that I love to quote, which says, 'Just begin to weave and God will provide the thread.' You have no cloth, no thread, you just picture this beautiful tapestry and what you need. You start to weave, and then the thread comes, just as you need it. That's what's happened to us the whole way through. But when you commit, you have to commit in your heart. You have got to give everything and say, 'This is going to happen, no matter what.' There's no room inside for failure. No matter how great the fear is, you just go forward.

When you commit, you have to commit in your heart. You have to give everything and say, 'This is going to happen, no matter what.'

And so with our building and our 400 plastic chairs, we got our call centre friends to phone 350 applicants and tell them to come. We welcomed them very, very warmly. We introduced them to the founders, to the academics, to the manual labourers, to the administration staff, and they quickly realised that they were all the same five people. The next day we lost 100 students, so we had only 250 students, and then we started. We started this little virtual university, with 400 plastic chairs, 250 students and five of us, and we had absolutely nothing. After a few weeks, we came up with the idea of practicum. We said, 'Why are we doing all the work, and they're just sitting in the seats?' So we said to the students, 'We've created a wonderful new leadership development program in CIDA. You guys are now going to manage the whole university.' That's become a beautiful tradition in CIDA, that our students help to run their own university. Going forward, they will build universities, they will grow their own food and manage our own energy needs.

Extraordinary growth

Then we asked ourselves, how do we start to impact on this tidal wave of AIDS and HIV amongst the youth, and the message not getting through? How could we multiply the five of us and turn us into 5,000? We came up with the idea of the Extranet, which is an extraordinary network. We realised that through our students we would be able to reach many more people in the communities, and they would teach people, peer to peer, and become positive role models. That was our idea. We approached PriceWaterhouseCooper and asked if they would teach accountancy. We asked Monitor to teach strategy, and the biggest law firm, Bowman Gilfillan, to teach commercial law. All of a sudden the best accounting firm in the world, the best strategy firm in the world, the best law firm in the country, now became the faculty of this new university. We thought if these brilliant people could give their knowledge to these 250 kids, and if they in turn can go out and teach 1,000, then we'd reach 250,000 people. And then if we could grow that, we could get to the point where hopefully we can reach millions of people a year.

That was our dream and our vision. It's always this idea that just a few people changing could then influence the lives of many people around them and create a network — everybody pulls each other up the mountain. So that's how CIDA started and seven years later we're working with 3,500 students a year, 1,500 across the university programs, 2,000 across the vocational programs and we have 10 colleges, schools and academies in various facilities in Johannesburg. We've helped to start a little campus down in Nyasa, Malawi, and we've also given a lot of input into the starting of a little university in Cape Town and one in Ethiopia as well. We hope, over time, to expand this model across Africa and the developing world.

Education innovations

We offer a very holistic education. We draw on principles of consciousness-based education, we draw on the best we find in traditional education, and we've invented a lot of our own things, and put those together to create an educational approach that is loving but disciplined, that develops intellect and also wisdom, and that develops managers and also leaders. We want to develop the whole human being.

The components include the development of the student within, academic knowledge, skills, and values. Then there's the application into what we call practicum, where the students have to run the university. They do cleaning, cooking, administration work and gardening. We're starting two hectares of organic farming now on one campus, and they help with construction. This year, we're building a double-storey classroom block with eight classrooms and 27 offices. The students will dig the earth themselves, with giant machines, they will make their own bricks, put in the foundations, build this huge double-storey block. All of that will be done by students, just under guidance, so that's the experiential learning component. They also start a business every single year, or a social venture where they can do something for the community, and then they work in a real company, or have more experience in building their own business.

Then we've got what we call Love of Life. Everybody's got to find their own uniqueness, and whether that's poetry or climbing Kilimanjaro, we want to help our students realise their dreams. We also have the Nelson Mandela Extranet, where students go and give back to their communities. We call it 'positive youth

When you start to see that you can change the world, it impacts back on you again. It's like throwing pebbles in a pond.

revolutions', so in the same way that the youth helped to end apartheid, we want our youth to help transform the country. Our students have taught 700,000 people throughout the country about entrepreneurship, about how to live a life, about AIDS and HIV.

Funding

Funding is the biggest challenge of the non-profit. Social enterprise makes a lot of sense where you're selling a product, but where you're trying to provide a service to people who cannot pay for it, you become very dependent on parties outside of that community.

In the beginning, no one wanted to support us except Monitor's founder, Mark Fuller, who's a great visionary — he sent a cheque for $25,000 in the mail. He didn't know what we were going to do, but he just said, 'If you're that passionate about it, I want to support it.' A big breakthrough came when Investec Bank gave us their former head office building in Johannesburg. Since then, we've been able to get the support of the most amazing corporate sponsors, such as Investec Bank, First National Bank, MTN, DaimlerChrysler, T Systems and Transunion ITC. The Dell computer corporation has been amazing to us. Oprah Winfrey has become a great supporter of ours. Michael Dell is building a men's dormitory, and Oprah built a women's dormitory. Dell has donated all of our computers and servers. Sir Richard Branson really gets what we're doing and has been the most wonderful fairy godfather to us. He started the Branson School of Entrepreneurship at CIDA.

So that's how we've generally funded it. The Kellogg Foundation has been very supportive, and we won a $1 million prize from the Skoll Foundation in 2006, which was very exciting, and the Gates Foundation are giving us money to plan a replication process. That's short-term. Our real goal is long-term self-suffiency and we hope that from the year 2011 onwards, CIDA in Johannesburg will be fully self-sustaining, through black economic empowerment transactions, through buying stakes in companies, and building companies that are for profit. We hope to use the monies from for-profit operations to fund our non-profit operations. It's a big strategy and it's going very well. Another strategy is that every student, within five years of graduating, would then fund another student from their community to go through the university, if they're earning more than R5,000 a month. We're coming up with a number of other strategies. Our most innovative strategy is the eco-campuses that we want to start creating in semi-rural areas, where we literally grow our own food, build our own campus out of the local materials, and harness infinity — the infinite energy of the sun and the wind and the waves. We'll create completely self-sustaining campuses, and then sell excess food and have beautiful African hotels that can bring in money to run the university campuses. We want to create these African learning villages all over the place. There's the one in Nyasa and we're just about to start one within two hours of Johannesburg as well.

Through the university, we're focusing now on building colleges and schools in industries that we think will have sustainable, competitive advantage for that area. We are looking at developing people for organic agriculture, eco-tourism, construction, trade, business process outsourcing, and then also microfinance and finance for the unbanked, and African heritage-related businesses. We're blind to the beauty of what we are as Africans. We don't appreciate it, and don't think other people appreciate it. So we want to bring up young people to deeply love their own culture, their country, their traditions and to learn how create to wealth out of that in a sustainable way.

CIDA's first incarnation

Before we started the university, for four years we taught Transcendental Meditation to 9,000 school children in inner city schools, in Alexandra, Soweto and Davyton. Their pass rates went up by 25 per cent across the board, across over 100,000 school results. We tracked 12,000 students in a control group, and their marks dropped by 1 per cent over that same period of three years. We had incredible results, and students who had been addicted to alcohol and drugs started to go clean. Every week there would be stabbings in the schools, and in one of the schools, there had been eight suicides in two years. After we worked with these kids, teaching them to meditate, it all stopped. We had these incredibly beautiful results and it was the most magical and amazing time of my life, seeing this transformation through nothing other than teaching people how to be the change within.

We then started to find that of these 9,000 school children, many of them had come through school and would end up on the streets, with no money. The universities are expensive, so they're excluded from public higher education. They didn't really know how to start businesses and they weren't able to get any kind of reasonable job, and so these beautiful, amazing, fantastic young people would just end up walking the streets for six months or a year. They'd come back and see us and say, 'Could you offer us a job?' We'd say, 'But we got you through school, that's the magic ticket.' We quickly realised that it's not the magic ticket, it means very little. The Millennium Development Goals talk about universal basic education. It's important, but it's only a building block. We've got tens of millions of people who've got a high school leaving certificate, but so what? Across sub-Saharan Africa, they're unemployed.

We've got a political democracy, but we are very far from an economic democracy. There's an inter-generational poverty where the children of the poor stay poor. If you were the child of a wealthy person, you'd come out of school, your parents would send you off to any university, you'd get a great job, and you'd be set. But the child of a poor person cannot do that. They might have just as much ability, they certainly have just as many dreams and aspirations for their life, their families and their communities, but they have these obstacles in the way that they don't know how to get past. So we decided in 1999, after doing a little pilot project, a self-development project in Alexandra and Soweto townships, to try and create the first free university in sub-Saharan Africa.

Being the change

I think I kind of fell into it. A few years previously, I was about to emigrate, and then at the last minute I decided not to, because of the crises we were facing in the country. I thought, if we all run away from the country, what kind of a country will we have? So in 1995, I gave up being an actuary and earning R1.3 million a year, about £90,000, and joined CIDA. CIDA was teaching Transcendental Meditation in communities, and I really believed in what they were doing — helping people to find themselves and to manage stress and to use more of their potential — and I asked if I could join them. Once we started on this work, it just got so addictive. I think when you start to see that you can change the world, it impacts back on you again. It's like throwing pebbles in a pond, the ripples go out and then they come back again. You change yourself, you start to change other people, and the ripples come back to you to affirm that this is the most beautiful thing you've ever done. It gives you so much meaning in your life, and then you just want to do more, and do more and more and more. You end up spending your whole life thinking, 'What more can I do, how more can I change myself, change the lives of others, have more integrity, have more love, more power, more ability to do good?'

I've been enormously inspired by people like Gandhi and Maharishi, who brought out Transcendental Meditation, and Nelson Mandela, these great people in the world that show us that it is possible to overcome all odds and all obstacles, and that it is completely possible to create a better world. If you know that, how can you live a little life any more? You can't, it's just not possible. And I really believe that if you grow yourself, it's like you open up the box, there's no way you can push yourself back into a little box again. Life would be so cramped, and what more is there to do than to love, and to serve, and to find the meaning of it all? I could never go back any more, ever again, to being on a little treadmill, taking care of myself and my own selfish interests. There's no happiness in that. There's only happiness, I believe, in serving. So in a way, it's the most selfish thing you can ever do. You should have to pay to have this much growth and fun and love and dignity in your life.

Man was not born to suffer, we're just not using our potential. We're using only about 5 per cent of our innate human potential, psychologists tell us. I see it as a great calling to help people develop more of their potential, so we don't have to be 5 per cent mothers or fathers or sisters or brothers, husbands or wives or teachers and so on, but 10 per cent or 15 per cent or 20 per cent, whatever we could get to, to build a much more enlightened, loving, humane and creative society. I firmly believe that's there's a solution to every problem, it's just a question of awareness. However wide our awareness is, that's from where we can pluck the solutions. The broader our awareness, the broader our ability to find solutions to our intractable social and economic problems in the world. So I com-

There's only happiness, I believe, in serving.
So in a way, it's the most selfish thing you can do.

pletely believe that change has to begin within; education has to begin within. Instead of just being outside in, where you learn a whole lot of facts from outside of yourself, it should be inside out and as you change yourself from within, transform yourself, you will transform the world. There's no other way to change the world in a sustainable way. If we can make every tree in the forest green, then the whole forest will be green.

Nothing is more powerful than your own dreams. The only truth you can ever hold onto is that little voice inside. No one else can hear it, and it's so silent that if you're not very quiet, you will not hear it yourself. But that little voice is guiding you every step of the way, that absolutely true and straight compass, on what you should be doing. The vast majority of people are not doing what they really believe in, they're just trying to pay the bills and put their kids through school and things like that. I'm not saying it's easy, I'm not saying it's simple, but if you listen to what you know to be true, you will be protected. There's a wonderful quote about how the universe will support you. 'Jump, and the ground will rise up to meet you.' And life is so exquisite, so beautiful, so infinite, that to just give it away is like throwing away a diamond. So know who you are as a human being. You're one of a kind, no one else can do what you can do. You're a critical part of the jigsaw puzzle, so it's vital that you stand up and do whatever your duty is in life. Only you know inside what that duty is.

Inspiration

Nothing is fixed and anything is changeable. You can look at the most intractable problems that seem so completely unsolvable and you can solve them. Just drops of water can dissolve the hardest rock over time, and so it is possible for us to create a safe and prosperous, and healthy, wealthy, successful, happy world. Even if you can do it in the life of one person, it's worth it. You start to see, 'Gee, I did help that person, and their life has changed...' It inspires you. Every day I see our students coming back. They've come from nothing, and now they've built a house for their parents and brought them out of poverty and they're putting their brothers and sisters through school. They're happy and fulfilled and their eyes are shining, their lives have meaning and purpose, rather than being just empty and dull and self-hating. This is deeply inspiring, deeply inspiring. People inspire me, people who fight against the status quo and go for a better future. It's never easy, but you know what? You've got one life and so many years and you shouldn't waste it.

When I was at school, I always thought history was something that happened to us. But now I know that we can change history, we can change the future. Every one of us has the right, the God-given right, to change history in the direction of what we want it to be.

www.cida.co.za

www.cidafoundationuk.org

David Constantine

*It never really crossed my mind what happens to disabled
people in developing countries. I can't claim ever to have said,
'I think we need to go out and help the disabled people
of the developing world.'*

David Constantine co-founded Motivation in 1991, and as Chief Executive
of this organisation has gone on to improve the quality of life of many thousands of disabled people in dozens of developing countries. Motivation
provides mobility — through provision of appropriate wheelchairs and
prosthetic limbs; economic empowerment — through vocational training
and employment opportunities; advocacy of disabled people's rights; and
capacity-building in local organisations to meet local needs. A wheelchair
user himself, he has a great understanding of disabled people's needs, and
a strong desire to help those in developing countries whose needs are
underserved.

As a wheelchair user in the UK, I've been able to go to college, to get a job, to move around and take part in society. That wouldn't have happened here 40 years ago, and it doesn't happen in developing countries now. In developing countries, disabled people can't do any of that. Not only do they not get decent rehabilitation or medical input when they need it, they also have no mobility, because they can't get wheelchairs or prosthetic limbs. There are no services and no support. They are dependent on their families and stigmatised in society. It was only when I started travelling in Central America, eastern Europe and Asia that it struck me how privileged I'd been. Then you think, why? So we work towards improving these conditions.

There's a statistic that says there are 20 million people in the world who need a wheelchair and haven't got one, which is a figure I find hard to believe. The reality is it could be more than that. One in five of the world's poorest people are disabled, and then about 80 per cent of the population in developing countries live in rural areas, and only a very small percentage of them can travel to any sort of rehabilitation. So there's a huge need for better mobility and better services to back that up. When you have a mobility disability, if you haven't got some simple basics, like a device to help you — a wheelchair or a prosthetic limb — and the back-up, then you're pretty stuck. That's what we're trying to change.

Beginnings

Our first programme was in 1991. There were three of us, myself, Simon Gue and Richard Frost. I met Richard when we were both studying for a degree at Oxford Brookes University, and several years later I did a Masters in computer-related design at the Royal College of Art, and that's where I met Simon. On the course, there was a design competition that everybody had to enter. Lord Snowdon had set the brief — to design a wheelchair for developing countries. Simon and I teamed up. I had experience of using a wheelchair and he had experience of travelling around Asia and Africa, so we put our heads together, we came up with a design and we won. There was some prize money and the college encouraged us not to let it drop, so we took them at their word, and asked if we could go off and research it in India and Bangladesh over the Christmas period. They said yes.

In Bangladesh, we visited a centre called the Centre for the Rehabilitation of the Paralysed, which was founded and run by an English physiotherapist . She

Once you've got someone mobile and you've got them supported by a local organisation — then what? If they don't work, they won't have a very good quality of life.

asked us if we'd come back and build wheelchairs for them when we finished college, and we said, 'Yes, why not?' We finished college in 1990 and then raised the money in the States to go off to Bangladesh for six months to build wheelchairs. I came back to the UK briefly in the middle of it, and when I got home to my flat, there were two messages. One was asking us to go and work in Poland, and the other to go and work in Cambodia. That was the next two years' work, and we've never looked back.

We've never had to look for work since — it's all word of mouth. We've built up a series of networks and connections with individuals and other NGOs, and it's just built up and up and up over the years. We started by doing one programme at a time, and we'd all go off to that country and come back, and then we'd go off and come back again. After three years, we realised we needed to set up a UK base, rather than operating out of my flat. So we took an office in a grotty old building in London, hired an administrator, and I stayed back in the UK a bit more to start it off and build a fundraising base. That was in 1993, and it was the first year that we took on two programmes. Richard ran one in Romania and Simon ran the other in Cambodia. We started building up staff, taking on people to work on the projects, some of whom are still with us. And then it built up from there.

In those days, the programmes tended to consist of going to work with a local partner in a developing country, setting up or refurbishing a small wheelchair workshop, designing a low-cost wheelchair that could be made locally there, training local staff how to do that, and putting in place the services — the assessment, prescription and follow-up. We don't just go and make the technology, we teach people how to do assessments and fittings properly. We spent seven or eight years doing that, and building up a lot of programme experience.

In the meantime we'd been asked a lot to go to Africa, and we hadn't done it at all. We'd worked in Central America, eastern Europe and Asia and we'd done different things, such as programmes for people with spinal injuries, for people who are amputees in Cambodia, and supported seating projects. In Africa, we felt that we needed a longer-term vision, so we set up a one-year wheelchair technology training course and an orthopaedic training school, using all the knowledge we'd built up over seven or eight years, and they're still running. The school is the only place in the world that you can get a qualification in wheelchair technology that's accredited by the International Society of Prosthetics and Orthotics. The students come from small workshops all over Africa and we then support them when they leave. So we changed the style of the programme slightly — rather than us going to workshop after workshop all over Africa, which would have taken us the next 40 years, this is another way of doing it.

Each project is always slightly different from the last — different design, different partner, different user group — and then over the last five or six years, because we've built up this core skill of design and training, we've been requested by other NGOs to go and work for them. For example, we're training staff from the International Committee of the Red Cross physical rehabilitation department, so 80 of their worldwide staff are coming to trainings that we've prepared especially for them.

We've got various programmes running throughout Asia, supported by our team in Sri Lanka, and then all the Africa work is supported by our team in South Africa. The programme office here in the UK is for finance, some technical work, administration, fundraising and programme management. This is the HQ here, but all the real work goes on overseas.

Development

After we got to ten years old, we looked at the way we'd been working and what we'd achieved. It's never really been about numbers. The workshops we set up tend to make about 300 wheelchairs a year. It's more to do with the quality of the service and the programme you put together, and its sustainability. If you made loads in one year and then they break down two years later, what good have you done? It needs to be a sustainable service that the local partner can run.

We were taking on more work and bigger projects, which meant a much bigger staff and more funding to find. The most expensive component was setting

We've had our struggles, but generally, whenever it's been bad, something good has come out of it.

---

up the workshop, doing the design and then production. We could do that standing on our head by then. And we had all these different designs and all these different ideas, which we knew worked. So we took the best of everything we'd done, and realised we could actually put these very sustainable technical solutions into a range of wheelchairs — no one wheelchair is going to be the answer — and produce them cheaper at a consistent quality, en masse in China, and then set up a training so we can hand the knowledge to the staff in the local organisations.

This became a flat-pack wheelchair range, called Worldmade, based around the knowledge and designs that we've done all around the world. It's still low-tech, still repairable in developing countries, and designed in such a way that it can be used on rough ground, on the different sorts of terrain that we've learned about over the last 15 years. It means that organisations that want to deliver wheelchairs but don't want to produce them have that option now. We also insist that they have the training to go with it for basic wheelchair services and fitting. We've become quite well known for our training and our wheeled mobility work, both in supportive seating and various different types of wheelchair.

Key issues

We deal with four key issues. One is products and services — we link those two very strongly together to teach other organisations that you can't do one without the other. There are lots of organisations that hand out wheelchairs or equipment and think that's it, and they can walk away from it. Well, that's not the case. It's essential to have the service — that's the assessment, the fitting, the prescription, making sure it works for the user, and the follow-up. Then there's the rights aspect, which means working with disabled people's organisations to help them become stronger — we show them how to run themselves better, how to govern themselves, and how to raise money themselves so they don't need to keep coming to us.

And then there's economic empowerment, which is a range of different things like income generation activities for disabled people's organisations, for individuals, and vocational training to get into mainstream employment. We team up with different companies too. One example is in Sri Lanka. We've got a small centre which trains disabled women how to sew to commercial standards. M&S have a scheme called Marks and Start, and they're strongly supporting the programme. They've put their weight onto their trading partners and said they should be employing disabled people. So these women go into very good jobs, and it's a very simple programme that has a major effect on their lives. We visited the M&S factory in Sri Lanka last year, and we had tea with nine of the women who'd got jobs there. One of them said, 'This has completely changed my life.' For a disabled woman to get a job in a developing country is pretty rare really. She said, 'I'm the now the major breadwinner in my family. I make decisions now.'

Once you've got someone mobile, and you've got them supported by a local organisation because you've built that up and made it stronger — then what? If they don't work, they won't have a very good quality of life, and will be reliant on their family. So in a developing country where there is no support and back-up, it's really important that they've got some sort of income. So those are the four areas — mobility, your ability to do things, knowing about support and your rights as a disabled person, and having the economic empowerment to improve quality of life. That's really what we are about.

It's really important to make chairs that are suitable for people's local environment. For example, if a chair's for a rural area, with rough terrain, we'd make it with three wheels, so with a wheel sticking out at the front. My own wheelchair is made of aluminium, but in a developing country you'd only make a wheelchair of steel, because aluminium is much harder to weld. If a frame does break, the likelihood is you wouldn't be able to find someone to weld aluminium because you need the right equipment or the skill — it's not easy — whereas with steel you can easily find someone to fix it.

We also make chairs propelled by a pedalling system like you have on a bike, but using your hands in front of you. It's really good for longer distances, because it's actually hard work to push a chair, and it's not very good for your shoulders either, in the long term. Also, in countries where you either pay extra for your

The surfing, the photography, and the sense of the world, made me want to go away a lot. Suddenly I was faced with not doing that any more.

---

wheelchair on public transport or it's just a bunfight to get on, then the hand cycle gives you the option of going from A to B much more easily. This model has a shelf on it, which means that you can carry a lot more and you can go to a market and set yourself up as a stall of some kind, so all sorts of possibilities can begin to open up.

Luck

Throughout Motivation's history we've had lots of little bits of incredibly good luck, like meeting people at the right time. I only applied to one college, not quite realising I was applying to the best in the world, and I nearly fell over when I got a place. I really didn't think I would get one and I did, and it was there that a million doors opened. At the Royal College of Art, you are opened to a million choices, to amazing things that all connect up. I did computer-related industrial design. But you could get involved in a bit of fashion or a bit of textiles and a bit of film and all sorts of things and they would all fit together in some way or other. It was brilliant, very inspiring. And then there was this competition, for the Frye Memorial Award. It came to the college every year with a different brief, and usually it was for the greater good of society, something that would help people, rather than just another jug kettle or something like that. And the year that I happened to do it was the year they chose a wheelchair.

We've had our struggles as well, but generally, looking back over the years, whenever it's been bad, something good has come out of it. The biggest challenge is funding. Funding, funding, funding. Large funders and large donors think that they can delay things by four or five months, and that a small NGO like us can survive. We can't. If we had a decent amount of money, we would be able to achieve so much more. Not that much money, just enough to stop struggling all the time. The funding comes, with difficulty, from all sorts of different sources —

USAID, the EC, DFID, trusts, foundations, companies, individuals. We sell Christmas cards and greetings cards; we talk at schools and rotary clubs. You name it, we'll try it. So it's anything from a big programme grant for several years, to a fiver that Mrs Smith sends in.

You realise it's all worth it when you know it's making a difference. There are lots of little stories, like Porimol, a young boy in Bangladesh. He's got severe cerebral palsy. He couldn't speak, but being seated properly with the seating system that we designed, he was able to sit up properly. We heard recently that he'd started to talk, and that's partly due to him being able to interact with life and with people, thanks to the postural support the chair gives him. Otherwise he'd just be laid on the floor in his parents' hut or on the bed.

Circumstance

I didn't really decide to do it, it sort of decided itself. I don't think about it very much now, 16 years later. But on quite a few occasions over the years, I suddenly think, 'This is what I was supposed to do.' And although, yes, we decided to do it, it was never a grand plan of mine, or Richard's or Simon's. It fell in our laps through various circumstances and decisions we'd all made to get to that point. I didn't have an injury in 1982 and then suddenly say, 'Right, what can I do with this that's going to be really good?' Not at all. And although I had travelled a bit, it never really crossed my mind what happens to disabled people in developing countries. So it wasn't like I had an epiphany. I can't claim ever to have said, 'I think we need to go out and help the disabled people of the developing world.' It had never crossed my mind before we started. It was a series of circumstances that channelled me and the others into this point where we had this thing sitting in front of us, saying, 'Are you going to take it or are you going to leave it?' And we took it.

My family emigrated to Australia when I was 11 and came back when I was 13, much to my dismay. Also, I'd been to South Africa and seen apartheid and no one else had really done that. It gave me a sense of the world, and I always felt a bit different at school after that. I suppose that prepared me for feeling a bit different after I had my accident. Having a sense of the world made me want to travel more. I'm very interested in photography, travel photography particularly, and so

*I wouldn't call us your typical charity-type guys by any means.
We're not do-gooders.*

that drove me, partly because I was not supposed to travel any more, in theory. And I'd been a surfer before I had my accident. So the surfing, the photography, and the sense of the world, led me to want to go away a lot, and suddenly I was faced with not doing that any more.

So when this opportunity first came up, it seemed like a perfect thing to be doing. The three of us all wanted to travel and see the world, but doing something constructive was important, rather than just being a tourist. So we had a similar sort of drive, we had some basic core values. But I wouldn't call us your typical charity type guys by any means. We're not do-gooders; we just had a sense of wanting to do it differently, to do it properly. And to be given the opportunity to go away to India, when everyone said, 'Oh, you can't go to India in a wheelchair,' was very exciting. I do travel a lot. Last year I did ten trips, and this year I've been to Sri Lanka, Cambodia and Ethiopia.

Accident

I had a diving injury in 1982, in Queensland, Australia, on Fraser Island. I dived into a shallow pool of water in an exuberant moment of stupidity. The result is I'm paralysed from the shoulders down, C4-5 level. I've got no grip in my hands, and no use of my legs or trunk, so I need an assistant to help me day-to-day. But I live independently in the community, run my own care system, and work full-time.

Like many things in life you get to a fork in the road. You have, say, an injury or a disability or a marriage break-up or whatever it is. You're going along quite happily and suddenly something happens. You either take the road which takes you downhill, and you just sit around doing nothing and it slowly spirals down into more and more depression — you're not doing anything so you don't feel you can, so you don't, so you feel you can't, and so on. Or you go the other road. You either take it on or it takes you down. I have a very low boredom threshold, so lying in bed and sitting around the house is not an option.

Being the change

You don't need to be thinking big things particularly; you can do plenty of little things just in your own life to make change for the better. Simple little things like turning off lights or saving your compost or whatever it might be, being nice to people. It can be really small things or it can be lots of small things that build into a bigger thing. I've just been very lucky to have the circumstances to do that. So everybody says, 'Oh, it's amazing, what you're doing', but you know, I'm just doing a job I love. And I know for a fact that I can't do something I don't really, really love. I've been there and I just can't. It takes a disabled person a lot more physical and mental effort to get up in the morning than most people — not that I fight that ever — but it means that I need to do something that I really believe in.

www.motivation.org.uk

James Dakin

It's not rocket science. Happy, inspired teachers have happier pupils who are far more engaged and remember a lot more information.

James Dakin hit on and developed a concept that is now transforming learning for primary school pupils and their teachers. Through the specialised application of storytelling as a teaching tool, children are having more fun in class, performing better across the board, and gaining in confidence and self-esteem. Meanwhile, teachers find their love for their work is renewed through the capacity to be flexible and creative. Dakin calls his approach Teaching Freedom, and set up a non-profit company of the same name in 2004 to spread the message. Forty primary schools in Leeds are now using this methodology, and there are plans to expand elsewhere in the UK and beyond.

Teaching Freedom works with respect and inspiration as crucial educational tools. We reconnect teachers with their passion for their vocation, through the powerful medium of stories. The teachers inspire themselves in the delivery, and the children respond because they're fully engaged.

I didn't start out to create Teaching Freedom. It happened after I was commissioned to run some stress management and personal development courses for teachers in Leeds. One of the head teachers called me up to say that a member of her staff had taken the techniques into the classroom and was generating highly significant results, and that I should go and have a look.

So I did, and I witnessed a 37-year-old male teacher with a broad Geordie accent using visualisations and storytelling with a fairly difficult class of boys. He was captivating these children's imaginations through stories. Something very profound was happening. I showed another teacher at the school the same methods, and within three months, both of their classes had completely outperformed the ones on either side of them. From there, Teaching Freedom was born. I went to the Chief Executive of Education Leeds and said, 'Will you part-fund this project to run a pilot?' On the third request, he said yes.

So Teaching Freedom happened. It's something I tried to give away three times. On each occasion it came back to me with a resounding clang. I saw its potential being so great that it frightened me, so I tried to give it to the local authority, and I wrote to the government twice. Nobody took me up on it, so it stayed with me. Then I decided that actually this was something that really appealed to me.

It goes back to when I was a child myself. My father wasn't around very much, and when he was, he wasn't the most caring, sharing kind of person. I felt a need to be valued and loved by him, and it never came. I think that's given me a desire to help other people feel good about themselves; to have other people feel validated for who they are; to give children the ability to be themselves in their uniqueness, in their individuality, and to help them realise that that's absolutely OK. In fact, it's not just OK, it's essential. Teaching Freedom does all of that, for children and for their teachers as well.

For something to be memorable, it has to stand out —
it needs to be engaging, it needs to make
an impact and it needs to be relevant.

Creative visualisations

The cornerstone of our approach is creative visualisations, which are like guided meditations. The teacher carefully combines all the key learning points of a lesson into a story, and then takes the children on an adventure, so each child learns the information by playing the lead role in their own story. If we wanted to teach the children about rocks and soil, one of the most effective ways of doing that would be to take them down a mine, so they could physically see, feel, touch and smell what it is like to go underground and witness the rocks and soil and the different strata in person. We can't actually do that in real life, but we can if we go inside the mind. If we say to children, 'Close your eyes and imagine…,' all of a sudden we have the entire world open to us, to discover and to explore.

These visualisations allow teachers to become much more creative again. So many people go into primary education because they're naturally creative and have a flair for stories, for being responsive and spontaneous. With the national curriculum, with all the measuring and testing, this gets crushed out of them and they lose a lot of their flair and creativity. But through creating the visualisations and telling the stories, they do get to express their creativity, and the majority of teachers also tell us that when they're running the visualisations, they themselves are having a lot more fun, and as a direct result, the children are far more engaged. It's not rocket science. Happy, inspired teachers will invariably have happier pupils who are far more engaged and will remember a lot more information. These are the two things which for me drive everything. So many teachers fall out of love with their work. Teaching Freedom represents a wonderful opportunity for them to be creative again, while still hitting all of their targets.

The visualisations deliver a number of impacts, one of which is obviously academic. The academic improvements that we've witnessed, which have been considerable and consistent across all subjects, are a by-product for me of the teachers and the children having a better relationship, and having more fun together.

Bringing learning to life

For something to be memorable, it has to stand out — it needs to be engaging, it needs to make an impact and it needs to be relevant — and yet so much of the curriculum simply doesn't appear to be relevant to the children. So we create experiences in which children are able to learn by becoming personally involved in the subject.

If I want to teach you about paella, the most effective way I can do that is to take you Spain, introduce you to a chef who's passionate about it, get you to touch and taste all of the ingredients, see it, hear it and smell it being made, with the chef describing it to you in wonderful detail and with infectious enthusiasm, and then letting you taste it at the end. You have seen it, tasted it, touched it, smelled it and felt the whole experience. It's whole-body experiential learning. You now have many ways to anchor the experience and remember it. This is the real crux: it's bringing the learning to life. Young children have got the most fantastic imaginations, and we work with them rather than force them to come out of that magical realm and conform to learning.

In this way, more children retain more facts for longer through a visualisation than through more traditional methods, across the board from the most able to the least able. Teachers regularly tell us this. So it works with children of all learning styles and abilities, and also across a range of subjects. Literacy is the most popular, but over the last couple of years, we've seen a big increase in the number of teachers using them for science, history, geography and religious education, and also in some cases for IT, and design and technology.

With Teaching Freedom, the children come back from the experience with a lot of information and an excitement to write. So first the quantity of their writing improves, and then, consistently, teachers report that the quality of writing and the vocabulary gets significantly better too. We train the teachers to use visual, audio, kinaesthetic, olfactory and gustatory vocabulary, so that when they are creating a story, they are actively making sure that the children can see, hear, touch, smell, and taste experiences along the way, so they are engaged on all sensory levels. After a visualisation, many children are absolutely bursting to talk about and to write down what they've been doing, so the teachers can spend less

You have seen it, tasted it, touched it, smelled it and felt the whole experience. It's whole-body experiential learning.

---

time just persuading them to write, and more time helping them improve the standard of their writing.

Also, speaking and listening skills are significantly enhanced through this process, as it creates a lot more discussion, often of greater depth and breadth than usual. For example, in their imaginations, the children have experienced being bullied, or witnessed someone else being bullied, but without being told what to feel. In the discussion afterwards, the children have come out with their own views and comments, and teachers have regularly been surprised by their sheer depth. Or perhaps they've been learning about deforestation and captivity by pretending to being a gorilla in the jungle, and having the forest cut down around them, and being caught and being put in a zoo. Without being told it's right or wrong, the experiences are offered to the children, and they then make up their own minds whether they like this or not, and they discuss it afterwards.

Social benefits

So we know that the creative visualisations impart facts very well; they also help to develop social skills. The teacher can put the children in places where they have to learn manners, where they have to show respect to adults. They're opening doors for people, they're getting off chairs so that a pregnant lady can have a seat, and they're picking up litter. We have a large social context. Once a year in schools, they will celebrate the Chinese New Year — it's part of the syllabus. But in this case, rather than just talk about it and see pictures of it, with a visualisation they are able to travel, via their imagination, to China, to celebrate the Chinese New Year in person. When teachers do this, they introduce the children to a Chinese girl or boy of the same age, who will be a guide to show them everything that's going on. So during the experience, the children are not only learning the facts in the curriculum, but they are also getting a feel for what it's like to be there, to hear the firecrackers going off, to see the Chinese people celebrating, to go home with their new friend and have grandma cook them some dumplings, which they eat with chopsticks. Then they have fortune cookies. It gives the children a sense of another culture.

Unlike some traditional writing exercises or numeric exercises, where children with learning difficulties may not be able to join in, with these visualisations all the children are involved at the beginning of the class. It generates a sense of coming together, a sense of enjoyment and shared experience. We encourage teachers to get the children talking about the key learning points immediately after the visualisation. Then every child gets a sense of achievement and inclusion, of being able to contribute to the class as a whole. They're all equal, regardless of academic ability, all able to have their own experiences of what's happening, and to share them with the class. So not only do they all join in together, but they all know that at no stage are they going to be told that they're wrong.

A sense of value

Even children with low self-esteem, even the most frightened and fearful ones, who don't usually tend to join in very much, learn that what they have to say is right. Because it's theirs, it can't be wrong, which helps them develop a greater belief in themselves. They're feeling welcome, they're feeling accepted for who they are, and they're allowed to have fun with their learning, so they engage a lot more and contribute more in the lesson afterwards, either by discussion or through the work set by the teacher. So they get more positive feedback, which helps them feel better about themselves and this reinforces the positive behaviour and their desire to learn.

By giving them an opportunity to experience being valued, accepted and appreciated, I feel we are playing a significant part in sowing the seeds of confidence in these youngsters at critical early ages of six or seven, when they're still quite open and their characters are still forming. We're really helping to give them a sense of being accepted, a sense of play and freedom within the classroom, and allowing them to express themselves openly and creatively.

They learn to value themselves, and they learn to value others as well. As a result of seeing other cultures through the visualisations, discussions begin about the differences and similarities between the one they've just visited, such as China, and our own. This enables children to develop a greater understanding of themselves and their community, a greater sense of their own culture, of their

The real passion that motivates me is when I see teachers come alive with what Teaching Freedom's about, and I see the joy in the children's faces.

own place within it, how they behave, how they perceive things… So one of my hopes is that the children who are experiencing Teaching Freedom will grow up valuing diversity, and with a greater sense of community and acceptance of others.

Our system really reaches out to everyone, even the so-called 'difficult' ones, but children who are labelled like that often aren't difficult at all. They are bored, fed up, disenfranchised, disinterested in what they're learning about, or they're not being challenged. The moment you can engage them, a lot of the disruption will disappear. Children don't try and stop having fun. Other children are disruptive simply because they need attention, and the creative visualisation is another medium through which they can get positive attention, because they can join in a lot more.

So really, Teaching Freedom has a great deal of potential, and is indeed already working very well for the teachers we've trained. Over the last four years we've trained 266 teachers in Leeds, so in that time approximately 10,000 children have been taught using our methods. In September, at the start of each school year, a teacher will assess their new class to see where they are academically, and then make a prediction on what they believe each child will achieve by the end of the year; they monitor them through the year. Then we ask the teachers how many of their children have surpassed their expected grades, or overachieved, at the end of the year, and we've discovered that it depends on how often the teachers use our approach — the more often, the better.

The results that they've given us show that when creative visualisations have been used at least once a week, 54 per cent of children have surpassed their expected grades in writing, 60 per cent in reading and 44 per cent in numeracy. Teachers tell us that they would expect between 10-20 per cent of their class to overachieve in any given year. That wouldn't be surprising. Once you start getting up to 20 and 30 per cent, that's unusual, so to be reaching over 50 per cent is really quite remarkable, and these figures are consistent over the four years.

Learning freedom

The training courses are highly experiential and they have two distinct themes to them. One is the practical application of developing and running creative visualisations, and becoming more aware of how the vocabulary we use engages children. The other part builds up self-confidence. So many teachers in primary school education are so fearful of doing something different that we have to work with them to develop their confidence levels, so they feel able to engage in something which is brand new for them, or which is going to stretch them. The courses are very respectful of those attending, and yet they are all challenged to be willing to discover more of their own potential. Every person on the course has the opportunity to be stretched and to grow.

The learning that I've had through this process has been so intrinsically linked with the development of the project that actually they are the same thing. It's been instrumental in helping me to grow and develop in my own way; it's challenged me on so many levels, including my own belief in what I'm worth and able to achieve. 'Am I worth going out there and being taken seriously by leaders in education?' I'm not a qualified teacher, so it really challenged me to ask, 'Could I offer experienced head teachers something which would make a fundamental difference?' I discovered that I could.

Then when Teaching Freedom began to evolve, the challenge was, 'Will teachers and head teachers take me seriously?' And they all did. So again, my belief grew. Then it was a question of 'Well, how do I fund this? Am I worth people giving money to me? Is the project worth giving money to?' Again my belief in myself and what I was doing was called into question, as I was forced to go out and ask for and to justify the money. So I learned how to speak to fund-holders, not from a place of fear and need, which is where I started, but from a place of being inspired by what I'm doing. That is an ongoing lesson, and a truly staggering leap. Over the past four years I have raised £251,000 to cover all of the costs associated with running the project for this length of time, through corporate loans, personal loans and donations.

If I'm coming from the heart,
with clear intention, people respond.

One of the fascinating journeys about Teaching Freedom for me has been the fact that throughout the whole process I have been, financially, completely insecure. At no stage have I been in any comfort zone in terms of having money behind me. And so that has been one very real motivator, to actually generate an income. But the real passion that motivates me is when I go into classrooms and I see teachers come alive with what I've taught them, with what Teaching Freedom's about, and I see the joy in the children's faces. The teachers give me stories of children whose behaviour was appalling suddenly behaving very well; children who didn't write anything suddenly writing pages; children who misbehaved a lot now working through the break voluntarily because they're so on task. It thrills me when I see teachers in their 50s, who've been in teaching for 30 years, who've got bored of creating lessons, suddenly becoming inspired again and excited and laughing and joking and being spontaneous and creative.

It's an immensely humbling feeling. It's awe-inspiring, it's amazing; to me it's what living's all about. To witness that degree of change and to see people taking it seriously is a truly remarkable experience. It's exhausting, stressful, trying, challenging — all of those things rolled into one, with some very tough times and some times of immense joy. It's a rollercoaster.

Being the change

It is being the change. And with the greatest will in the world, I had no idea that I would be called upon to be the change in this respect. I'd always wanted to make a big impact, but at no stage had I thought it would be through schools. I wanted to make a difference and an opportunity presented itself to me. Everything that I've been doing with this project has required me to walk my talk, and that's what's made the difference, along with an absolute determination to see this through to the end. And intuition — a lot of this was based on blind faith and a belief that there was a calling for me, which didn't have a business plan, didn't have a business model; it just said: 'You can do this. Do this.' And so I did it.

Where to now? Well, in the 2007-08 academic year, Birmingham County Council has agreed to run a pilot with a small number of teachers from a cluster of their schools. And in 2008-09, Manchester County Council is also looking to run a similar project using whole-school involvement. They will be prepared for it this year. My number one drive is to make Teaching Freedom viable and available to every single primary school and every parent within the UK. Beyond that, my vision for Teaching Freedom is truly global. The techniques are simple and profound, and they translate into any culture that embraces the ancient art of storytelling — they transcend all boundaries and create enormous opportunities, especially for third world cultures where technical resources are limited or non-existent.

And what have I learned? It's basically that I am a lot less important than I always thought I was! The most powerful thing this process has got me to do is to walk my talk with authenticity and integrity. I've discovered that I no longer want fame and fortune. When I'm absolutely on mission, that's when I'm at peace with myself, and that's when I feel my greatest joy.

www.teachingfreedom.com

Paul Dickinson

*I had become convinced that climate change was something
I was going to be condemned or blessed
to work on for the rest of my life.*

Paul Dickinson left a well-paid job in design in order to investigate climate
change. When he understood the gravity of the problem, he decided to
dedicate the rest of his life to averting climate catastrophe. Recognising
the significant contribution of corporate activity and greenhouse gas emissions, he created the Carbon Disclosure Project, an unprecedented coalition of institutional investors worth trillions of dollars. Together, they
demand that the world's largest companies declare their emissions and
their responses to climate change. These findings are then made freely
available to the public online.

I for one am certainly not very worried about small amounts of gradual climate change. Humans are inherently adaptable and if the climate changes a little bit, it gets a bit warmer here and there or whatever, it probably wouldn't be the end of the world. But what extensive study of the science will tell anyone is that the earth's system is not linear and we do not face the risk of some mild discomfort from gradual temperature change but a very real risk of abrupt climate change. The history of the earth's system shows that there have been changes of 10 or more degrees centigrade, changes that can occur perhaps even in a single decade. That might be the result of some kind of terrible volcanic eruption, or a meteorite, or a tipping point. For example, the Amazon may begin a die-back, or a thaw of permafrost in Siberia may lead to great releases of methane.

I think we have to fight for the next generation right now and I do see the climate change challenge very much in terms of a war. Roosevelt asked Churchill in 1944 what to call the war. It was simply referred to as 'the war' at that time, it wasn't called the Second World War and they were scouting around for names. Churchill said, 'The entirely avoidable war. There never was a war more easy to avoid than that which had laid waste of what was left of the world after the previous conflict.' That's the crux of this. Not only is climate change threatening the lives of millions and, God forbid, billions of people, but it's a problem that is in fact in organisational terms relatively easy to solve. It follows from this that the change that we need to see involves two fairly simple concepts: a very large-scale reduction in the production of greenhouse gases, and an end to deforestation. In combination, those two actions may be sufficient to withdraw for the foreseeable future the risk of abrupt climate change.

Beginnings

In the year 2000, I had become convinced that climate change was something I was going to be condemned or blessed, depending on which way you look at it, to work on for the rest of my life. I was trying to make contact with people who had power and influence who I could work with. I had to this end made contact with Tessa Tennant, who was the founder of the environmental investment movement in Europe in 1988. She and I were talking in the summer of 2000 and we took a view that you could get a hundred people in a room who could stop climate change, and those hundred people would be the heads of the hundred largest fund management institutions. Those hundred institutions collectively control more than 60 per cent of the shares of the all world's companies, and therefore they could instruct those companies to do pretty much whatever they wanted. That's the big idea behind the Carbon Disclosure Project in a sense — to utilise the power of institutional shareholders.

We advanced and tested our ideas and finally settled upon the fact that in the first instance, the most that institutional investors could do collectively would be to ask for information on greenhouse gases from corporations. We then set about a process with my colleague Paul Simpson. Paul and I and Tessa really led this until Tessa moved on and now Paul and I are at the centre of the efforts. We wanted to get a lot of large investors to sign a request for information, for disclosure of greenhouse gas emissions from the 500 largest companies in the world. We spent two years developing a set of questions that was fit for purpose and a covering letter; in fact a whole series of documentation, all of which we had to agree many months in advance of it being used. We then managed to persuade a group of 18 investors, not to sign it, but we promised not to change a word of it and we said, 'Can we tell other investors that you are intending to sign it?' And they said, 'You can say that.' So, 18 investors put their necks out a little way.

We then sent out our documentation to 100 investors saying, 'We're not going to change one word of this. You've met us, we're reasonable people. Will you put your name to it?' And strangely and wonderfully, a number of them did. The very first signatory was Legal and General Group who are an enormous asset manager. They very kindly and intelligently in my view took the view that this was a good thing, that data feeds efficient markets, and others joined us including Allianz, Credit Suisse and UBS. With these giants we went out on 31st May 2002, we wrote our letter to the chair of the board of the 500 largest companies on earth. We got that delivered by UPS with a signature. It cost us £5,000 just for delivery. So, we sent out this letter, 45 per cent of the companies answered our questions, and we launched the responses.

Capital growth

On 31st May 2002 we represented $4.5 trillion of assets, which we thought was rather a lot, a few years of UK GDP. But there was more to come! We spoke to the signatory investors and said we'd like to carry on doing this, and they said, 'That's a good idea.' So we then sent another information request and this was backed by 100 investors with $10 trillion. And we then sent another information request a year later. We'd now moved onto an annual cycle. This time we represented 155 million investors with $20 trillion. The response rate was going up to 71 per cent answering the questions. What this means is that 71 per cent of the world's largest companies send an answer to our website, and not only is this available to all the investors, but it's also available to the public, so anyone can see what these corporations emit. Today, if you want to see what McDonald's or Coca-Cola or Disney or Ford or BMW or IBM or Shell or Exxon — anyone — if you want to know what they emit, just go to our website, you can download and you can see it free of charge. In fact I was told that someone from Swiss Re Insurance once said at a conference, 'In any future litigation on climate change, Exhibit A will be the letter sent by the Carbon Disclosure Project, 31st May 2002, because how can a corporation say they didn't know about climate change when so many shareholders were getting together to talk to them about it?' There's an Italian phrase that says, 'It takes the union to make the force.'

In 2006, we did something rather unprecedented: we expanded. So instead of writing to just the 500 largest companies in the world, although we carried on doing that, we expanded in Canada, the United States, Brazil, France, Germany and Japan, Australia and New Zealand, and also with electric utilities, in partnership with various other organisations. That was a big success and we then represented 200 investors, with $30 trillion. And then good things happened. We launched all over the world, bigger than ever, this time representing 280 investors with assets of about $40 trillion.

Accountability

We felt a degree of frustration that we had put together an absolutely unprecedented coalition of investors, we'd done something that no one had ever done before, and we had got half of the world's largest companies to report on their greenhouse gas emissions in a public and transparent way, and then people would say, 'So what? What really happened? It's just greenwash.' Our view is that corporations are formally, legally accountable to their shareholders. There is a different character to a unified request from a large group of shareholders to a large group of companies, where they're all compared to the same set of ques-

I think we have to fight for the next generation right now, and I do see the climate change challenge very much in terms of a war.

tions in a single process — that is hard to greenwash. Corporate CSR reports are somewhere where the corporation can set its own agenda and talk in its own voice about the things it wants to talk about. We don't permit that. We ask the same questions of everybody and we expect answers. Hermes, the UK's largest pension fund suggested that they might vote against the adoption of the annual report and may even vote against the re-election of directors to companies that don't respond to the Carbon Disclosure Project. Let's be in no doubt, sometimes journalists ask, 'First of all, how do you know they're telling the truth?' And we say they wouldn't want to lie to their shareholders, especially to so many large shareholders because that would be in breach of various securities laws. And then people say, 'Well, why do they answer to CDP?' And we say if they're not answerable to their shareholders, who are they answerable to? There has to be some kind of accountability for performance.

Having said that, it is not the habit of major multinational corporations to put on their websites, 'We were bad and then some people wrote to us and so we changed and now we're good.' So such successes that the Carbon Disclosure Project has had are very frequently unsung. But I was with a large US investment bank recently and a senior member of staff told me that the CDP had an enormous impact on what they do and they'd now inspirated climate change into all of their main business streams, including mergers and acquisitions, asset management and research. We have very large amounts of evidence to suggest that when corporations are called upon to account for their behaviour in a public and transparent environment, if you will in an enormous fishbowl, they then start to compete with one another about who can do best. Marks & Spencer, Tesco and Sainsbury's all launched green initiatives in the same week. So although a lot of people haven't heard of the Carbon Disclosure Project and although we can't every day present some kind of accounting for the impact that we have, we are reasonably confident of the effect of our work. We draw attention to the critical question: which companies are part of the solution and which companies are part of the problem?

Corporations can save the world

If I wasn't doing this I would probably be focusing more on waking up the great information and communication technology sectors to how significant they are in the solution rather than the problem. I got to spend a morning at Davos, this extraordinary World Economic Forum thing where all the world's most powerful people seem to go. And there in the corridor was Arun Sarin, the chief executive of Vodaphone. I said to him, 'Mr Sarin, do you know that your company produces 200 times the profit per ton of carbon dioxide in comparison to British Airways? Surely any right-thinking government would not just tax air fuel but would remove all taxation from mobile telephones and telephone operators?' I don't know if he took any notice of what I said but I stand by the comments.

And more broadly within the context of climate change, I would without doubt be particularly interested in seeing if we can dematerialise our economy through an expansion of the infinite resource of microelectronics, software and content, which in a very real sense is art, culture and other people, as an alternative to shipping all sorts of physical things around the world. Keynes put it better than I ever could when he said, 'It's better to export recipes than cakes.' And somebody else said, 'Sell carbon and buy silicon.' I certainly think there's another world possible.

I wrote a book called *Beautiful Corporations*. I certainly think that they can do beautiful things. They are the organising entities within society for the foreseeable future and therefore they are capable perhaps of being the change required to get us off a suicidal course of action. So I am hopeful that they will serve the interests of their customers, which is what marketing means, and yes, they will save us.

Progress

So where are we today? We have somewhere between a quarter and a half of human emissions reported to our website from company operations, product use and disposal. We have a globally recognised system whereby shareholders are holding corporations accountable for their impact on the problem of climate change and we are also now to some small degree funded by four of the world's governments, including the US federal government. It's an exciting time for CDP.

It is possible to organise and manage a global system for dialogue between institutional shareholders and corporations, in a process which is safe and trans-

We wrote our letter to the chair of the board of the 500 largest companies on earth… It cost us £5,000 just for delivery.

parent for all parties and independent. We've established that. We are excited about the level of recognition that our organisation has obtained, the level of trust and support we've received from very many different authorities, and the willingness of all sorts of different stakeholders and participants in our work to consider this change of gear. It is universally accepted pretty much that emissions are completely out of control, and nothing's being done about them and we are losing this war. And so what we are interested in doing is helping to develop, with others — because we're a tiny organisation of eight people — the case, the academic, economic, legal and fiduciary investor case for increased action to protect citizens from the risk of climate change. The big idea can be encapsulated in a joke I'm fond of making. It's not very funny but it's not meant to be serious either. 'Destruction of the world through unmitigated climate change is against the regulations.' We live under this enormous burden of law, thousands of regulations. It is not in my view possible to blow up the world and comply with those laws.

Research

Now I have to confess to the hand of fate, in as much as an aunt of mine died and quite unexpectedly I received about two years' salary which allowed me to withdraw from my previous job and read up on climate change. I'm not a kind of superperson, I actually had some good fortune. It gave me more confidence to trust my judgement, but maybe now that climate change is all over the newspapers, people wouldn't need quite so much support to do that.

In 1999 I stopped working and sat at a little desk and looked into climate change for about six months. Then I took a view that there were a whole bunch of graphs that I'd looked at and they were all going in one direction. That the political consensus had been reached and was secure, and if I spent the rest of my life working on climate change, I would not be wasting my time. And I think also the leisure time that I had — I did spend six months not setting my alarm clock — in that time I did kind of allow my guts to help me decide what I was going to do with my life, and they helped me decide 100 per cent climate change and nothing but. Until I'm about 70, when I don't know if I'll be quite responsible in the discharge of my duties. At that point, I may go back to doing those things that people do when there isn't a war on.

The obvious question is, 'Has there been an opportunity cost to doing this?' I think it's probably true that over the last five or six years, I've earned quite a bit less money that I used to. That's kind of OK because, to be honest, there's not that much you can really do with money that's all that useful, except maybe fly around the world on exotic holidays, and I've not flown on holiday since 2001, so that particular adventure is lost to me. So should I be living in a bigger house? Should I be having a normal life and kids and things like that? It didn't feel that difficult for me to decide to really focus on my work, and I could have combined that with having a family, but I took a view that I would have to give up either leisure or a family. I decided to give up having a family, working on the assumption that there was no shortage of children and that I have eight nephews and nieces.

I am, I would say, completely fulfilled. I'm never ill and I consider myself to be a living embodiment of the Confucian maxim that when you get the job you want, you never work another day in your life. I leap out of bed in the morning, rush to my computer and couldn't be happier. The system is kind of set up to make people think that if they're not earning absolutely as much money as they can all the time, they're going to die, whereas probably the reverse is true. And people also think that if they give up one afternoon a week to help their local Green Party, they're going to be booted off the career ladder. I do think that there's some utility value in keeping some balance in your life, and for example I am actually only paid 90 per cent of my salary by the Carbon Disclosure Project. Half a day of the week, I sell video telephones, because I believe that video telephones are going to change the world. I don't think that one has to be a tycoon with a top hat and a cigar, or a monk. I think the modern world with the internet and email can permit us to live a portfolio existence that suits us personally, so being the change for me, I think, has been about being richer in every sense — healthier, certainly happier — and it doesn't really get any better than that.

Being the change

You have to be absolutely sure that what you are doing is right, and you have to be sure that if you've been convinced that what you are doing is wrong, that you're going to change it. There's nothing to be admired in being proven wrong, accepting that and then not changing. You have to be flexible. You know, in some senses, I've sent the same email all day every day for six years, and at times it hasn't been that interesting, but if you can remember why you're doing it, if you can smile at the joys of nature and people and if you can be endlessly impressed with what you're trying to conserve, that will give you the strength to do some of the fantastically dull repetitive work to deliver on what you need to do. You know I say that Confucius says when you get the job you want, you never work for another day of your life and that is true, but at the same time your desire to enact and protect and do what you need to do is sometimes going to find its expression in things that aren't terribly interesting. I've met people from NGOs who want to launch a new campaign every week and have lots of exciting meetings, but you know, fairly substantial amounts of graft are the centre of the implementation of anything. Crucial to our success has been a good idea and the laser-like focus on its implementation, combined with a wide gene pool of advice, a plan which is set and followed but also flexible, and really good colleagues. If you put those together you can't really fail.

It really isn't that difficult to solve this problem. What gives me hope is that just because we've not had an apolitical global enemy before, it doesn't mean that we, the world community, cannot rise to slay this dragon. It requires nothing more than logic, intelligence, self-preservation and cooperation, all of which have been demonstrated on a considerable scale in other circumstances in other times. And it is the overwhelming interest of parents not to make the lives of their children miserable, or indeed to end the lives of their children, and so, drawing upon the deepest purpose of living and replicating beings, I am confident that the intelligence and capability of the human race who have got us into this mess are going to get us out of it.

www.cdproject.net

Beautiful Corporations, Financial Times/Prentice Hall, 2000

Scilla Elworthy

We're shining a spotlight on these pinpoints of light all over the world — people doing incredible things with their courage, rather than with a gun.

Dr Elworthy has devoted her life to preventing and resolving conflict. She founded two of the UK's most pioneering and influential peace NGOs, the Oxford Research Group and Peace Direct. ORG's work grew out of the anti-nuclear movement, and its most significant innovation has been to bring together and facilitate dialogue between all stakeholders in the nuclear arms debate — policy-makers, the military, scientists and civil society. ORG was awarded the Niwano Peace Prize in 2003 for its promotion of disarmament and non-violent conflict resolution. In 2004, Peace Direct was created, to address the issues of conflict on an immediate, grassroots level. Peace Direct supports thousands of peace-builders around the world and brings their lessons to both government and public attention.

If one goes right down to the root causes, the challenges facing the planet, the biggest change I'd like to see is a massive WAKING UP. At the moment, so many of us are sleepwalking into disaster, and so the change that's going to make the difference is when — on critical issues — people are alert and in action. The change is not going to come from what governments do and it's not going to come from what international organisations do. We can't rely on them. The problems are bigger than that, and the problems can only be solved by people acting in concert, across cultural, religious, and particularly national lines.

A particular part of that 'waking up' that I'm concerned about is conflict. At the beginning of last century, 80 per cent of people killed in conflicts were military. At the beginning of this century, 80 per cent of people killed in conflicts are *civilians*. Much of the suffering we see on our TV screens is caused by conflict. For example there are currently 8.4 million refugees in the world — homeless people, who've had to flee from their land, who've lost all they had and are unable to feed their children or care for their health — because of war.

Therefore I'm investing effort into spreading knowledge of how conflicts can be prevented. And if they happen, how they can be resolved without the use of superior force. Governments tend to rely on armaments to boost their national power, to threaten others, and in their view, to deal with conflict. Anybody who's had any experience of the world knows that violence simply breeds more violence. If we didn't know that before, we've seen it in Iraq.

People won't stop buying and selling arms until they realise that they can depend on a better way, a more effective way of preventing and resolving conflict. Some governments simply want to have armaments to increase their own power, but once really large numbers of people are weaned off the idea that superior force is the way to deal with conflict, once really large numbers of people realise that, then we will get a step change, and billions of dollars that are now devoted to armaments can be put to useful things. A fraction of what we spend on armaments could deal with hunger, disease and education across the planet.

Beginnings

I lived in Africa for 10 years after I graduated. I was working on nutrition then, in Africa, and then I moved with my husband and small daughter to France. I started working for UNESCO as a consultant on women's issues and they asked me to prepare UNESCO's contribution to the 1980 UN World Women's Conference. The contribution they asked me to write was about the role of women in peace research and in peace-building, about which I knew at that point absolutely nothing. So I went off to find out and I got hooked. That was when I really started thinking hard about weapons issues and security and nuclear weapons as well. That's how the one thing led into the other.

The Oxford Research Group started around my kitchen table. I'd been involved in various anti-nuclear protests and I realised that they weren't working. My conclusion was that we must enter into a dialogue with the people who actually make decisions on nuclear weapons. That means from the drawing board, the laboratory, right to the deployment. We set out to map out how those decisions are made in all the nuclear nations. In my optimism, I thought it would take six months, and it took four years before we published our first book. But in that period we really learned a lot about how the whole process worked, and about the attitudes and assumptions of people who fill those positions. I did my doctorate based on a series of interviews with people who made those decisions, and I listened to them at great length. That enabled them to begin to trust me and then we were able to invite them to very confidential meetings, where they would meet, for the first time often, their opposite numbers from other countries, countries who were their enemies during the Cold War years. They would also meet with their critics, people who had maybe been in the nuclear industry and decided it was disastrous, and knew the technical necessities for getting arms treaties to work. So the work became a question of providing a safe enough container, where people could really take their masks off and talk to each other as human beings.

Building trust

At first, of course, nobody trusted us, because nobody knew what we were up to. They'd heard about it, it sounded a bit suspect. But the way it happened was, the first group of British military began to trust me because of the interviews that I did for my doctorate, and they told other people. Then at a conference I met some Russians and a Chinese delegate and then took the bull by the horns and went to China and met a lot of other Chinese policy-makers, and just started gradually talking to people about whether they would be willing to come to this kind of meeting. Then we held the first meeting, and it was successful in that people were relaxed, although they thought it was a bit odd because it wasn't in

Anybody who's had any experience of the world knows that violence simply breeds more violence.

---

a five star hotel, it was in a Quaker retreat centre where they had to make their own beds. People did find it a bit odd, but they were intrigued by it and the majority of them at any rate gave us very positive feedback. So when we wanted to hold the next conference, we would say to them, 'We want to invite so-and-so who's a colleague of yours, will you phone him up and tell him that it's OK to accept this invitation?' That's the way it worked. And still we found we had to invite four people for every one who would accept.

We were working with all the nuclear powers on negotiations to get rid of or build down nuclear weapons, which soak up such vast sums of money. It was compelling and demanding and often nerve-racking, like when we went to China. The Chinese generals that we had to deal with were intimidating and it was a question of trying to find a way through their formality and hectoring and find a way where an actual communication could be opened. I was leading the delegation, which had two British generals, an admiral and an air marshal and various other very accomplished people. It became a question of trying to mix a combination of insistence and standing our ground with a warmth and an openness. So, not being prepared to be hectored, but at the same time really stretching out our hand of mutual interest, and getting to issues of actual discussion that they wanted to talk about as much as we did, rather than spending the time in political grand-standing. It's now become much easier to talk with Chinese officials. The higher you go, the easier it is.

The policy-makers who've been involved in these discussions say there is no other opportunity where they know it is safe to relax, to talk as human to human, to explore possibilities for the détente and disarmament that so many people want. In some of our meetings the base has been laid for future treaties.

I've had the good fortune to work with and alongside the most remarkable people, with whom I've had stimulation and great adventures. Adventures like when we were going to hold a meeting in New Delhi. I phoned up the Indian general who's in charge of the Indian Armed Services Institute, the biggest military think-tank in India. I'd met him once and so I asked him if we could come and hold a conference there. Then we went from there down to a fort in Rajasthan. We transported all these nuclear weapons policy-makers from Britain and America and Russia and China, as well as India and Pakistan, in a bus down to this absolutely magical fort in the middle of the desert, and kept them there for three days to talk to each other — until they really understood each other's point of view. That was such an adventure, and there have been lots of adventures like that, but they were nerve-racking. We didn't know if we could afford it, we didn't know if the bus would crash with all these important people on it, we didn't know if key people would walk out. In fact on the last day there was a massive electric storm, everybody got soaked, but all ended up back in the bus, laughing.

Peace Direct

Dialogue and conflict resolution have been passionate interests for me since before I worked on the nuclear issue. In other words, I want to go down to the roots of conflict. That's what really fascinates me — what are the methods that work?

A few years ago I set up an organisation called Peace Direct, which links up people in safe parts of the world with people at the sharp end of conflict. We can learn from them. These are people who are acting non-violently and effectively to prevent or resolve conflict, and we can learn from them — how they do it, how much it costs — so that we know and can prove the cost-effectiveness of a non-violent approach.

These are incredibly inventive and efficient people who are risking their lives to gather people around a table, to listen to each other and resolve their differences; this sounds simple but it takes courage and endless patience. People like Sami Velioglu in Kirkuk in northern Iraq, who set up a centre for listening and documentation, so that the wrongs that would otherwise drive people to pick up a gun or drop a bomb, can be righted through a sort of citizens' advice bureau.

There are people active all over the world, I mean literally hundreds of thousands of grassroots initiatives, which are completely unrecorded and largely unfunded, that Peace Direct is now getting behind, and making people aware of. We're shining a spotlight on these pinpoints of light all over the world — people

*A fraction of what we spend on armaments
could deal with hunger, disease and
education across the planet.*

---

doing incredible things with their courage, rather than with a gun. And we're linking them up with ordinary people in this country who can support and encourage them, like a group in Oxford who support peace-builders in the Congo, and a group in Bristol who support Sami's work in Iraq.

That's part of it. The other part of it is dialogue with governments to inform foreign offices and ministries of defence about these amazing initiatives and the fact that if more government money were channelled their way, they could become more effective.

It's not only due to us, but I do notice that a lot of other NGOs have taken on the principle of dialogue as their main method of working. Dialogue is very different from lobbying, for example. Lobbying is when you're trying to convince somebody of your point of view and get them on your side, whereas dialogue has to imply a genuine willingness to listen to the other side.

A wish

In my journal, I devote the back page to ideas of things I would like to do if I wasn't doing what I am doing, and there are about ten of them at the moment. One thing I would love to do is set up a kind of MBA in the Middle East, to enable postgraduates to spend a year learning the skills of negotiation. So each Middle Eastern country would send, say, 20 graduates, and at the end of a year you would have a cohort of 400 people who all understood the skills of mediation, non-violence, and resolving conflicts without the use of force. So they would have a shared language, so when their respective countries got into dispute, there would be these people on either side who would know how to talk to each other. I'd love to do that.

Non-violence is very different from pacifism. Pacifism is passive, non-violence is active. It's the training of the intellect, the mind, the emotions, the body and the spirit, in the resilient knowledge of how to resist superior force, and replace force with other methods of reconciling differences. Gandhi trained people in non-violence, but since Gandhi there hasn't really been an established training course in this and I'd like to introduce that as a formal training course. I have already designed a curriculum in non-violence which would be a training, not only obviously of the intellectual side of things — all the theory, there's plenty of that — but also training people's emotions.

You need to have a very strong psyche to be able to do good non-violent work. You have to know yourself very well, you have to have a lot of self-awareness. The physical training is also vital, because if you are going to be doing conflict resolution for example, sometimes you have to travel for days in very uncomfortable situations, and you have to be able to stay up all night and work through the night for two or three nights on the trot. You have to be able to absorb very unfamiliar conditions and eat unfamiliar food and so on. Also you have to learn both an inner and an outer martial arts, in the sense that you have to learn when to take the metaphorical punches and when to respond.

It's a fantastic discipline, but I'm not aware of anywhere that actually teaches it at the moment. Sometimes you have to back off, and let the person who's feeling very aggressive come towards you. Sometimes you do have to stand firm, and that means asserting something that you feel to be the truth. One is a definite assertion and the other is the backing off and letting that aggression bend itself.

Whether it's actual war or conflict in the living room, we need to understand how the cycle of violence works. It has various stages, and it works in the human psyche at the level of the emotions. It starts with an atrocity — within a family that might be a hurt or a misdeed — followed by shock, fear, grief and anger. And if nothing is done, the anger hardens into bitterness, the bitterness into the need for revenge, revenge into retaliation, and that breeds a further atrocity.

So let's say that somebody in your family or your lover or your friend has hurt you. If nothing is done to alleviate your feelings, you may well go and hurt that person back, whether intentionally or unintentionally. Or you may hurt somebody else. Intervention is needed at the point before anger hardens into bitterness, revenge and retaliation.

Dialogue is very different from lobbying… it has to imply a genuine willingness to listen to the other side.

Terrorism

I think the immediate concern for most of us in the West at the moment is the issue of terrorism, and what we can do about that. To my way of thinking, it's a question of enquiring deeply into what makes people take the route of terrorism, and not succumbing to simply branding anybody who uses violence as a terrorist, but rather to actually understand why they're doing it. Nelson Mandela, when he was sent to jail on Robben Island in 1964, was the world's number one terrorist, and now he's the world's number one hero. Now, he's the same man…

I'm not saying that people who are branded as terrorists now are all Nelson Mandelas in hiding, but it is our business to understand the very high ideals that a lot of people who commit terrorist acts have, and to listen to them, to really listen to them. I'm a great believer in talking to terrorists, listening to them, not putting anybody outside the pale, and that we should encourage our leaders to do just that.

For example, we should have encouraged them to be talking to Sinn Fein and the IRA long before they were openly doing so. Right now we should be encouraging the Americans to be talking to Hezbollah and Hamas because nobody should be outside the pale. We should try and understand everybody's point of view, just as Nelson Mandela insists on doing in all the conflicts he's been involved in.

It's also crucial for us not to be pushed into an intimidated stance in our own country, when our government tries to bring in laws that are manifestly unjust, like arrest and questioning without a formal accusation. There are a lot of laws at the moment being passed which are taking away our civil liberties and we have to resist them. Our civil liberties have been so hard-won and it's disastrous if we sit back and allow them to be taken away from us. We should be using all the means at our disposal in our democracy, right from going and talking to our MPs about it, to manifesting in the streets, demonstrating, signing these massive online petitions. Hundreds of thousands of people signed the petition on the road toll. What difference do road tolls make, as compared to some of the things we are being asked to do in the fight against terrorism?

I don't think we should stop marching. I think we were all so abashed by the fact that it didn't stop the war in Iraq that we've backed off from public demonstration, and I really don't think we should. But I think we should use the internet in more imaginative ways. It's offering such a lot of possibilities right now for people to get together with people in other countries that they wouldn't have normally done, to enter into conversations with people in cultures that we otherwise wouldn't understand. So there are lots of possibilities for that now, but in terms of protest, I think we can cause very striking news items as a result of massive petitions.

Challenges

On a personal level, my challenge has always been that at crucial moments, under criticism, my self-confidence will collapse. I've always been vulnerable to that, I think from childhood. My father was very critical and so I've got an internalised critical voice that jumps in at the worst moments, and it can cut me off at the knees. I've had to develop ways to reassure myself, and to deal with this critical voice, which I think affects a lot of people. It's been a prod to self-knowledge, and to develop as best I can as a human being. It's been very humbling, and it's also been a very much a constant reminder of the need for self-awareness, and the need for quiet times, reflection and meditation.

On a political level, each bigger challenge that I took on always terrified me. For example, when I first had to go to the United Nations, I was absolutely intimidated by the building, and the people. They seemed so smooth and superior, and now it doesn't frighten me a bit. Then the next challenge was the military — I was very, very frightened of going and talking to generals and people like that; I thought they would think I didn't know what I was talking about and dismiss me. And now I don't find that the least bit frightening. I enjoy them as people. I might disagree with them, but I like talking to them, I like listening to them.

What I've learned is to do one's very best, but not to take responsibility for the outcome. Because what I tend to do is think that if something fails it's my fault, but actually it's in the lap of the gods. So I suppose it's that — to do one's absolute utmost, but then let go. That's one thing, and the other is to try not to take oneself too seriously. To do one's very best, but then to realise that ultimately we are all very fallible and we do silly things.

A quality I'd really like to have, and I'm sort of working my way towards it, is the presence of mind to be able to stand up in the instant when it's required and do the right thing. Aung San Suu Kyi did when she was leading the protesters in the streets of Rangoon. They came round a corner and she saw this line-up of machine guns pointed at them, and she heard the safety catches click off. She turned round and said to the students behind her, 'Sit down,' because she knew they were afraid, and she knew they would get shot if they were afraid. She walked on up to the soldiers until she got to them and put her hand on the barrel and lowered it. I would give my eye teeth to be able to do that. To be fearless enough in the moment that one does the right thing, that's the quality I'd like.

How to be the change

First of all, be absolutely assured that you have it in you to do whatever you want to do, and if you can allow your creative ideas to emerge without squashing them, just go for them. If you have a creative idea that says, 'Let's crochet images of coral reefs to show people how they are being destroyed,' do it. There's a woman, a mathematician in America, who did exactly that, and she's got an exhibition going around the States now, showing people how coral reefs are being destroyed through beautifully crocheted sculptures. You know, anybody in their right mind would say that's mad, but she did it and it worked. So whatever your creativity suggests in the dark of the night or when you're out on a walk by the river, go for it. Go for it. Somebody will join you, and maybe thousands of people.

www.oxfordresearchgroup.org.uk

www.peacedirect.org

Making Terrorism History, Scilla Elworthy and Gabrielle Rifkind, Rider & Co, 2006

Unarmed Heroes: The courage to go beyond violence, Peace Direct, Clairview Books, 2004

Jeremy Gilley

If we want to move from a culture of war to a culture of peace,
then we've got to create a moment of peace — we've got to
unite, we've got to come together as one.

Jeremy Gilley is an actor turned filmmaker, who in the late 1990s became preoccupied with questions about the fundamental nature of humanity and the issue of peace. He decided to explore these through the medium of film, and specifically, to create a documentary following his campaign to establish a globally-recognised day of ceasefire and non-violence. He founded Peace One Day, a non-profit organisation consisting initially of friends, family and volunteers. In 2001, Peace One Day's efforts were rewarded when the member states of the United Nations unanimously adopted this annual day of global ceasefire and non-violence — 21st September, Peace Day. As well as being an inspiring symbol of hope and goodwill, this day now offers life-saving opportunities, for example to bring humanitarian aid to areas of conflict.

I'd like to see a world that comes together as one, a united world. It's fairly obvious why we need to come together. I'm concerned about the starvation and the killing of innocent people, and the way we treat each other and our environment, as indeed we all are. That's what's driving this Peace One Day initiative, and as a filmmaker, I want to use the medium of film as consciously and as constructively as I can.

The idea

I had read in a book by Frank Barnaby that the media had a special responsibility to be very careful about what kinds of images and thoughts we string together, because so many people take them in. That was interesting, and it inspired me to think, 'What can I do with a film camera? How can I use the form to somehow make a change in the world?' I really wanted to make a film about peace, and my research led me to realise that there was no day of peace. That's when I had my idea — could I make a film about trying to establish the first ever day of peace on the planet with a fixed calendar date?

I was also reading that the academics were saying that the key to humanity's survival is 'intercultural cooperation', and that fascinated me. That notion has stuck with me for the last nine years. It makes sense: if we are going to move forward, if we are going to lift the level of consciousness around the fundamental issue — the protection of each other and our environment — then we are going to have to unite and come together as one, in a moment of intercultural cooperation. Therefore, it makes total sense to me to have 21st September as a starting point for individuals' actions for a more peaceful world.

There are lots of charities and organisations that we can back. However, I think that until we actually shift the level of consciousness around the way we behave with each other, then we won't move forward; we'll always be coming up with nice ideas that will relieve the suffering for a small amount of people but actually aren't going to change the world, which on its present path is going to destroy itself. I'm much more interested in some kind of serious global shift. Humanity's never come together as one in its history, so what Peace Day is there to do, adopted by every member state of the United Nations, is to facilitate that process of unity.

First steps

Effectively, we just wrote a series of letters, right at the very beginning. Once the idea had formulated itself as a film about trying to create the first ever day of peace then, when you sit down and think about it hard enough, it's fairly obvious what you have to do in order to achieve it. Very quickly I realised that the United Nations had the structure to be the foundation for a moment of global unity. It wouldn't have been sensible for me to say, 'This is going to be Jeremy's Peace Day,' or 'Peace One Day's Peace Day'. It had to be 'the world's Peace Day', and therefore one had to penetrate the closest organisation that we have to holding the global community together, and that's the United Nations. I started writing very early on to the UN, as well as every government, every intergovernmental and non-governmental organisation I could think of, and all the Nobel Peace laureates.

Very quickly, I was invited around the world to meet key individuals like His Holiness the Dalai Lama, Oscar Arias, Mary Robinson, Kofi Annan and others, and they supported the idea — they wanted the day to become a reality. Humanitarians were telling me it could save people's lives, and educationalists were saying this could inspire and empower young people to become the driving force behind the vision of a united and sustainable world, and that this day must be created. And so ultimately, it was a question of time before it was going to have to happen, because it makes total logical sense — you had an Earth Day, a No Smoking Day, an AIDS Day, a Mothers' Day, a Fathers' Day, but you didn't have a Peace Day. It made sense to everyone to make it happen.

The campaign was launched in 1999, and the UN resolution was passed in September 2001, so it took a couple of years. In order to create a ceasefire and non-violence day with a fixed calendar date, you need to get a government to sponsor that idea. You can't as an individual put an idea forward to the United Nations General Assembly, obviously. You have to find a government to sponsor your idea, and that government needs to find a co-sponsor. And once you have the two governments in place, then they can put that forward to the United Nations General Assembly and a vote can occur.

Gathering evidence

The role I played was as if I was going to court, on behalf of the global community,

I had an idea. It's turned out to be a good one, but ideas are nothing without people to support them becoming a reality. I'm well aware of that.

trying to put the case forward for the creation of this day. In order for this day to make sense, I had to prove categorically that it was going to mean something, that it would be practical, that it wasn't just a symbolic gesture. So that was my approach — in order to create the day, I decided that I was going to court and I would have to present to the United Nations General Assembly some really hard-core evidence that this day should be created. And along the way, we heard from some of the greatest thinkers on the planet, as well as men and women who were in the field every day saving people's lives, saying, 'Yes, this makes sense. This has got to happen.'

I travelled to Somalia, Burundi, Gaza, the West Bank, India, Sri Lanka, North America, Europe, Central America and Australia, speaking to men, women, children, humanitarians, teachers and UN staff. From all of those different people, I heard about lots of very practical steps that could be taken if a peace day was put into place. Educators could inspire children on the day, humanitarians could immunise, faith leaders could bring people together in places of worship.

I'd never been to Somalia before, I'd never been into an area like that. There was no real government structure in the country in any way, and what I saw and what I smelled was horrific. It blew my mind. I realised at that point how lucky I was, and because I was that fortunate that I must do everything that I possibly could to make sure that this film succeeded, and that this day was created.

I saw people starving, dying of hunger. I saw hospitals where there was no medication and no hygiene. It wasn't the doctors' fault, they just didn't have anything to clean with. Everyone was in serious pain. I saw displaced people, hundreds of thousands of them, living under plastic sheeting and nothing else. I saw malnourished children, men and women whose children had been murdered, women who'd been raped and seen their daughters raped and their sons killed in front of them. When you speak to lots and lots of people like that, and you see those things and you smell those things, it changes you. It made me very determined to continue, no matter what, determined that in some way my film camera and this idea, should it truly grow to be recognised by every human being in the world, would save people's lives and would inspire and empower people.

At first, I hadn't really cared whether the day failed or succeeded, it wasn't important to me. What was important was making a great film. It was through the course of making the film that I realised the importance of establishing the day and the benefit that it could have to the global community, and then that took over. So I made a decision halfway through the film, when it was getting tough, that I would never give up, no matter what, that if this was the only film that I made in my life then I was going to make it, and it was going to be a success in that the day would be created.

The film didn't change, it just kept on documenting what happened. It was a change within me, in terms of a decision and a new energy to make sure that the goal was accomplished — a real injection of enthusiasm and passion.

Raising awareness

The British government and the Costa Rican government took this idea forward, and it was put to the United Nations General Assembly and unanimously adopted on 7th September 2001. It was the best day of my life, without a shadow of a doubt. I'd spent a couple of years running around the world, and a year planning, so I'd spent three years working immensely hard, along with many other people and the support of lots of corporations. To sit up at the top of the General Assembly, in the little press box with my camera, and to witness it happen — it was a very moving, very exciting, very special moment.

Once the day had been created, the next job was to make sure that people observed it, was to do everything that I could to promote the day, to let people know that it now existed, that there was now a Peace Day with a fixed calendar date, a starting point for ordinary individuals' actions for a more peaceful world, as well as an opportunity for governments, NGOs, schools, unions, faiths, UN agencies and so on to get involved themselves. We needed to inform all sectors of society that the day existed, in order that they could then make a commitment to the day in whatever way worked for them, whether it was an individual holding a minute of silence, or a humanitarian agency organising an immunisation campaign.

If you've got something that you want to accomplish,
just don't give up.

It's a lot of travelling, a lot of meetings, a lot of letter-writing, a lot of telephoning. In order to really make it work, you have to become very active as an organisation — a lot of people sending a lot of emails, making a lot of telephone calls, pushing as hard as we possibly can. The way we see it, it's a global networking exercise. We're trying to manifest a moment of global unity, trying to create global awareness of a day. We have to be strategic about that. We use music, we have concerts, we make films, we work with sports organisations, fashion icons, we have our website and we recently put an education resource into the schools of the UK and beyond. We carry out a lot of processes that raise awareness and engage people.

Peace Day

All kinds of things happen on the day. Aid is moved, people are immunised, ammunition and landmines are destroyed, children are educated, people are praying in their places of worship. Families are coming together, people are saying sorry, football matches are created, all kinds of different activities are going on. Governments are acting and raising awareness of it; the UN system is very, very active across all its different agencies, and so it's endless in terms of what does go on, on the day.

When I travelled the world, I was told that on this day, we could immunise children; if there's a cessation of hostilities or a marker for efforts to immunise, then you have a starting point. It's like if you're going to get married, you have to choose a date — otherwise how can you plan? It's impossible. In the same way, if you're going to immunise some children, you need a moment to say, 'That's the day when we're going to immunise those children.' If it's a particularly dangerous area, then you're going to need to speak to both parties involved in that conflict and say, 'We're going in there, and we need to go in safely in order for this to be

107

carried out.' Those are the kinds of things that happen and those are the kinds of successes we've seen. We've just seen 680,000 mosquito nets given out in the Democratic Republic of Congo; each mosquito net saves someone from malaria. It's all the very practical things that I'm interested in.

For example, the World Food Programme deliver aid every day — thank God they do — but their way of acknowledging Peace Day and placing importance on the issues of peace was to organise the delivery of aid into an area in southern Sudan on the day. They orchestrated, they organised and they delivered that aid. The International Rescue Committee reunited a young girl soldier with her family in the Democratic Republic of Congo on that day. She went home and met her family for the first time in many years. Star Syringe have created a single-use, auto-disable syringe and that was being used in 14 different countries on Peace Day this year, immunising children. Those are three specific examples of how the day works, and there are many, many more like that.

All kinds of things happen here in the UK as well, in our educational establishments, in our homes, in our workplaces and in our communities. You can be as creative as you want to be. Some people hold a minute of silence, some people get their family together, some people say sorry to their dads or their girlfriends or they plant trees — whatever action means something to them. In whatever sector of society you look at — government, NGOs, education, unions, sports, faiths — you will see different examples of what people do. The UN figure this year was 100 million people marking the day. It's an opportunity for individuals to celebrate and act on the day in whatever way they want. If they log that on our website, that commitment will then inspire others to do the same.

We just put an education resource into around 85 per cent of secondary schools in the UK, sponsored by Ecover, which was an incredible thing that they did. That resource is about inspiring and empowering young people to become the driving force behind the vision of a united and sustainable world. There's a component about bullying, which is a key message for young people. I've spoken to 33,000 young people and recorded 417 hours of their thoughts. I probably know better than anybody what the day means to them because I've relentlessly, tirelessly documented their thoughts around this issue.

It's a very simple process technically to carry out,
it's not a dream or an if or a but or a maybe.

Young people

Young people don't know where to start, they don't feel they can make a difference because of the way society speaks to them — it does everything to disempower them and not empower them to know that they can be the change. So we've created a tool for them to learn about conflict prevention skills and conflict resolution, about the great peace-makers and individuals who've made a change in the world, and about bullying and its relationship to Peace Day. It's not just a day where it's all about guns, it's actually about the violence in our homes and in our schools, and in our communities.

Young people feel disempowered with what they see on the news and what's going on in their communities, and we need to change that. We need to provide a moment of hope, we need to give them a starting point for their actions for a more peaceful world. We need to make it real. We need to provide that opportunity. If we don't do any of those things, what kind of a society are we going to create? Not a good one.

The teachers think it's great. We have something called Citizenship, which is relatively new to our curriculum. That's all about being a global citizen, so Peace Day fits that like a glove. Peace Day is all about empowering the individual to take responsibility and act in a constructive way towards a more peaceful world, a more peaceful home, a more peaceful school, a more peaceful community. That's why we created the educational resource. Teachers and children love it. It works.

This day inspires and empowers young people, giving them a starting point for their actions for a more peaceful world, which up to today they didn't have. If we want to move from a culture of war to a culture of peace, then we've got to create a moment of peace — we've got to unite, we've got to come together as one. If we don't do those things, then we're never going to move forward. What's the alternative? The alternative is catastrophic. The alternative is that we live in a culture of war, that we're never going to change. That's a form of madness, and I'm not joining in on that gig. I'm not interested in that.

I am totally convinced that if we don't come together as one around the fundamental issue — the protection of each other and our environment — then we won't survive, and I truly believe that it's something that we can do, that 21st September can unite the world in a way that we've never known in our history before. It's a very simple process technically to carry out, it's not a dream or an if or a but or a maybe. It's based on human resources and technology, with a lot of creativity, through music, film, fashion, sport and digital media. It's a great idea, it saves people's lives, it inspires young people, and it's highly creative and extremely interesting. I'm focused and committed to spending the rest of my life, or until the goal is achieved, bringing the world together, on behalf of every member state of the United Nations that adopted this day. It's a great thing to be doing.

Hope

It gives me hope. If the day hadn't been created and we'd failed, then I don't think I'd have any hope. When I began the journey, I was wondering whether humankind was fundamentally evil and the destruction of the world was inevitable. I've spent many years now travelling the world and I don't believe that it is. I have hope because the world came together and created a day of peace, and I have hope because I'm seeing people do extraordinary things throughout the world. Many of those things are saving people's lives and that gives me hope — that what we have done has worked, and it's growing so quickly.

The UN said that 100 million people were active on the day in 2007. We thought that about 27.6 million people were active in 2006, so if our figures were semi-accurate and their figures were semi-accurate, then it's tripled in a year. If it continues to do that, we predict that by 2012 about 3 billion people will be aware of the day — that's almost half the world.

I used to have all kinds of different aspirations — I don't any more. There's nothing more important than this that I will ever come across in my lifetime, not anything more important than playing a part in trying to make sure that every

The individuals change this world,
that's how it happens.

human being on the planet knows about the day of peace. We're not talking about something that's my idea that I had in my bedroom, and I've called it my day — it's nothing to do with me. This is a day for every human being on the planet to act as one. All that's important to me is to play a part in making sure that everybody knows about that. There's nothing else.

The power lies in the hands of the people. That's the opportunity. It's not about government, it's up to you, it's up to me, it's up to anyone who receives this message, who understands that Peace Day exists. It's up to the individuals. The individuals change this world, that's how it happens. And collectively, if we act together as one, we can lift the level of consciousness around the fundamental issue — the protection of each other. If we could truly do that on a scale that humanity's never known, we can't even predict or pretend to know what would occur. It's huge. That's what it's all about.

If we live in a democracy and if democracy follows the will of the people, and the will of the people is for peace, then we'll have it. It's a call to action to each and every one of us to say, 'Man, we're in this together.' Do we have that within our capability as human beings to come together as one, to accept our differences in colour, in politics, in religion? It's a small planet, let's do what we can to protect it and each other, because they are intertwined, they are one, they are the same thing. That's what we have to do. It's incredible to even be talking about these things, because they will become a reality.

What'll come next is whatever comes next, but we need to get there. Let's just get to that place, and then let's see what happens next. 'If I get to the top of this mountain, what about the next mountain?' Forget about the next mountain, let's just get to the top of this one. Let's just think about what's in front of us, and what's in front of us is a moment of global unity, and we can't give up on that. We can't ignore that and say it's not worth fighting for. We need to make that journey. We have to move there, and then let's see what happens. If we want 365 days of peace, which of course we do, then first we're going to have to have one. If we can have one, maybe we'll have two. Let's get to one first, and then see where we're at.

www.peaceoneday.org

Peace One Day, Putnam Publishing Group, 2005

Peace One Day DVD, 2003

Roanna Heller

There are different levels of change, but I get inspired by what you can do in your own community, on a face-to-face level.

Roanna Heller's love of community first manifested itself when she started throwing street parties for her neighbours in Sheffield. From this grew a new sense of kinship and solidarity, which prompted an idea. Could you create that kind of relationship with people you've never met, on the other side of the world? In 2006, Freedom Road gained two twin communities, Dundas Place near Melbourne, Australia, and Monte Sinai in Esteli, Nicaragua. Jointly-held, simultaneous parties have ensued and a true bond has developed between these otherwise completely unrelated neighbourhoods. Emails, gifts and photos are exchanged as the relationships continue.

There are a lot of changes I'd like to see in the world. On a personal level, I'd like to see people treating each other with more respect, being more open to the potential for friendship, and supporting each other in the communities they live in. I think we need change on a wider level as well: we need to create an equal and just world, and to prevent environmental catastrophes. So there are different levels of change, but I get inspired by what you can do in your own community, on a face-to-face level. I don't feel driven to go into politics or campaigning, I want to make changes where I can see them, changes that give me immediate positive feedback. And I'm interested in making global connections as well, and seeing how we can make those links friendly and intimate.

I want to see these changes because I notice that even though I live in quite a friendly part of the country, people don't necessarily know their neighbours, and aren't willing to take a risk in terms of befriending other people. In the street-twinning project we're doing, having strengthened our community cohesion here, we're able to make links with other people on the other side of the world. It's not just about having a strong community here, but using that strength to be able to look outwards and form new relationships with other communities.

Community spirit

There was a garden halfway up the street. There was no house there, it was an abandoned piece of council land, and it had become totally overgrown. I thought this could be a potential place for people to get together. I'd only lived on the street for a couple of years and I was keen to meet more people and share things with my neighbours. I thought having a party in the garden would be a good way to start. I talked to the people I did know on the street and they thought it was a good idea so we decided that yes, we would go ahead. We sent an invitation to all the neighbours and put adverts up in local shops. The party was lovely. People brought food to share, and tables and a gazebo, and I thought, 'Wow, this is actually working, people are enjoying this!' Some of them were meeting for the first time, and others were catching up with neighbours they'd not seen in months. Two women who live on the street decided to become long-term gardening volunteers, and suddenly we had this little oasis halfway down the street.

Over the years, we've had more parties — bonfire parties, carol singing, picnics. We've got to know more of our neighbours and some of them really well.

We've got this unusual community spirit on our street —
maybe we can do something with that to make
a change in the wider world.

One lovely result for me has been that I now know people of lots of different ages, including older people and families with children. Before the street parties began, most of my friends were of a similar age to me. It's opened up my world.

A couple of years down the line, I was thinking, we've got this quite unusual community spirit on our street — maybe we can do something with that to make a change in the wider world. I was doing an art and design course at the time and I was looking for a community project as my final piece of work. One day, I was out walking with my husband, and we came up with this idea: what if we could twin Freedom Road with another street somewhere else across the world? We could bridge the ocean without actually going anywhere, without getting on a plane. That's the beauty of new technologies.

It seemed daunting at first. How do you find a street on the other side of the world? What would you type into Google? Originally, we thought it would be nice to twin with another street called Freedom Road somewhere else but it wasn't very easy to find and link up with one. I researched the twinning that was already happening in Sheffield and discovered an active link with Esteli in Nicaragua, which had been going for 20 years. I contacted the Sheffield Esteli Society and they put me in touch with Peter, the twinning coordinator in Esteli. He was cautiously optimistic. They don't have street identity in the same way, they have *barrios* — neighbourhoods — so it was more likely to be a cluster of streets that we would twin with. That was absolutely fine with me; I didn't want to create a mirror of what we've got here, that wasn't the point at all. So he spoke to some of the community leaders in a new *barrio* called Monte Sinai. People were just moving in, and they were living in shacks while they built their own homes on a small piece of land. As they didn't know each other, the twinning could be a way of bringing them together. Peter spoke to the community leaders in Monte Sinai, and they really liked the idea.

We made a second twinning link with a street in Australia, Dundas Place in Port Phillip, which is near Melbourne. This came about when I was searching the internet for street parties and street activism, and I found a page on the merits of street parties and a toolkit of how to hold your own on a council website! Their city council actually had street party workers who were paid to encourage street life and neighbourliness as positive social change. I thought this was incredible and inspiring, so I got in touch with them and asked them if they knew of a street that might like to be our twin. I thought two twins would be better than one in case one of the links fell through. As it was, we were able to create a three-way twinning — triplets!

We set a date for a twinning party, which would take place on the same day in all three communities. We did all the planning through email. I suggested we exchange street decorations to brighten up the parties and help us think of our twin streets. We made bunting because we thought this was quite a nice English thing to do, and we hand-printed onto it images that were inspired by the street — railings, birds, houses and bricks. We made enough to send some to Dundas Place and Monte Sinai and some for ourselves. Monte Sinai made us a huge banner which read, in Spanish, 'The Twinning of Freedom Road with Monte Sinai'. And Dundas Place made us a beautiful piñata in the shape of a tram, as both Port Phillip and Sheffield have trams, and they filled it with little koalas and sweets.

So we all had our party on the same day, Sunday 21st May 2006. Unfortunately it rained in all three places. We were united in appalling weather, and each party went ahead in good spirits. We didn't have any kind of posh video link-up or anything. We just knew that on the other side of the world they were having their party thinking of us, and we were having our party thinking of them. It was a great feeling.

We decided to have another twinning party in April 2007 and it was more successful as the weather was good. We had food from all around the world. Someone made Australian cakes called lamingtons, with coconut on them, and someone else made a spicy black bean dish, a typical Nicaraguan food, and we had a display with photos from Monte Sinai and Dundas Place, so people could actually see our twins. The Mexican dancers were the highlight of our party. We couldn't get Nicaraguan dancers, but it's a similar style of dance. They wear very

We could bridge the ocean
without actually going anywhere.

wide skirts of amazing colours, which make lovely shapes as they move. It was really stunning. Although most of our party took place in the garden, we did close the road so we could all spread out a bit more and not worry about the cars. The dancers actually performed on the road, which was quite a challenge for them because it's a fairly steep slope.

At Monte Sinai, the main focus for them was planting trees. Esteli lost many of its trees in Hurricane Mitch in 1998, and with the loss of the trees the soil became poorer and crops failed, so tree-planting is a matter of survival. They said they planted trees in honour of the people of Freedom Road and Dundas Place, so with each one they planted they said, 'This in honour of our brothers and sisters.' They cooked Chinese food, and we saw photos of huge pots of chop suey. For entertainment, they had a clown and gigantonas — giant papier maché puppets. The downside was that there were only two parties. The residents of Dundas Place felt too partied out after a big celebration in February, and didn't feel they had the energy to plan a twinning party. By April, the weather in Australia turns much chillier. We are keeping in contact though, and there's a possibility we can have a party with them again next year.

Growing closer

We tried to think of ways to get to know our twins better. We came up with the idea of making an album about our street and the people who live here, and this could be the catalyst for penpal links, so we could get to know each other even more. The Freedom Road album is a collection of profiles that people on the street have filled in, and there are Polaroid pictures and messages for the twin streets. We wanted to keep it as simple as possible so as many residents as possible could join in. About 45 people contributed to the album. That's certainly not everyone on the street. Sometimes I've felt pretty down that some people on the street don't seem interested in the twinning, but I don't let this worry me too much.

Anyway, we were thrilled with the album. It's really colourful. Each page is decorated with a collaged border and the profiles are interspersed with recipes and drawings by the children on the street. We were very eager to see what we would get from Monte Sinai. A beautiful album arrived a few weeks after we'd sent ours off, and it was full of letters and photos. Now, I should say something about the language barrier here. I've not found anyone on our road who speaks Spanish! But there is a local Spanish-English conversation group who've been very helpful; they translated the album for us. We've all been so moved by the letters and the lives they describe, by their enthusiasm for the twinning and their new neighbourhood. One of the roads has been named 'Calle de la Libertad' — Freedom Road! Each letter is warm and intimate; we are their 'dear friends', their 'sisters and brothers', and they say they hope the time will come when we can come and visit and rest in the shade of one of their newly-planted mango trees.

So that's the stage we're at; we've made the albums, we've exchanged them, and we keep in touch through email. I've not spoken to any of these people in Australia or Nicaragua, which is quite weird. We'll have to see how it progresses. You can't predict that, it really depends on the ideas people have, so it's quite fluid and organic, which is what I like about it. As for the development of it, I don't know which direction it's going to go. It's not for me to decide. The point is it's a community project, it's not just me working individually. It makes me laugh every time I think about it, the fact that we've done this. It seems quite a bizarre thing to do, but it's not actually that difficult. All you have to have is a little bit of perseverance and it's amazing the things you can do.

Building community

The people from Monte Sinai have said that it's been a fantastic catalyst for getting them together. There were people who had been living in all different bits of the city before, and a lot of them were in really poor housing. They all came together for this new housing project, and they didn't know each other. They've said that having the twinning makes them feel special and valued, and the fact that there are people in the western world interested and caring about them is great for them, and we feel the same way. And in Dundas Place, they've had street parties for years, but the street-twinning changed their outlook and showed them another possibility. They didn't have to have a party with just their

It seems quite a bizarre thing to do,
but it's not actually that difficult.

---

friends and neighbours, they could look to other places around the world. It's funny, people keep on asking me whether I'm going over there, and I say, 'Well, probably not.' Sometimes I do think, 'Wouldn't it be lovely to go to Australia and Nicaragua?' They're great places for holidays, or to spend a year working. But then I'm very committed and tied to where I am, so I think it's quite exciting to make those links without having to up sticks and abandon all my friends and the place I live.

In Monte Sinai they have a lot less materially than we do, yet they have such strong communities and such passion and creativity. It makes me feel very grateful for what we've got, but also aware of all this material stuff. Some of it's great and I'm really glad to have electricity and clean water and everything, but I don't necessarily need gadgets and fancy holidays and maybe I shouldn't be buying so many clothes. It puts things in perspective and makes you think — what's really important is people. It's not the things, when it comes down to it. We get such warmth and friendliness in the emails from Monte Sinai, and although there's only so much I know about them — it is a relationship at a distance — it's lovely to feel that warmth when they talk about us as their brothers and sisters. And they organise themselves really well; they break down into committees to plan different areas of the party. I've seen photos of them looking really passionate and sometimes really serious when they're planning the party. They're really into it. It's inspired me a lot and fired my enthusiasm. It's great to have that connection, and find out what life is like through them. You can watch documentaries about people all over the world and that can give you some insight, but actually having a personal relationship, even if you've never met the people before, can show you a lot more. That's very inspiring.

Teenage activism

When I was a teenager, I was involved in a lot of direct action. I was rebellious and wanted to change the world in quite a different way. I went on lots of demos and marches. I had similar concerns about the environment and social justice, but I was a bit of a fundamentalist really. I actually felt quite angry towards people, that they weren't taking action like I was. After that, there was a bit of a weird period of going through some tunnels and working out, 'Who am I and what do I want to do with my life? Is there a way of making changes in a more positive and kind and loving way, rather than being angry?'

I don't think campaigning and demonstrating is a bad way of going about things, but I think it suits different people, and it can be quite exhausting — people burn out. I was never particularly good at it, basically. If I'd persevered, I'm sure I could have been a better activist, made some positive changes, but part of my problem was that I was a teenager. I wasn't able to think through my actions very carefully. It's a very emotional time, there's often a lot of instability, so people do get drawn to those kinds of movements sometimes for not necessarily the right reasons.

There was a period after I graduated from university of not knowing what to do, of being lethargic and sitting around the home feeling miserable. Then I went to Berlin for a month. I had a friend over there who was very inspiring. She took a lot of photographs and was fascinated by the urban environment and the visual world — colours, shapes and different ways of exploring space. When I got back to Sheffield I started taking photos and looking more closely at what was around me. Looking at the world creatively, through a camera, made me more engaged with the place, and I started being more positive about what I could do with my life. I started volunteering with a community arts organisation, helping to organise a small festival in one of the local neighbourhoods. I started to feel more hopeful — maybe there was a way I could combine my interests in the urban environment and creativity, to make some small positive change.

Creativity

Again as a volunteer, I started up an organisation, Art in the Park, which runs regular art projects for the public in parks and green spaces. This didn't happen overnight. It involved a lot of support from other volunteers and people with different expertise. It's been going for four years, and I get paid now and we have two other workers! We work with different creative materials, and people come along and have a go at things they've never tried before, like clay sculpture or

*I started to feel more hopeful —
maybe there was a way I could combine my
interests to make some small positive change.*

photography or painting. I'm passionate about people getting out and using the spaces around them, and engaging with them. And through doing all that, I became a lot happier and suddenly noticed I had this ability for organising things, which I didn't really know about before. Things evolved. Once Art in the Park became a little success I started thinking, what else can I do? And that's when I came up with the idea of the street-twinning.

I guess I'm passionate about meeting different people, finding connections and ways of working together, and inspiring other people. Art in the Park is an organisation that really has volunteers at the heart. One of the aspects I enjoy the most is building up the relationships with the volunteers and supporting them. A lot of them are in their early twenties or late teens and they're not quite sure what to do, a bit like I was. We give them the chance to volunteer, and it opens up different possibilities and puts them into contact with people, places and creative ways of working that they wouldn't normally come across. That's the ethos of Art in the Park — creativity and community — and it's the same thing with the street- twinning. We wouldn't necessarily be best friends with the people at number 33, say, but we do have things in common. We can build connections and learn from each other. It's the same ethos when you're looking at the whole world. There may be limits to the sort of relationship we can make with people that we never meet, but we can still make connections, friendships, and learn about each other's lives. We can broaden our horizons, so that the choices that we make in our lives are better informed. Whether that's buying a packet of vegetables or going on holiday or deciding to bake our own bread, or just being a bit more creative about our lives.

For example, it's quite easy to create some sort of community event, like a party in the garden or in the street. I think a lot of people get put off holding street parties because they don't know how to go about it, or they worry about the cost of insurance. But in fact, it's not that difficult. You just need to get talking to your neighbours and your local community forum or parish council. Usually they're quite supportive and could pay for the public liability insurance. And they'd point you in the direction of the local Highways Department who could give you permission to close the road. It's a great way of starting out. But everyone's different, there are all sorts of ways of getting involved. That's the beauty of it.

Sharing

Dundas Place made the tram piñata, and they also made one in the shape of a globe. They put a star on it for each of the three locations and joined them with a gold ribbon. Each point was about the same distance away from each other, and it was a very, very, very long way. It kind of makes you tingle. It's a lovely feeling to have, to be part of that community. And when it comes down to it, community is just about sharing, for me. There are all sorts of different ways that that can happen — the actual details of what you share and how you share and who you share with. It's so different for everyone; the idea of community is incredibly loose, but the sort of community we've created is this very particular connection between these three points that didn't have any relationship. I like the randomness of it. There's no reason why it should happen, or why it should be this particular street. It's just that we thought, why not make life more interesting?

www.streettwinning.org.uk

Gill Hicks

There is so much we can do for each other.
Let's not wait for a tragedy to do that.

On 7th July 2005, Gill Hicks was a passenger on the London Underground, when a suicide bomber blew up her carriage. She lost both her legs. When she was taken to hospital, nobody knew her name, and she was labelled 'One Unknown'. For her, the great love and care she received from those who rescued and looked after her, not knowing who she was, reflects a deeper truth: that we are all united by our common humanity, irrespective of our differences. After the bombing, she left her high-flying career at the Design Council, and is now an ambassador for the charity Peace Direct. Her experience has not left her vengeful or bitter; rather, she feels grateful to be alive, and is committed to sharing her message that we are all responsible for peace in our world.

The greatest change that I'd like to see in the world is for us to remember that we are all connected and that life is precious. To recognise that we have more in common than we do different — we are all human beings. That ultimate change would mean that we all would respect each other and all the many different views and beliefs that we all have, and learn that maybe there is more than one right way.

The key, for me, is to live this philosophy — to be the change that I wish to see, to use the words of Gandhi, who is a great source of inspiration. I've seen the effects of what love for a fellow human being can do — it radiates outwards and becomes infectious. Within my own personal world now, everything's based on love. It's quite powerful and quite extraordinary. I've seen this probably mostly with those who rescued me and cared for me on 7th July, and two years on, they are some of my dearest and closest friends. That is something born of unconditional love. I try and spread that word through writing and giving talks, and I speak about the power of my own story. I was labelled as an unknown person. My label was literally 'one unknown'. It didn't matter who I was. I was just a human life, and so many people not only risked their own lives to save me, but also they loved me and cared for me and cherished me. That's a very powerful reminder of how it doesn't really matter what wealth you have or don't have, or what religious belief you have or don't have. Truly, what connects us all is that we are all human beings.

The bomb

Things can change in the click of a finger, or a draw of the breath. That for me is what experiencing the bomb was like. I didn't hear a sound, I didn't see a flash. I was very, very close to the suicide bomber, and it was literally just a click of the finger and my world was changed — as I now know, changed permanently, changed forever. However where I'm fortunate is that I survived, and I have a life.

I was on a very normal journey. A commuter journey in a city like London is like a choreographed ballet sequence, where everybody knows what they're doing and where they're going, and you all fall into line and work your way through a station, onto a platform, onto a train, quite often without speaking to or having any contact with anyone else. That's the law of the land. For everything to be so normal, and then with a click of a finger, changing to something so surreal and unimaginable — that in itself was a very powerful reminder of the fragility of life. For me, my innocence was gone that day. I say 'innocence' in that I felt

Maybe there is more than one right way.

---

connected to the world before, but only through newspapers and watching the news. I was able to turn off and I was able to be separate. The troubles of anyone or anything happened somewhere else, and they didn't happen to me. I had no reason to ever believe they would happen to me. I was a busy professional, worrying about my own life, as indeed probably everybody is. Being thrown into the unexpected was the first powerful aspect of the bomb.

The second powerful aspect was the wait to be rescued. And understanding, like I could never, ever have appreciated before, life and death. In those 45 minutes, I was sitting there, having almost like a lightning bolt going through me, waking me up to the real possibility of death, and how actually death wasn't terrible. There was a very strong voice of death. There was a rather beautiful welcoming proposition, and what I've learned from that is that I'm not afraid now of death.

But I chose to survive. I think it's very important to not be afraid of being alive either. The big outcome of that for me was, if I'm lucky enough to have a life, if I'm lucky enough to have this gift, which I really believe it is, then I must do something with that. That's what's really been my driving force. That time in the carriage has really informed the way I've looked at my life since. That is the power we all have — to make a change, to make things different — and if we all did just one thing, that's what I'm interested in. What would the seismic shift be if we all made one contribution every day, every week? What if that responsibility of being alive, and being here, was something we all thought about?

Achieving peace

What I'm really interested in is how peace can be broken down, and I find the many definitions of peace fascinating. Because, peace full stop, sounds like an unattainable, unimaginable state of the world. And so I'm interested in seeing if we can break it down and make it not such a scary concept to achieve. Then perhaps peace could start at home. Maybe that's the contribution that we could all make today. If my home could be my land, my world, and I could do all I can to build peace within my own home, and that radiates outwards, and then if my neighbour did the same, and their neighbour did the same, then collectively we could start to say we have a very peaceful neighbourhood. As that starts to grow, you see the cumulative effect of things. We can look at our own lives to say, 'Well, I'm the commander of my own life, and my own home, and my own patch, so what can I do to effect a more peaceful and harmonious and beneficial world within my own space?'

We can start by resolving any immediate conflicts that are there. So if you've got teenagers going off the rails or you're having arguments with your husband, or you're fighting over the garden fence with your neighbour, it's really important to address that and to look at it and think, we're only here for a breath of time — does it really matter? Does it really matter? That's the big thing, to wake up every day and say, 'What really is important?' Because everything else can be pushed to one side, and you approach life with a very different grace. The aggression tends to go, or the fact that the fence is one millimetre on my neighbour's side loses its importance. It starts to lose its importance when you assess everything to say, 'Does it really matter?' What really does matter is that my world's harmonious, and that I'm not stopped from making a greater contribution, whatever that may be, by being clouded or halted by smaller aggressions.

Miraculous

I still look at my experience as not only quite surreal and unimaginable, but also miraculous. I'm in awe of my own self, so to speak. I'm amazed that I've gone through this and come out the other side, so filled with determination and love and all these other things which I think are quite surprising not only to me but to many others. There was no long struggle, there was no long journey, and I guess that's probably what's captivated me the most about the story. The moment my eyes opened and I was on a life-support machine, I fairly much knew my legs had gone in the carriage. I gestured to the medical team in intensive care, and they knew I was asking about my legs. They told me, 'I'm sorry, your legs could not be saved.' My very first reaction was, 'Show me my arms. I need to see my arms.' The moment I knew I had arms, I felt, 'Well, that's OK. I've got arms and I'm alive.' It was the complete absolute euphoria of thinking, 'How amazing that I'm here.'

We're only here for a breath of time —
does it really matter? Does it really matter?

And that stayed. That has genuinely stayed, with the appreciation and awareness and gratitude of it being the most amazing gift that we could ever have, and that is just to be alive.

It's the way you look at the world, isn't it? Because I was so excited that I was alive, everything else then became wonderful, became positive. I'd think, 'Wow, I can drink a cup of water on my own!' Rather than thinking, 'How horrific that I've been put in this situation, and I haven't been able to drink and I've only received water through the drip of a sponge.' Holding my own cup of water was a momentous occasion, and I've appreciated drinking water ever since. So, for me, the volume knob has been turned up. The sky is bluer, the grass is greener, all these things are very intense. Life is very, very, very intense and all built on the foundation of appreciation, gratitude and immense love. I feel that I am very much living proof of how different your life is when you build your life on that foundation, because the rubbish tends to not stick. If it does seep in, which is natural, it just slides away. There wasn't a journey or a struggle. That love came immediately. Equally it was a very immediate feeling of not harbouring any hatred or bitterness. These feelings of gratitude and euphoria at just being alive far outweighed, and if anything, ate up any feelings I had of hatred and bitterness towards the person who did this and those who led him to it. There was no struggle for me to come to terms with something.

I'm painting a very wonderful picture, but of course, if you were to ask me, would I like my old life back, my answer would very, very clearly in capital letters be YES. Because as much as I've had this wonderful insight and understanding of life in a different way, and understanding of myself even, of what I can achieve, not only physically but spiritually and mentally — I had no idea — I would love to have my old oblivious life back. That's what it is, it's ignorant bliss in many ways. I'd rather have my limbs and I'd rather have my old life. Perhaps the ultimate would be to have my old life but with a greater awareness and appreciation of the urgent need for greater peace in the world. But that is not the case and I'm very fortunate that I'm able to see things as I do now, because it is incredibly difficult to learn how to walk again. Effectively I don't know where the ground is, I can never touch the ground. And so all these things are incredible challenges but I guess I've chosen to take the route where I'm in awe at every achievement, rather than devastated by my loss.

What is it? What are the ingredients that can make people feel this way? I do feel like I've been, in actual fact, reborn on 7th July. My life started again; I was given something back. I do feel that strongly, and perhaps that's why I can feel so appreciative. I see that as a great shield and protector, feeling euphoric and feeling grateful and feeling all these things, against any perhaps of the 'natural' feelings of wanting retaliation for this. I think I'm very lucky that I don't harbour anger or bitterness. In terms of the cycle of violence, I would probably say that my intervention point is that the feelings of euphoria and gratefulness far outweighed any desire to say, 'Right, I want names and addresses, let's go get them.' I was just too happy to be here.

Faith

I've always been a person of great faith, and I continue to be so. I don't know, but I would love to believe that I have been the recipient of divine intervention. But equally I'm very interested in the power of people now. The whole idea of being labelled 'one unknown' has really captivated me, and made me think a lot about how it really doesn't matter, that there's no 'right way' to be, but that perhaps there are many right ways. I no longer believe strongly that it's an 'us and them' culture. I think there's an amazing power within people that, luckily, I've seen unleashed. I've been the recipient of that, and if that's being wrapped in divine intervention, I don't know. I do my roll call, where every morning, I thank each person that risked their life, each person that did so much to keep me here, and I then thank God on top of that for bringing them all to me, and for aligning everything as such that I had these amazing people on that day, and that these amazing people are now very dear and close friends.

Over time, my thinking matures, and because I don't know — I can't put myself in the bomber's shoes, I can't talk to him — I can only go on collected hearsay and assumptions, and I do believe every person is different. The moment

I've chosen to take the route
where I'm in awe at every achievement,
rather than devastated by my loss.

he detonated that bomb, I don't know what was in his heart. The picture I'm starting to paint and to understand as I journey further, is that he believed he was right. It's been a big leap for me to try and understand that there are perhaps many rights that can all sit at one table. And the greatest thing that I think I can say, is, 'OK, I will accept and try to understand that you have your point of view and you believe you're right and God is on your side. Equally, I ask for that same respect back, that I believe I'm right and God is on my side.' The greatest thing in this equation is, people should never be killed or have to die for a belief of being right, and under the name of God. It's a very, very difficult one, because I'll never have that conversation with him directly.

Humanity

The greatest thing that I've learned about and that I've shaped a lot of my thinking on, is those who risked their lives to come and get me out, and who did so not knowing or caring who I was. It was what I was — a human being. That's really, really affected the way I conduct my own life and think about the world. There is so much we can do for each other. Let's not wait for a tragedy to do that. And I think we see it in many ways every day, but it's just nice to keep reminding us that that is the connector, and it's very powerful, very strong. My memories were not just of a rescue. My memories are of being saved, but equally of being loved. It's the way someone would hold my hand. That is what's extraordinary. That is humanity, and it still touches me to this very day.

Many people who were strangers to me are now dear friends, through tragedy. That gives me great hope. We've been brought together by something, but it hasn't crushed us, and it hasn't torn us apart, and if anything it's reminded so many of us that there is so much good in the world and there's so much to celebrate, and that's what we concentrate on doing.

I guess on a very personal level, when I look down and see that my legs are gone, I just feel that is so senseless. Taking my legs, killing so many of not only my fellow passengers who were right next to me that morning, but so many across London that day, and so many who die every day at the hands of terrorism and bombs. And then there are those who are left maimed like me. There's such a senselessness to it all that I think for me, initially it was about, how do I make sense out of that, what does make sense any more? And the only thing that I could think about was, part of being grateful is equally for me to say, I will do something with my life, I will make this count, I will make what's happened to me count. That's the only way I can make sense of it. That's what drives me to say I must make a difference. If I'm so lucky to be here, then I must use that wisely. It's had a huge impact. I was an absolutely committed workaholic before, and now I've left my job, left my career. I'm still scratching my head about how I'm going to make a living, because of course I still have a mortgage and bills to pay. But somehow it doesn't matter. Somehow the world just looks after me. All that does matter to me is that I make sense of this and I make Gill Hicks being saved make a difference.

Strength

I like to move about very quickly, so for me to be challenged by my own personal speed sometimes gets me down, because I'm just not able to move fast enough. Once again, I have a great layer of people that are always there to lift me back up and say, 'Come on, it doesn't matter. You just walk slower now, that's how it is.' And that's fantastic. The support and love from family and friends have helped me enormously. But apart from that, really I have to rely on myself. I have to rely on the strength from within, and not rely too much on any external intervention.

The death of my mum and dad really affected me, because it was my first understanding that we're not here forever. I think we don't quite understand ourselves not being here, and that had a huge impact on me. But I had a toughness in other ways. I was tough on myself in business and very determined to get ahead, actually to make a difference within architecture and design and art. It's just that now I've swapped that for, 'What can I do for humanity? How do I give back and make things count?' So I guess some of the work practice, coupled with the very real wake-up of Mum and Dad going, have somehow toughened me. Maybe tough is too strong a word, but somehow given me a strength to do what I do now. But I'm very much a newcomer to it, and it is odd. If anyone had asked me on 6th July 2005, 'Do you ever see yourself working in peace?', after a great bout of laughing, I probably would have said, 'No!' I love it that I always wear black, so I still look very much like I work in architecture, but I fool all the peace people by not wearing white!

We're all here and it's a responsibility for each of us, what we do with our lives. Someone, somewhere is feeling the effects of something you have said or done. That's a great responsibility. You could have someone floating around today thinking, 'Oh, I'm brilliant!' because you've told them they are, or you could have the opposite effect. I think what we do carries a great responsibility, and equally with the environment. The environment and peace are the two major things that we all need to be responsible for on the earth. I see it as beyond government responsibility. There's not one single body that can, in inverted commas, 'fix it'. It is up to all of us.

www.peacedirect.org

One Unknown: A powerful account of survival and one woman's inspirational journey to a new life, Rodale International, 2007

Rob Hopkins

*I like to think of this process as
unlocking the collective genius of a community.*

Rob Hopkins has created a local, yet worldwide phenomenon — Transition Initiatives. As a permaculture teacher in Kinsale, Ireland, he was well-placed to lead an investigation with his students into how the community could respond to the impending problem of peak oil — the point at which demand for cheap oil outstrips production. This led, in 2005, to the world's first Energy Descent Action Plan for the town, a ten-year strategy to reduce oil dependency and recreate a more vibrant, localised community. He then moved to Totnes in Devon and engaged the community there in the process of becoming a Transition Town. Since then, 21 places in the UK have already followed suit, and over 200 others around the world seek to do the same.

The change that the Transition Initiatives movement wants to see is that we engage in the process of moving to a lower-energy society as a positive move, rather than as a disastrous collapse or as some hair-shirt exercise. The environmental movement has been extremely lucid at arguing what it doesn't want, but never quite so good at arguing for what it does want. The converging challenges of peak oil and climate change mean that we have to rethink lots of very basic assumptions. With Transition Initiatives, rather than wait for top-down imposed solutions, we're looking at developing mechanisms whereby communities can engage in this as a positive transition and really see the huge potential and benefit that there is in making this move away from cheap oil. Because just as easily as saying, 'How terrible to be leaving oil and gas behind,' you can argue that the age of cheap oil has made us fatter, more stupid, with worse food and less exercise; that actually if we really plan that move away from cheap oil to something more localised and resilient, that could be one of the best things that ever happened to us.

The approach grew out of work that we did in Kinsale in Ireland, where we developed what we called the Kinsale Energy Descent Action Plan. That was the first time anywhere a community was invited to take part in a process of exploring what a lower energy future might actually look like as a positive transition. It began in September 2004. I was teaching permaculture at Kinsale Further Education College, and on the first day of term we had Dr Colin Campbell come In and talk to the students. He's an expert on peak oil. And we watched a film called *The End Of Suburbia*, which is very good on this whole thing. So the students had both of those in a single day and it was a huge double whammy shock to the system — for me as well, I'd not really come into contact with it before. So, with the second year students we designed a project where they looked at how the town of Kinsale, if Colin's projections and forecasts were right, might actually prepare for this transition away from fossil fuels, and embrace this downward descent as a positive move, what we call 'energy descent'. We spent about eight months working with people around the town. We visited existing practitioners who'd been doing green building, gardening and forestry and so on for a long time, trying to engage people in visioning how that could actually be.

Out of that emerged what we called the Kinsale Energy Descent Action Plan. We put it on the website for people to download for free. We finished the plan and then I moved to England. A couple of the students went to the town council with a proposal that the council adopt the Energy Descent Plan, and they were expecting it to be talked out or not really grasped. The council adopted it unanimously.

Transition Town Totnes

I moved to Totnes in Devon in September 2005. What we had started in Kinsale had a lot of potential and needed to be explored and developed further. I met a fellow peak oil activist, and we spent a year doing lots of film screenings and events and talks to try and build up a groundswell of interest in this as a subject and then in September 2006, we ran an event called the *Official Unleashing of Transition Town Totnes*. We had 400 people come to that. That was very, very powerful.

Since then we've started up lots of small groups exploring different aspects of this — food, energy, housing, psychology of change and so on — which are very vibrant and the process has really developed an extraordinary momentum that's driving it forward. A lot of the groups have emerged from different particular events. When we wanted to launch a food group, for example, we ran an evening in Totnes called *Feeding Totnes: Past, Present and Future,* with three speakers, and then we followed that up with an Open Space day. (Open Space is a method of bringing large numbers of people together to explore complex ideas, in such a way that they design and run the event.) The food group arose out of that. So some of the groups have arisen because we've engineered them, and others have emerged spontaneously, like the local government group and so on. It's a very broad spectrum of people. We've just taken on two part-time administrator-coordinators.

There are various projects coming out of it now in terms of large things like a community renewable energy company, and a local currency. We've printed 10,000 Totnes pounds and we're selling them into circulation. People can buy 10 for £9.50, and they can spend them in 70 local shops. It's about plugging the leaks within the community, so you actually have money that's loyal to the town and isn't going to leave. The amount of work it can do to support the community is increased. Then there are other things like edible nut tree plantings throughout the town, and a local food directory. We're running oil vulnerability auditing

The scale and the speed of change that we're going to see in the next ten years is going to exceed what we've seen in the last 100 years. It's the most extraordinary, exhilarating period to be alive.

with local businesses. It builds up a very thorough picture of where a business relies on the availability of cheap liquid fuel, for transportation, for manufacturing, for lubricant, industrial materials and so on. It exposes the areas of risk. All kinds of initiatives are emerging.

The main objective is to develop an Energy Descent Plan for the town, which is a 20-year plan, a timetabled roadmap of how to get from here, where we're so dependent on imported fuel and food and so on, to a point where it's a more localised, vibrant, abundant and pleasant place to be. That's something we're building up to creating next year. We've done the awareness-raising phase, we're now in the design phase and then once we have the Energy Descent Plan, we'll enter the implementation phase. But seeing as we've only been going for a year or so, what's been most extraordinary is how many other towns around the country are starting up doing this process too. This idea has gone viral. There are 21 towns in the UK that are on the list of official Transition Initiatives, and there are over 200 around the world that are in the early stages of exploring it. It's popping up all over the place.

A better future

A key concept to this whole process is that the future with less fossil fuel could be preferable to the present if we design sufficiently in advance, and with sufficient creativity, and if we can engage a broader spectrum of people than we've ever engaged before. A number of people who write on peak oil and climate change use the term 'wartime mobilisation'. We've never seen anything like what we need to do now, apart from in 1938/39 where the whole economy was re-geared, where we shifted from centralised agriculture to 10 per cent of the national diet being grown in gardens and allotments and so on. It's an enormous thing but when the energy goes into doing that, things can happen very, very quickly. Transition Initiatives are about stimulating that as a positive process.

As a society we've always looked forward and tried to envision the future. We're very good at imagining, in our popular culture, future scenarios that are disastrous and catastrophic — robot wars and nuclear holocausts and things — but we're not very good at imagining a low-impact, more localised future. So, my vision for what Totnes would be like in 20 years, for example, would be that there would have been a massive programme of energy conservation and our housing stock would have been made a lot more energy-efficient. People would be working nearer to where they live, there'd be fewer imports and a lot more local manufacturing, so you have a much more vibrant local economy. I think we'd see a lot more food production coming in to where people live. The idea that food is grown in the countryside and people live in the towns will be blurred beyond recognition from today, I think. In terms of energy, you'd be looking at a whole spectrum of local energy sources from hydro, wind, solar, all in and around the town. The town might be on its own grid by then; and the money generated through the consumption of that electricity could be cycled within the community rather than leaving it.

Young people will be growing up much more skilled. Our generation are possibly the most useless ever to walk the planet in terms of the skills we have. People will become a lot more practical again, and a lot less specialised. People could have a lot more time for each other, more time to come together rather than all dashing about insanely all over the place. We'll probably have less technology around but more useful technology. I think we'll live a lot more in rhythm with the seasons, in particular in terms of our energy and so on. I look forward to it, actually, and I think it's really important to enable people to get a grasp of what that might be like, almost so that you could smell it. We can't expect people to embark on this kind of transition without it being a really exciting collective adventure. People say to me, 'How do I tell my children about climate change?' That's where this comes in. You tell them this is the potential for the greatest cultural renaissance that has ever happened. This is the potential for a world that is almost unimaginable. I think the scale and the speed of change that we're going to see in the next ten years is going to exceed what we've seen in the last 100 years. It's the most extraordinary, exhilarating period to be alive.

Reaching out

We try to design the programme so that different events appeal to different interest groups within the town, such as the farming community, local schools, chil-

People know that things aren't right,
and they know continual economic growth
for the next 5,000 years is completely insane.

---

dren and parents. We're working with the older people in the town, doing interviews with them and getting their memories of life in Totnes before the age of cheap oil, and how that transition was between the 1930s and the 1960s when cheap oil came in. We're trying to engage all the different sectors of society here — the people who environmental projects don't normally get to. If we're looking on the scale of this being like a wartime mobilisation, this really has to reach out.

This work engages people in a way that I've never seen in any other environmental process. There's something about it that people find really exhilarating. When you see people really get the idea and they really engage in it with passion and they put their energy behind it, it's extraordinary. There's a huge amount of energy there that we're only just starting to tap. People know that things aren't right, and they know this can't carry on forever, and they know continual economic growth for the next 5,000 years is completely insane. But no one's done that good a job of trying to draw people into it as a positive process. It's all been about campaigning against climate change rather than working positively to create what we do instead.

One of the things that I find amazing is when we run Open Space days and we have 100 people together in this huge hall, brainstorming about food, for example. You go from feeling like you're one person on your own, out on a limb, the only person who really understands the scale of this problem, and feeling completely alone and scared, to feeling like you're a part of a buzzing hive of people sparking all these ideas off each other. You go from thinking, 'My God, I don't know how to grow food!' to, 'Yes, but here's Bert, he does, he's been doing it for 50 years, and this is the person next door to you, he does it too.' You start to reweave all of these things. All the different parts in a town, those are what make it strong, all the links between the different things. This process of Transition Initiatives is looking at the web that kept communities vibrant, strong, able to withstand shocks of all kinds, that we've cut because cheap oil has allowed us the luxury of thinking we don't need them anymore. It's a process of picking up and re-tying these connections, of re-weaving that web again. It's incredibly exciting to see that process happening. People understand it. It makes sense and it feels right.

I like to think of this process as unlocking the collective genius of a community, and trying to get away from that idea that in order to overcome our problems, we have to bring in lots of experts from outside. Occasionally they have a place, but a lot of the time those answers exist around us. One of the things that has surprised me has been how true that is, particularly when we run these Open Space days. People come out of the woodwork, who've been doing these things for years, and are incredibly gifted and incredibly generous with their energy and with their time. There's so much that we're told in the media about everybody being selfish and out for themselves, and that that's normal. At every turn, this process confounds that expectation and brings out the best in people. It brings out their altruism and their desire to make things happen.

In the long term I think the Transition concept has huge potential as a way of meeting government halfway. Government is incredibly nervous of saying to people, 'The future will mean less stuff but a higher quality of life.' But now the communities are coming up saying, 'We don't need all that stuff actually, we've designed this transition and this is what we want to do and this answers all the questions that you're asking but are unable to find answers to because you think we can't cope with the implications.'

And more locally, the town council have been really supportive all the way through. One of the Transition Town groups is the Liaison with Local Government group, with people who are much more involved in that local government world. They invite key people from the district council to come to certain events. There's a district councillor who's very involved in Transition Town Totnes. They can see the energy that's being galvanised, and I think they find that exciting and want to be engaged in it.

Permaculture steps up

In theory it should be utterly exhausting and occasionally it is, but it's so nourishing that there's nothing else I'd rather do instead. It feels a little bit like being in the eye of a hurricane. It's what I've wanted to do for years. I've been teaching permaculture thinking, 'Well, we're slowly building up to changing things,' but

We don't have some birthright, because
we happened to be born where we were, to just
shovel down resources as if they were popcorn.

---

when you meet peak oil, you can't just bimble along, this is big-time. For the permaculture movement, my challenge is, are we ready? In permaculture you basically have a system for the design of sustainable human settlements. You have the design system for societies that no longer have cheap oil to do all the things that cheap oil does for us. It's permaculture's time to step up to the plate really. So I'm saying, 'Are we ready? Let's go!' It feels like the culmination of a lot of different things but in such a way that it's really shifting up a gear, like a wartime mobilisation. In my own life and in my own work I've had a kind of inner wartime mobilisation, if you like. A huge push: how do we step up from where we are now to where we need to be? It's very exciting.

The thing that really resonated with me about permaculture was the ethics, which are earth care, people care and fair shares. Earth care is the care of the earth and its systems and conserving what's already there — healing the earth, basically. People care is that you can't do that independently of the human communities that inhabit the earth, so it's about engaging and supporting them. Fair shares is about living within our allotted footprint on this planet — one planet living, living within our carbon allowance, however you want to look at it — recognising that we don't have some birthright, because we happened to be born where we were, to just shovel down resources as if they were popcorn.

Being the change

My outlook is a very strange mix: growing up around the ethic that emerged out of punk, of do it yourself, be the change in that sense; being involved in Buddhism for quite a long time and that ethic of service and right livelihood; having been involved in loads of protest things in the early 1990s, having a certain degree of rage about all the fantastic places that were covered in tarmac during that time and how heartbreaking that was; and a sense from being involved in permaculture for a long time of how if people have the tools, then they can act, but if you take all the tools away then they can't do anything. When people have those tools and they're shown how to use them, it totally changes their outlook on life and what they do. And, being a father. All of a sudden all this talk about seven generations actually has some tangible meaning. I can put a face to those generations and there's a reason for doing it all.

I've always felt very driven. I always had a very strong sense that change starts with the individual and that you can't wait for anybody else to do anything. It's about living as an example of the change that you want to see, really. I've always been really inspired by those people who have done that. There've been some key people through my life who have really been like that. And I think once you've spent time around those kinds of people, the idea that you could not dedicate your life to leaving a better situation than the one that you came into is inconceivable really. I saw Bill Mollison, the co-founder of permaculture, speaking in 1992. He had this amazing gift to speak to a hall full of people and mortify and profoundly offend half of them and totally change the life of the other half. He gave me an enormous kick up the backside, which has propelled me forward ever since. He was basically saying, 'You know all of this, so what are you doing? What are you doing?' And leaving you in that place of, 'Yeah, what am I doing actually? I know the problems, I know what's wrong and I know now, having listened to what he's said for the last couple of hours, what I can do about it, so why would I not? Why would I not?' Having kids really ramped it up a gear in terms of it all having much more meaning and implication.

It's a bit like allowing a whirlwind into your house. Things will never quite be the same again. But it's fantastic, what else would you do? You kind of swallow it down and it becomes a part of who you are. The main thing is to pace yourself, and not beat yourself up for not doing everything, and to recognise that you can't do it all on your own. Bill Mollison used to say, 'I can't save the planet on my own. It'll take at least three of us.' Find people around who you're drawn to. Celebrate as much as anything else. If it's not fun, then you're doing it wrong. If it's not feeding you and nourishing you on all levels then you're not doing it right. The other thing is to be really honest with it. If you don't know the answer to something, there's nothing wrong with saying you don't know it. What people engage with is genuine experience. You know enough about it that it's driven you, and it's that passion and that enthusiasm that people pick up on. You become an example of it in such a way that people can really see it and that it's really true within you.

I don't know all the answers to all of this. The thing is, the Transition process is not about putting forward all the answers, it's about asking the right questions. There's a degree of humility with that which I feel a lot happier with. We don't know, but it's important at this point in history that we ask the right questions. Once you've asked those questions, life's never the same again. You look at everything in a very different way, and then the whole process starts to roll.

www.transitionculture.org

www.transitiontowns.org

Small is Inevitable, Rob Hopkins, Green Books, 2008

Chris Johnstone

When people act for something bigger than themselves,
when they face challenges that are difficult enough
to really absorb them and grab their attention, that's
when they tend to be most satisfied in their lives.

Chris Johnstone is a specialist in the psychology of change, dedicated to helping people find their power to address both personal and planetary issues. Through his writing, workshops and clinical work, he encourages people to face their concerns, whether they be alcoholism or climate change, and take positive action. He has seen turnarounds happen frequently in his clients' lives as well as his own. As a junior doctor, he led the campaign in the 1990s to reduce untenable working hours in the NHS, and for many years, he has been a key figure in the 'Great Turning' — the movement to turn humanity away from its path of environmental devastation, and instead to head towards a life-sustaining civilisation.

My work is to help people find their power to move in directions important to them. That's very broad and there are different sides to this. One is addressing personal concerns. I work in the health service, helping people tackle addiction problems, and I teach adult education courses helping people make positive changes in their lives. But also a lot of my work is about helping people respond to their concerns about the world. In my writing, talks and workshops, I focus on the psychology of what helps us make a difference. What's really interesting is that whether you're looking at personal or planetary change, the things that help us find our power are pretty much the same.

The biggest change I wish to see is that when people feel troubled by disturbing information in their lives or in the world, rather than feel, 'My God that's too much, I can't do anything about that,' they see it as a challenge to rise to, and then begin the journey of a constructive response. I feel that most passionately about global issues, because a common response is avoidance. So if my life's work can be about supporting the process of facing bad news about the world and rising to the challenge, in a way that helps create a turning, then I feel my life will have been really well spent.

Suing the NHS

In the late 1980s, I was working crazy hours as a junior doctor. I asked my colleagues, 'What can we do about this?' A number of them said the same thing: 'We don't have the power here. There's nothing we can do.' I didn't believe them. I got very involved in the campaign to reduce doctors' hours and challenged the legal basis of my contract by taking my employers to court. The first lawyers I saw said I didn't have a hope in hell. A well-known barrister said it could be laughed out of court and that it could actually do our cause harm. Another lawyer said, 'Look, you can't do this, there's no precedent.' But I was talking with a friend at a party, who was also a lawyer, and she said, 'I don't agree, I think you're being damaged by your working conditions and that can't be lawful.' She helped me start the court case, and 12 other doctors each chipped in a fiver to pay the £60 it cost to issue a writ. After six years and ten court hearings, I finally won the case.

Initially it was just done as a publicity stunt. I issued the writ on a Bank Holiday. On a Bank Holiday, Parliament's closed so there's not much news about, and the journalists were hungry for a story. A friend leaked it to a radio station late at night as journalists tend to listen to late night radio. That weekend I was on call for 50 hours straight, my bleep went about 60 times and I don't think I got more than an about hour and a half sleep at any one stretch. When I came out on Monday morning after having worked since Saturday morning, there were six TV crews and 30 journalists waiting for me. It was all, 'Dr Johnstone, can you yawn this way? Yawn wider, wider!' It was on the front page of the newspapers, and friends the other side of the world told me they'd seen it on their television news.

I kept diaries of my working conditions, and so I had printed out for the journalists on that Monday morning a diary of what my previous week had been. 'Start at eight in the morning, still on the go at half past three in the morning, get to bed for about half an hour, called out again.' It was so ridiculous. But those diaries are what really convinced people. They also provided important evidence in court, and that was part of what helped me eventually win the case.

Crash

Shortly after that, after a working week of about 112 hours or so, I fell asleep driving and wrote off my car. That seemed to provide such a clear parallel to how my life was — if you drive yourself on and on and on, you're likely to crash. I thought, 'Well, that's what I'm doing, and if I just carry on driving myself on like this I'm going to crash in some other way, whether it be an accident or cancer or a bad mistake at work or whatever.' So I resigned at that point. When I left my job, I became homeless and jobless. I felt real fear. I remember a time I was staying with some friends and I felt my legs literally like jelly. I didn't know what I was going to do or where I was going to go. I went and sat in the hills and had one of those momentary insights, like a flash — aha! If you always know what you're going to do then there's no novelty or excitement in life. I didn't know what I was going to do, and another way of looking at that was that there's mystery in life. I felt like I'd discovered mystery sitting in those hills. One of the ways you can really wake up to life is by having that sense of enthralling mystery, by saying, 'Hmmm, I don't know what's around the corner, so it's worth being awake for!' From that moment I was able to relax into the uncertainty. If we have a need for certainty, it creates a lot of anxiety, but as soon as we let go of that need, we can just relax into what's happening.

*I became homeless and jobless.
I felt real fear.*

Some friends had a caravan on the west coast of Scotland, and they said I could stay there. So I stayed in this tiny little caravan for three months, and it was my rehabilitation. I used to go and climb up the hills. Contact with nature really helped. I was depressed at that time, and it helped my recovery from the ghastly hell I'd been through. At that time, some people said it was brave to take on the Health Authority, but actually, from my side, I'd been thinking about killing myself. I'd got to the point when my life was so awful, I was thinking about suicide. I thought, well if I'm going to go down, then really the kinds of fears that would stop me taking action — like it being bad for my career — don't really count for much. When you reach the point of having nothing left to lose, there's a great power in that.

I've been working in the addictions field really ever since then, on a part-time basis, but also every now and again coming back to the idea of wanting to write a book. I'd had a few failed attempts until about six years ago, where I was having a conversation with a friend and I heard myself say, 'The thing I most want to do before I die is write my book.' I wanted to write a book that would help people find their power, drawing on the experiences I'd had. Once I'd made that decision and committed myself to it, I made it the main thing in my life. I cut down my working hours to make room for the writing and I got it done.

Turning things around

One of the things that makes life really rich is when you're living a good story. The stories I'm drawn to are stories of turning things around. That's pretty much the core of most great stories. It may seem pretty dismal and ghastly at the beginning, but the characters find their way to a happy ending, and the story is how they do that. I'd been through that a number of times. I was severely depressed, thinking about killing myself, and now I run courses on happiness. I went through a personal hell in my working environment, and people said, 'No, you can't change it.' And I somehow rose to the challenge and took part in this story of turning things around. So both on a personal level but also on a larger system level, I've lived the story of: 'No you can't, no you can't.' 'Well, let's try anyway.' And then finding that you can. And it's a process that I work with in the addictions field. Exactly the same thing goes on: 'No I can't, no I can't.' 'Well, let's try anyway.' And we find, yes we can, and life gets much better. I believe in the story of turning things around, and when I'm part of that story, it's as though the story acts through me and amazing things happen. The story can unfold in terms of your own personal life, and we can all join together and engage in it at a collective level.

At a collective level, things are so dismal, it's difficult to believe. I call it the Titanic Syndrome — we are heading towards a major crash, and when people look at that, sometimes it's so horrifying that they say, 'I don't want to even give my attention to it, I want to look the other way.' But what I see as an essential part of the turnaround story is looking and seeing how bad things are, in a way that shakes you up. That's when you say, 'Right, I'm going to do something about it.' In addictions recovery, we talk about that as hitting bottom.

When I work with clients, I'm always interested in their crunch points — the points where things got so bad they made a decision to change. When they describe these times, they remind themselves of their reasons for change, and this deepens their motivation. A young alcoholic man I was working with described how getting beaten up had become a turning point for him. He knew it wouldn't have happened if he hadn't been drinking, and the more he talked about this, the more he made his own argument for change.

I use a similar principle when running workshops addressing global issues. When people have space to talk about their concerns for the world, they remind themselves of their motivation for change. When we talk about the things that really alarm us, it has an activating effect. It is when we're stirred up that we begin to look for a new way forward.

I'm very involved in positive psychology, which is a scientific approach to looking at how people increase happiness and feelings of satisfaction in their life. Research shows that when people act for something bigger than themselves, when they face challenges that are difficult enough to really absorb them and grab their attention, that's when they tend to be most satisfied in their lives —

I've lived the story of:
'No you can't, no you can't.' 'Well, let's try anyway.'
And then finding that you can.

and that's been my experience. There's also some research that shows that on the whole, people who are involved in acting for addressing global issues tend to be happier, which is so different from what people would expect! There are self-help books that actually say, 'Avoid negative thoughts.'

What I'm much more interested in is how we respond to the negative thoughts we have. You can have a negative thought that leads to a positive response that leads to an amazing life. I see that particularly as an addictions specialist. So much of addiction is, 'I don't want to look at that, it depresses me, so I'll have a drink and cheer myself up.' Whereas the learning of recovery is that the way to feel good about your life is to do things you feel good about, and that often involves facing difficult challenges. When you face a difficult challenge, and you rise to it, then you're left with the inner glow of true gratification.

Bouncing back

I wrote my book to show people how to find their power to do this. There've been some failures along the way. I sent quite a lot of book proposals to publishers that got rejected. The whole process of writing my book was one of rising and falling and rising and falling. I spent a year working on a book proposal and sent it to somebody, and after two months I got a bland response saying they didn't think it was suitable for their list. I thought I was sending them an offer they couldn't refuse. But each of those failings, each of those mini-disasters along the way has been part of my training. So each time you fall — splat! — there's a bruised period where you pick yourself up, but then you say, what do I need to find out about, in order to do better next time round? And then after working with a publishing consultant, within two months I had a publisher sign me up. What I'm learning from this is that things that seem like major failures at the time can later be looked on as important learning experiences that helped me succeed. At the time they felt awful and it felt like the end of everything, but you get up, you continue the journey and you learn from that.

My book meant so much to me. I'd had this little voice inside my head for years saying, 'I want to write this book.' It was 17 years from my first book proposal until it finally came out. I remember when I finished the first draft I was on an incredible high, and then when I finished the final draft, I was floating. I was so delighted. It was an amazing feeling to have. I have a number of questions I ask myself every day. When I'm going out for a walk, I say, 'What am I really happy about? What am I really pleased about? What am I thankful for?' And one of the things that keeps coming up is I'm really pleased I got my book done.

What was surprising was the way my whole being really engaged in this project. I'd wake up in the night and I'd have ideas. When you're really filled with a project, creativity acts through you. It's a bit like white-water rafting — you're swept along by something. There've been a few times where big flows like that have happened. The court case was one of them and the book has been another. I feel like there's something bigger going on and all I can do is be a loyal servant of it. There's a thread that I'm following and it feels right inside. Sometimes it's a bumpy journey, but I suppose what I'm learning is to trust those threads more, so I'm less likely to dismiss something because it seems like a hare-brained scheme. If it feels right inside, if I really get that signal inside like this feels like the right thing to follow, then I'm more likely to do that.

The Great Turning

The main thing that keeps me motivated is the idea that I'm playing a part in an amazing story. I think of it as the Great Turning. It's a story that's difficult to see when you're in the middle of it. But when you step outside something you can see it as a whole. When astronauts look at the earth, they can see it as a whole. We need to step outside our own period in history to see what's happening. We don't know how it's going to go. It might be that this is going to be looked at as the great unravelling, the great vandalism. This is how people in the future might look on the current moment. They might look upon it as the period of the great trashing of the planet and where we wrecked things so much that all the generations after us were picking up the pieces and making the best with a damaged planet and a disturbed climate and all the rest of it.

That's one version of how things could go. But another version of how things could go is: this is the period in history where we woke up to what we were doing

*You can have a negative thought that leads
to a positive response that leads to an amazing life.*

and put the full weight of our lives behind creating a turnaround. If that happened, then maybe 400 years in the future they'll look back at this period and say, 'That was the time of the Great Turning.' I like that story, and the idea that I could become part of it is one of the things that feeds me with motivation. I produce an email newsletter, the Great Turning Times, and I get people emailing me from all around the world telling me ways in which they're part of the Great Turning too. It becomes a story that reinforces itself. The more I become part of the story, the more evidence I see that the story is happening, and the more I want to become part of it and the more confidence I have. It becomes like a snowball rolling down a hill — the more it rolls, the bigger it gets. Also, it's what I feed myself with. The diet we feed ourselves will influence what we become. It's not about avoiding negative information, it's about taking in the negative information, but also feeding ourselves with stories of a positive response. Positive stories are like fuel for positive vision.

What I most want at the end of my life is to feel that I've really played my best role in the Great Turning. I constantly come back to that question — what's the best way of doing it? One of the major hold-ups is the blocked response to the difficulty. People look at what's going on and they say, 'This is too much, it's too overwhelming, I can't do anything so what's the point?' And they switch off. Those decisions: Do I rise to the challenge? Do I give up? Do I even look at the problem in the first place? Those are the points where I want to give my energy and attention because they're leverage points. We have incredible creativity as humans. If we were to really notice what's going on and give our full attention to finding and constructing the best response, we just don't know what could happen! And at the moment, generally, we're not even on the case. How does society think? What does the media focus its attention on? One of the biggest uses of the internet is pornography! We are so off-track. If we were to use our fantastic brains and hearts and find ways of working with each other to address the issues like, 'How do we carry on living?' and, 'How do we create lives that are worth living?' I think it's amazing what could happen.

Being the change

There's been this false split between selfishness and altruism, and it's so unhelpful. The research shows that, on the whole, more materialistic people have less satisfying lives. Somehow we've got on the wrong program, and I'd say that if you really want an enjoyable life, then finding some way to contribute towards positive change in the world is one of the best ways of doing that. What I would also say is, pay attention to ways you can make it more enjoyable. Because sometimes I think we can do work for the world in a way that's about duty and suffering, rather than about enthusiasm and joy. It's actually strategic to make what we do enjoyable, because for a start we're more likely to keep on doing it. There's a high burn-out rate in people who are active for causes bigger than themselves. But also, if we make what we do enjoyable, it's more likely to become infectious. I think what's needed is to make the process of being the change so contagious and infectious that everybody wants to do it. Many people are missing out on this great secret that actually this is a really enjoyable way to live. If you want to live a life where you feel more alive and you have that bright light in your eyes, this is the way to go.

I think that who you hang out with does make a difference. We base our sense of what an appropriate way to act is on comparing ourselves with other people. If the people we spend time with all have one particular set of responses, we're more likely to follow that response too. It's tribal behaviour really. So if you find that your reference group doesn't support positive change in the world, then look for recruiting new friends, and spend time with people who are having positive responses because you're likely to catch it from them. Whereas cynicism and disbelief and fearful shutdown can also become contagious responses.

Optimism and hope

My garden used to be just concrete slabs, and now it's a mass of green. It's just a tiny corner of a city, but it's part of the Great Turning. It's a tiny step in a bigger shift towards a life-sustaining culture. There are apples, blackberries and roses, and I've got over 30 different types of fruit, herb and nut. I make my own Ribena from the blackcurrants. I find hope in the amazing regenerative power of nature. You can have something that looks like a desert, ecologically, and yet seven years later it looks like paradise. And what also gives me hope is my own personal experience of turnaround. I know that it's possible in my own life, I see that it's possible in my garden, I've seen that it's possible in a large, seemingly stuck organisation, I see it happening in my clients, and I see it happening in lots of places around the world. Every time I see that story happening, it reinforces my confidence in the process of turning things around. People say, 'Are you optimistic that it will all work out fine?' No I'm not, but I am optimistic about engaging in the journey of finding our best response. I know that it can make a difference and I also know that when we are on that journey and engaged in it, it makes life a lot more fun and a lot more satisfying.

www.findyourpower.org

www.greatturningtimes.org

Find Your Power, Nicholas Brealey Publishing, 2006

Van Jones

***It's not just about saving polar bears,
it's about saving urban kids too.***

Van Jones is an environmental and social justice campaigner based in Oakland, California. He co-founded the Ella Baker Center for Human Rights, which focuses on keeping young people out of prison. He has devised a win-win strategy to address the problems of poverty and climate change: green jobs. He identified the need for a workforce qualified to create a clean, green energy infrastructure, to retrofit housing stock; in fact, to build a new, green economy, that can protect the environment and lift people out of poverty at the same time. A green jobs corps is now being established locally by the City of Oakland, and Jones has gone on to great success nationwide. In August 2007, the Green Jobs Act was passed, allocating $125 million in funding to train thousands of people across the US for green jobs.

We have to transition to a green economy that is strong enough to lift people out of poverty. The first industrial revolution was horrible for people and it was hard on the planet, and I think we need, for lack of a better term, a second industrial revolution where we proceed with much more wisdom and care and caution with regard to our impacts on living systems, human and non-human. I think that we've begun that process in the United States, finally. We're beginning to see a strong counter-current in the direction of more sustainable economic activity. The challenge now is to continue to expand that consciousness and expand that coalition politically to include the people who most need a cleaner economy and a more robust, labour-intensive economy. That's what I'm committed to.

I founded the Ella Baker Center for Human Rights eleven years ago, and our mission evolved to essentially be working to get kids out of jail and into jobs. That created a real moral dilemma — what kind of jobs do we think our young people should accept? There's an assumption that if somebody's low-income or they're a person of colour or they have a conviction on their record, that they should take any job they can get, and they shouldn't have any moral standards. We saw that as very problematic and contradictory. If some kid in the neighbourhood is engaging in economic activity that hurts people, say selling drugs or stealing cars, society puts that kid in prison. That same kid gets out and gets a job at a factory that's polluting everybody, or working in some industry that's toxifying the groundwater, you call that kid a success story and a role model. We thought that was bizarre.

Green pathways out of poverty

We decided that we would only advocate to get our young people into what we call green-collar jobs. That term's becoming fashionable, but we just grabbed it to mean vocational work, work with your hands that would be good for the health of the community and for the health of the planet. We recognised that the old blue-collar jobs were the old stepping stones out of poverty for people. The bad thing about the blue-collar jobs was they were often polluting and the workplace conditions were unhealthy. But they were there for workers and to climb that pathway out of poverty. Well, most of the blue-collar jobs in the United States are leaving. There's a lot of downsizing, firms are moving to India and China and other places, and a lot of those rungs that you would have been able to climb out of poverty are just no longer there. So it's almost like we're expecting a whole generation of people who've been born into poverty now to climb a six-storey ladder out of poverty, but the ladder only has four rungs on it. It's literally not possible.

What we know about jobs in the more environmentally-friendly parts of the economy is that they're very difficult to offshore. You've got to put up solar panels here, you've got to build wind farms here, you've got to weatherise millions of buildings here. You've got to grow organic food locally, if you're going to do it really in a green way. All those are jobs that aren't going to leave the country. So we saw an opportunity to advocate for young people to be trained for these jobs of the future, that could be stable, dignified, living wage and long-standing. We thought it was important to do that rather than accept any old pollution-based, poison-based job, and/or put people on tracks for jobs that are going to disappear very shortly.

So what does that mean for us practically? Practically what that meant was that we decided, having had a fairly adversarial relationship with municipal governments in the Bay Area, that we needed to find some common ground, to change our relationship in some ways with local governments, with the business community, even with the labour unions, to say, 'We need a different economic strategy for these kids.' It's one thing to advocate to reform policing, and reform the juvenile justice system. We continue to do that. But once those kids come home from jail, from prison, getting them securely into the job market is a big task that everybody has to play a role in, and especially in jobs that we can all be proud of. So we decided that we would create a Green Jobs Corps here in Oakland, to train young people to put up solar panels, to weatherise homes, to manage wind farms. To do all the work of the future.

The exciting thing about it for us is that if you teach a kid to put up solar panels, that kid is on the way to becoming an electrical engineer. That's a green pathway out of poverty. If you teach a kid how to weatherise a building, maybe double-glaze it so it doesn't leak so much energy, that kid is on the way to becoming a glazier. That's a green pathway out of poverty. Similarly, teach a kid how to repair a hybrid engine, the kid's not ever going to be hungry, because here in northern California there are so many Priuses on the road. Or, you have a lot of people who want to buy organic food. Can you get the kid in that industry? And

We don't live on a throwaway planet
and we don't have any throwaway people.

now, some of the people who are in construction are realising that certain kinds of homeowners want very special materials, for instance, bamboo. We thought to ourselves, what if you taught some of these young people from the beginning how to work with some of these specialised materials? Then you're giving them a competitive advantage in the labour market. If you give somebody a competitive advantage in the labour market, they can go from the back of the line for the last century's pollution-based jobs to the front of the line for the new clean and green jobs.

So that became our strategy. We have 25 people that work in this organisation and a few of us took this challenge on. Ian Kim and Jeremy Hayes decided they were going to pull together a city-wide coalition to make this happen. Now if you know anything about Oakland politics, we have a city council that has eight members and ten factions. It's a very divisive town, and very hard to get things done. But Jeremy and Ian walked to all four corners of the city and talked to everybody they could. More importantly, they listened to everybody they could, and by listening to people they gained their trust. And they were able to identify in every bureaucracy in the city, one or two people who really passionately believed in this idea. They pulled those people together to begin meeting and talking and planning, and they were so happy to have found each other and to have a common purpose, we were able to get a unanimous vote out of the City Council to fund this green jobs corps. We had the support of every conceivable kind of person. That was a big victory for us. So by the summer of 2008, we will have a green jobs corps in Oakland.

Green jobs nationwide

Because we were so passionate about creating this win-win opportunity in Oakland, fighting pollution and poverty at the same time, some people in San Francisco just across the bridge heard about our work and they investigated it and thought it was good. It turned out that those people were working for Nancy

Pelosi, the Congresswoman representing San Francisco, who also happens to be the Speaker of the House. That makes her the third most powerful person in the United States, according to our Constitution. If George Bush and Dick Cheney were to choke on a pretzel, she'd be President. She's got a very powerful role in our system. And her staffers really liked what we were doing. Not just what we were doing but the spirit that we were going about the work with, that we were reaching out to lots of different people, that we were sticking up for people who were left out, but we weren't doing it from a position of being righteous or mad at anybody. We just wanted everybody to cooperate. So we wound up getting a meeting with the Speaker herself. I asked her if she would do something on a national level that would give young people in urban America some help and some hope.

There's a whole generation of African-Americans, Latinos, Asians, poor white kids, in rural and urban America — nobody's ever told them anything except, 'Don't do drugs, don't shoot anybody and don't get pregnant.' And then they just walk away. They don't give them a vision of the future, they don't tell them what their contribution can be. I knew that Speaker Pelosi was very passionate about climate change and I said, 'Why don't you reach out to this generation of kids and tell them, "We have to retrofit a whole nation. We have to rewire, reboot, retrofit an entire nation's energy infrastructure. We're going to have to put up millions of solar panels, thousands of wind farms, weatherise all these buildings. I want you to help us. I want to give you the tools and the training for you to lead this effort, for you to do that great work."' I said, 'If you do that, not only will you secure the Democrats' hold on Congress for a couple of decades, you'll expand the coalition against global warming to include people who right now feel, "It has nothing to do with us," and you'll give real hope and real help to the people who have been thrown out and left behind. To me, a green economy is an economy that doesn't just focus on reclaiming throwaway stuff, it's also about reclaiming throwaway people, throwaway communities, throwaway neighbourhoods. That's a green economy, when you really are reclaiming the totality of what's sacred and what's precious.' And she agreed.

On 4th August 2007, in the House of Representatives, an amendment was passed with her support, to amend the Energy Bill to include $125 million a year for five years to do job training across the country, following our model. There'll be about 30-35,000 people trained each year with that money. And the special part of those dollars will be designated toward low-income people, people who have barriers to employment, meaning they went to jail or they haven't finished high school. We call it our Green Jobs, Pathway Out of Poverty Bill. Hilda Solis, a Latina environmentalist and Congresswoman from Southern California, carried that legislation. So this is a very important year for the green economy in the United States.

Bridging divides

I think fundamentally that we don't live on a throwaway planet and we don't have any throwaway people. We all need each other. When you get involved in progressive politics, it can become very divisive. People on the left are notorious for being righteous and smartypants and know-it-all. Sometimes that's good. Sometimes you need somebody to stir it up a little bit, challenge the status quo. But at the end of the day, rebels oppose, revolutionaries propose. I feel the politics of opposition has to yield at some point to a politics of proposition. At some point, the intellectual faction of deconstruction has to yield to an intellectual push of reconstruction. I feel that that's where we are now. At this point, given the severity of the social and economic crisis in urban America, the severity of the ecological crisis at the planetary level and the severity of the spiritual crisis at the human level, I think that we need more friends and fewer enemies, all of us. There are sometimes irreconcilable differences and conflicts and clashes; when you find yourself in a situation like that, sometimes you just have to fight it out. But I think you want that to be your last option and not your first assumption about every challenge. I come out of a part of the left that assumed that there was going to be a big fight, and we just wanted to be the most belligerent people in the fight, and I'm at a point in my life where I try to find common ground and see if I can build out from there.

Sometimes I've found, dealing with somebody who should be opposed to you — maybe they're an incarcerator, maybe they're a right-winger, maybe they're racially antagonistic, maybe they run a big corporation — you can sometimes persuade that person to do something completely opposed to their entire life story if you show them love and respect and remind them of who they really are. And all of us are really the same person in terms of wanting to be loving and wanting to do generous things that are maybe beyond our comfort zone, but that are meaningful. It's important, I think, for people to recognise the possibility of miraculous outcomes in every encounter, and to conduct ourselves as if a miracle is about to happen. We can have a politics of hope and optimism, as opposed to a politics of cynicism where we create what it is we say we don't want, which is antagonism from other parties.

Social and environmental issues

There's two ways to look at finding common ground between social and environmental activism. One is more of a deep, spiritual, moral piece that says we won't have a human society on a dead planet, and a human society on a living planet that's divided by race and class is probably not worth saving. And that takes you so far. But I also think there's a practical, strategic, hard-headed, political set of calculations that also have to be taken into account. Take the growing carbon reduction movement in the United States, probably the most important movement on the planet.

The United States is still per capita the biggest emitter of carbon, the biggest driver towards ecological catastrophe. The only way to fix it is for America to act right and hopefully convince India and China to act right. That movement is going to be derailed by polluters and poor people, because the polluters are going to spend a lot of money scaring poor people that any move away from the carbon path is going to cost them a lot of money — in their heating bills, their gas bills, in food costs. There'll be a backlash alliance between polluters and poor people, unless the carbon cutters reach out to the poor people first, and say, 'We want this movement to be a movement that's about asthma-free cities. We want it to be a movement that's about green-collar jobs, putting your kids to work. We want to be a movement that's about fixing our schools, so that there's clean technology training centres in every public school and green-collar vocational training in every community. We want this movement to be about solving your problems.'

If there is that spirit that it's not just about saving polar bears, it's about saving urban kids too, then there'll be a basis for this movement to continue to grow. But if the eco-elite just assume, 'Well, all my friends are driving hybrids, and I put up solar panels on my second home, so we've got this thing licked,' then all the people who can't afford to buy a hybrid, maybe who can't even afford the bus

Rebels oppose,
revolutionaries propose.

---

fare, and all the people who don't have a second house or even one house are going to, rightfully, feel resentful and fight back. So from a purely practical point of view, the idea that the mainstream mostly white environmental community can get this job done by itself is false.

So there's a real practical level there. Similarly, on the social justice side, we can't get any of our problems solved unless we are in league and alliance with the environmental solution drivers. Why? Our fundamental problem is that the de-industrialisation of America has stranded millions of poor people with no upward mobility through the legitimate economy. We've got to jumpstart the US economy. If you jumpstart it in a dirty way, with low wages and dirty energy, you put a dollar in a worker's pocket as a wage, you take it right back out in health care costs, for asthma and cancer and everything else. You're on a treadmill to nowhere. The only way to grow the economy that will make a lasting, meaningful difference is to do it in a way that creates more jobs, more wealth, more health — in other words to build a green economy, strong enough to lift people out of poverty. When you look at all of it together, you realise it seems like there are a lot of issues, it seems like there are a lot of constituencies, it seems like there's a lot of different interests, but at the end of the day, there's only one solution. The solution to all of it is a green economy strong enough to lift people out of poverty. That's the solution. Everything else falls into that.

The last thing I'll say about it is this: if you think about it, if we go along as we've been going along, poor people and people of colour in the United States will get hit first and worst with everything bad that's coming because of the ecological crisis, and will be benefited last and least for all of the positive ecological changes that are coming. And that's not acceptable. That's what we call eco-apartheid — a society with ecological haves and ecological have-nots. Eco-apartheid won't work. It will just be a speed-bump on the way to eco-apocalypse. If you have an eco-apartheid society, the backlash between the poor and the polluters will sink whatever little tiny percentage of the green economy you've got going, and then you're down the same tubes, you've maybe just delayed it by five years. So what we're saying is, poor people and people of colour have to engage with the mainstream white and affluent environmental community, and say, 'We want equal protection from the worst of the environmental crisis, and we want equal opportunity and equal access to the best of the ecological solutions. On that basis, we'll be your best friends, we'll be your best partners. We'll vote, we'll march, we'll work, we'll consume, we'll invent, we'll invest, we'll start new businesses. We'll be a part of a green growth alliance that can save the US economy and save the world. But if we can't have equal protection, if we can't have equal access, because of either our unwillingness to work with you or your unwillingness to work with us, our grandchildren are not going to be here.'

The greening of America

I feel called to do what I'm doing. The next revolutionary change in American society will be the greening of America. It can either succeed and include everybody, or it can fail by including only the eco-elite. I see that very clearly, and I feel that my calling is to make sure that the greening of America succeeds by being as inclusive as possible. Now, that's a very easy sentence to say, and it's a lot of work. It's tough, but it's not complicated.

I know that we as a country and as a species have only just begun to do the good that we can do. Sometimes you need a big challenge, like the one that we're facing in the new century, to bring out the best in people. I say a crisis is a terrible thing to waste. It's an opportunity for us to really find each other in a new way. I really believe if we say that not only are these young people in urban America and these lost kids on meth in rural America, the canaries in the coalmine for all the dysfunction of our system, but they're also going to be the sources of the genius and the creativity and the inventiveness and the resourcefulness to solve these problems. Then I think we're going to be in good shape. Let's put these young kids who've been thrown to the margins, let's put them in the centre of all of our movements and say that the green movement is successful when those kids have a green future. If you've fixed it for these poor kids, you've fixed it. If they can get up in the morning and breathe clean air and drink clean water, and go to work someplace that's not polluting anything, and then go and have a good

The only way to grow the economy that will make a lasting, meaningful difference is to build a green economy, strong enough to lift people out of poverty.

evening, you can be guaranteed that everybody else is going to be enjoying those benefits. You can be guaranteed that you've actually then transitioned over to a truly green society. If you don't do it that way… There is no 50 per cent sustainable economy. There's no 20 per cent. That's just not sustainable. Unfortunately this thing, it's like pregnancy — you're either pregnant or you're not. This is like that. It's either going to be sustainable, and you're going to be able to be here, or you're fixing it with one hand and you're undoing your successes with the other. That's the danger we have to avoid.

Gifts

Everybody is born with some gifts, whether it's for sports or science or social change, and the people I admire the most are the people who have found a way to express those gifts. Mine just happen to be in the domain of social change. I love Michael Jordan. I can't play basketball, I probably couldn't even dribble a basketball, but the artistry of his athleticism and the steely resolve of his competitive drive inspire me. I love excellence. I love people who have found what they can contribute and who are doing it. That's all I'm doing. I could make it be about, 'Oh, this is the most important work and everyone who doesn't do it sucks,' but I think that's for a younger man to say. At this point in my life, I'm just trying to make the best contribution I can make with the talents that I have, and I hope that everybody does that, whatever their talents are.

Everybody already knows inside themselves what it is that they're born to do. And then they do a whole bunch of other stuff. That's what humans do! We know what we're born to do and we find a thousand other things to do instead. The most important thing is to do what you love, do what you're good at, and do it with a spirit of generosity. But I can't tell people. I trust people to seek out their own inspiration, their own information and to do the right thing. What people most need is to be in community with other people who are trying to do beautiful, great things. I tell people, it's not what you should start doing, it's what you should stop doing. I'd rather have a conversation with people about what they should stop doing. What are you doing right now that's in the way of you being happy, that's in the way of you doing things that you know you could do? That's a much more fruitful conversation because 90 per cent of the problem is all the crap — all the relationships that aren't serving you, all the old patterns and habits that aren't serving you, all your own fears and insecurity. You disappear all that and then suddenly your sculpture or your radical circus touring festival or your website show up immediately.

A new stage

Most of the time, humans figure it out. Some societies have disappeared. Most societies persist, learn, grow, evolve, change. No matter how bad it is for me, I'm not an enslaved African here 150 years ago. I'm not living under segregation. So if you know your history and you know the kind of challenges that the human family has met, there's really no reason to despair.

We're in a new stage. Even looking at human history for the past 150 years, all around the world, there are so many people who have done so much incredible stuff against such difficult odds. No matter who you are, you're in a better position than they were. I'm in a better position than Dr King was, I'm in a better position than any African-American leader ahead of me in line. I'm in a much more enviable position, because I can look at their examples and build on their successes. I have technology. It wasn't possible 20 years ago to walk down the street and put your voice in the mind of somebody on the other side of the world, you'd be a wizard. Now, if you walk around with a cellphone and a laptop, you've got better technology on your person than the entire United States government had when it put a man on the moon. Every single person that's walking around is an individual superpower.

www.ellabakercenter.org

Craig Kielburger

*We quickly realised it wasn't enough just to kick down doors
and bring children out of factories. The challenge was
creating alternatives so these kids wouldn't end up
there in the first place.*

In 1995, when Craig Kielburger was 12 years old, he heard about child labour for the first time, and was determined to do something about it. He backpacked around south east Asia investigating the issue, meeting children working in factories and hearing their stories. With 11 of his classmates, he formed Free The Children, which has grown into the world's largest network of children helping children. Their Youth in Action groups have 35,000 members across North America, who get together to learn about global issues and raise funds for Free The Children's work overseas. Over a million children in developing countries have benefited from their holistic development model, which includes building schools, water and health facilities and alternative income schemes.

My hope is to see a world in which all children are free from the devastating effects of poverty. Free The Children's goal is to inspire and empower young people to achieve this by reaching out and taking action that creates lasting, meaningful change for their peers in developing nations.

We live in a time where over half of all people on earth live on less than two dollars a day and over a billion people are unable to read or write. An estimated 246 million children are currently engaged in labour around the world, many performing dangerous tasks in unsafe conditions. Meanwhile, global debt, military conflict, climate change and rampant greed have created almost unimaginable disparity between the world's wealthy nations and developing regions. It has been estimated that each year we spend $14 billion on ocean cruises, $18 billion on make-up, and $40 billion on golf. Yet the United Nations estimates that it would take as little as $7 billion to provide a basic primary education for every child in the world. While working for Kofi Annan, Jeffrey Sachs estimated that providing health care, water and sanitation resources and education for every person on the planet would cost only about $60 billion — and yet global military spending now tops $1 trillion annually.

For the first time in history, we possess the capability to eradicate poverty in the world. Yet it will require a massive shift in our global priorities. We believe that the key to freeing children from the cycle of poverty is through education. With the foundation of primary education, children are empowered to make informed choices about their health, their community and their future.

Beginnings

It all began back in 1995. I grew up in the suburbs of Toronto. Both my parents were teachers; I had a very traditional, comfortable, middle-class upbringing. For me, poverty was something that you saw either in the city downtown, or you saw it on the news, but it never affected my life. One morning I read an article on the front page of the *Toronto Star*: 'Battled child labor, boy, 12, murdered.' Learning about the life and death of child rights activist Iqbal Masih of Pakistan sent me on a journey that would forever change my life. It affected me more than any other story I'd ever seen. This first encounter with injustice, as experienced by a 12-year-old boy like myself, dramatically changed my ideas about the world. I remember being so angry that I ripped out the story from the paper, and kept

*I went to my grade seven class
and held up the article saying,
'I need your help. Who'll join me?'*

---

staring at the photo and reading the story again and again and again. I wanted to do something to help, and I went to my grade seven class and held up the article, saying, 'I need your help. Who'll join me?' And that's how Free the Children first began, with a group of 12 12-year-olds.

Iqbal Masih was a young boy from a community outside of Lahore in Pakistan, and when his family desperately needed money, they took out something called a *peshi* debt. Obviously in North America if you desperately needed money, you could pledge a house or a car or something as collateral; how a *peshi* debt is structured is that it uses a person as collateral. When they couldn't repay, Iqbal started to work to pay off this loan, as an indentured labourer — a modern-day form of slavery. He worked in a carpet factory, at the age of four, tying tiny knots — how hand-knotted carpets are made — and he would do this hour upon hour upon hour, six days a week.

When he was ten he managed to escape. He had to escape, because he found that his initial debt was worth the equivalent of about $16 when he was sold, and had augmented to more than $300 — they charged him for mistakes, and food. He quickly realised this was a cycle of bondage. At the age of ten he heard a human rights speech in his community saying that the *peshi* debt had been abolished, and he spoke to the leader there, who went on to help free him. Iqbal became famous in Pakistan, standing up in front of rallies, showing his scars, telling his story, explaining that he was now free.

He started travelling the world. He went to Sweden, he went to the United States, and when he was 12 he returned to Pakistan. He was riding his bicycle just in front of his home, and he was shot dead. He was assassinated. No one quite knows why, but it's widely suggested, and many believe, that it's linked to people who are in the import and export business in carpets in Pakistan, that basically he was assassinated for being a human rights activist.

I remember trying to sit down with my parents and I started by saying I wanted to take two months off school, which probably wasn't the best way to begin. I said that I wanted to go through India, Pakistan, Bangladesh, Thailand and Nepal, researching child labour. I told them that I didn't want them to go with me, and I asked if I could go. My mom said, 'Craig, we love you very much, but you're 12. You can't take the subway by yourself. So no, you can't go to India by yourself.' But every morning that followed, I kept asking the same question, until finally my mom said, 'You're not allowed to ask again, unless you already have half the money in the bank account and you can prove that you'd be safe. Then we'd talk about it.'

I started shovelling driveways to save up the money, and wrote letters to local organisations in Asia. I even pretended to be my own secretary at one point: 'Mr Craig Kielburger wants to come for a visit, will you help him?' And these groups wrote back saying yes. And I found a chaperone — a 25-year-old student from the University of Toronto. He spoke Bengali, he was from Bangladesh originally, and he wanted to learn more about his culture and his roots, so he offered to take me.

Researching child labour

The trip was from December 1995 to January 1996. And that is really in many ways why I'm still doing this all these years later. Not because of Iqbal. He was the initial inspiration, but it was realising that Iqbal's story was not just one story about a young boy who lived and died for what he fought for. It was understanding that there are millions and millions more Iqbals in the world, and having a chance to meet and spend time with some of them on that trip. I divide my life into pre-Asia and post-Asia.

While we were travelling, by luck, the prime minister of Canada and a Canadian trade delegation of 250 business leaders were travelling in Asia at the same time. While we were researching the issue of child labour, the prime minister and his team were signing multi-billion dollar trade deals that were making the front page of the papers, and they weren't talking about human rights.

So after taking part in a raid in India, out of desperation for the prime minister to raise this issue and talk about human rights and child labour, I decided to call a press conference. I went to the hotel where the prime minister was staying

*My mom said, 'Craig, we love you very much,
but you're 12. You can't take the subway by yourself.
So no, you can't go to India by yourself.'*

---

and started to slide notes under the doors of all the hotel guests, in the hopes that one of them would be a member of the press. Eventually security stopped me, but they kindly helped me to realise that there was actually a Canadian room where you could hold a press conference if you were Canadian. So I ended up holding a press conference with two freed child slaves, who we knew because we'd been volunteering at the centre where they had been undergoing their rehabilitation.

One was named Negashir, and he was 14 at the time. He had been branded all over his body with hot irons as a punishment for trying to escape. Mohan was even younger, he was 12, and he had witnessed a friend being executed when he tried to escape. These two boys told their stories for the press who were sitting there. Their photos went on the front page of the Canadian papers, and they ended up going round the world, and that forced the prime minister to sit down and meet with us, to talk about the issue of child labour. It had that immediate effect. It also had the larger effect of growing us from being a group of 12 12-year-olds. People around the world heard about what we were doing, especially young people, and they joined us in our efforts. Since then, a small group of concerned students rapidly expanded. Today, Free The Children is the world's largest network of children helping children through education. Our Youth in Action Groups encompass the globe.

In the beginning days of our organisation, many people were sceptical of our efforts. Child labour was not an issue on people's minds at the time, and the notion that children could make a difference in global issues was not one many took seriously. But as we demonstrated we could back up our message with real research and hard facts, we were able to convince people that we were serious about making a real difference.

Free The Children

Free The Children as an organisation started with anti-child labour campaigns, protest rallies, kicking down doors, rehabilitation centres for children once they had been freed from slavery. We were successful in passing various pieces of legislation in North America, often even internationally in developing countries to protect children's rights. We quickly realised it wasn't enough just to kick down doors and bring children out of factories. The challenge was creating alternatives so these kids wouldn't end up there in the first place.

We've implemented a holistic development model. Income-generating cooperatives for women are the cornerstone. We not only build schools, water projects and health projects — the women's cooperatives are what make it all economically self-sustaining. Within five years, we can actually start phasing out economic support.

The cooperatives are different in each country. In Sri Lanka for example, we run a vocational training centre where we teach skills ranging from sewing to basic carpentry to computer skills. In Kenya, where we're in a far more rural part of the country, the cooperative is usually based around animal husbandry and traditional Masai beadwork, that they can sell to earn income. We introduce financial literacy classes. We sit down with the women and talk about what industries already exist, what types of jobs or skillsets they think will translate into their economy. We find in a lot of developing countries, some groups come in and train 100 seamstresses for a rural community that really can only support three or four. So we analyse with each woman what her hopes are, what her specific skillsets are and what she'd also enjoy doing.

External capital is now introduced. This is not microcredit in the traditional system, because we don't ask for the original loan to be repaid. Instead it's almost a 'pay it forward' mentality, where as the women earn income, they put into a communal fund what they would have paid back as the capital with interest. That fund is jointly administered by all the women in the community, and then they help pay the teachers' salaries, do the repairs on the school, provide any monies that are needed to maintain the well or the water systems. Too often in the developing world, you see donations coming year after year after year in a model that is not really self-sustaining. I think it sometimes can be disempower-

I went to the hotel where the prime minister
was staying and started to slide notes
under the doors of all the hotel guests.

ing for the community, because it's constant handouts. But instead with this model, within five years, all of the projects, from the wells to the schools to the medical programme, are economically self-sufficient.

The organisation evolves

The second evolution of our network is Leaders Today. Free The Children has the mission of focusing overseas, and Leaders Today has the mission of creating that broader social shift, creating a generation of young global citizens among youth in North America. So Leaders Today runs camps in five or six cities every summer, to teach about social activism. We have speaking tours that go into the schools, and we have eight full-time people who write curriculum material for school boards that teaches about global citizenship, compassion and social justice. Leaders Today works with about 350,000 youth every year in North America, training, teaching, inspiring and empowering them to become activists, global citizens, people who have a different outlook on life.

The third and the latest incarnation is what we call Me to We. The whole idea is living a life larger than just me, living a life of we — our community, our nation, our world — reaching out to others. And Me to We for us became a broader philosophy; where Free The Children is looking at international development, and Leaders Today is engaging young people on international issues, Me to We opens it to include teachers and parents and adults and others of all walks of life. It's a way of living that feeds positively into the world. We can find a new definition of success based not on material gains, but in the way we reach out to help others. By making this shift toward 'We living', we not only improve the lives of others but also find new meaning and value in our own lives.

It reflects the evolution of our philosophy. The more global we wanted to become, the more activist we wanted to become, the more we realised we also had to return home to North America, shifting consumption patterns, voting patterns, volunteer patterns. On my first trip to Asia, when I was in Dhaka, the capital of Bangladesh, we were at a slum and there was a human rights worker there who said to me, 'You'll never end poverty *here*. You'll never end poverty just in the developing world. If you want to see the shift come about, you also need a shift in Europe and North America, the wealthy countries.'

It's not simply a question of getting more aid. It's also a question of looking at root causes — how we vote, how we shop, the careers young people pick, how they volunteer. It's really how you live your life. We need a shift dramatically in North America, because in many ways, the biggest challenge we face isn't a lack of education or clean water. The biggest challenge is apathy. There are so many issues, whether it be looking at giving anti-viral drugs at deeper discounts, dropping the debt, truly free and fair trade — you need to address all of these issues if you're going to create systemic change overseas. We need to look at how we live our lives in North America and Europe.

Driven by young people

The most amazing part about how we work is that the majority of the funds — 65-70 per cent — come from children, from our Youth in Action group members. Over 1,000 groups currently operate across North America, and they are the heart and soul of Free The Children. They come together in their schools and communities to learn about social issues and take action to help others. We do receive limited government funding, and we receive generous support from certain adult benefactors — Oprah Winfrey and her Oprah Angel Network among them, who are the largest and most generous supporters of our work. But it's kids, through bake sales and car washes, who are the ones who earn the vast majority of the money.

It's actually far easier to get government funds to build a school overseas, but the reason we put the emphasis on engaging youth in the fundraising campaigns is because we want to lead them in the education campaign. We see that as a fundamental part of our outreach in North America — educating, empowering, inspiring and challenging youth to get engaged in global issues. Each year, 1,200 students join us in volunteering overseas, actually travelling to help build a school in a developing country. We show young people that they can be world-changing leaders — not tomorrow, but today.

Young people are so often told that they are too young to make a difference; that they need to defer to the authority of their elders; that they will have to wait until they are older to begin seeking solutions for the world's problems. I strongly disagree. I believe young people of all backgrounds can assume leadership roles at any age — my own experience proves it.

When I began Free The Children in 1995, youth activism was a phenomenon that had yet to come into its own. The idea of young people taking action to help people on the other side of the world in conditions of injustice seemed an absurd notion to many of the adults with whom we shared our ideas. Apathy and cynicism on the part of many leaders and people in positions of power stood in stark opposition to the enthusiasm we found in the many young people who joined our cause.

People, particularly young people, are often led to believe that they lack the power to make a difference. Even when their passions are stirred, the widespread culture of apathy in which we live often curtails the ambitions of people interested in effecting change. All it takes is that first moment, that first impulse to do things differently. Great accomplishments can begin in small gestures. The only limit is one's imagination and ambition.

Being the change

Being the change can happen at any level. All it requires is a shift of one's mentality, actively striving to help others, whether it's through volunteer work in one's community, donating to a charity, making informed and responsible consumer choices, or simply performing daily acts of kindness. One of my personal goals is to show people that everyone wields the power to be the change — regardless of their age, background or circumstances.

Many people believe that the mysteries of achieving a meaningful life are complex and vast, or simply impossible to ascertain. I disagree. In our work with Free The Children and Leaders Today, my brother Marc and I have had the opportunity to travel the world, encountering fascinating cultures and meeting inspirational people — some well-known, some not so well-known. We've been able to discuss these questions with people from all walks of life and learn about their beliefs of what constitutes a life of meaning.

One consistent thread we've found is an emphasis on compassion and the reciprocal benefits of living compassionately. We've found that all widely-held philosophical and religious doctrines in some fashion touch upon the value of generosity and thinking beyond one's immediate self-interest. Regardless of one's personal beliefs, it cannot be denied that taking that extra step of reaching out to others can improve lives — both yours and those of others.

While the problems our world faces are enormous, I have witnessed how taking action directly creates positive change. We can't solve global poverty overnight; I'm not that naïve. But I have seen kids in resource-poor schools pool their efforts to help build schools in sub-Saharan Africa. I've seen ordinary individuals overcome obstacles to improve the lives of others. I've met young people who simply express the desire to feed the hungry and clothe the poor, and want to know how they can lend a hand. This innate sense of compassion and the willingness to help others — this is what gives me hope.

The most valuable lessons I've learned have come from children. I've met children born and raised in a trash dump in Manila who had never even seen a school, much less attended one. I've had a Brazilian child living on the streets of Salvador literally give me the shirt off his back. In so many places, young people have welcomed me as a friend, as I in return have cherished their friendship. The lesson I've learned from these children — and the thousands I've worked with through Free The Children — is that with giving there is hope, and with hope can spring forth change.

www.freethechildren.com

www.leaderstoday.com

www.metowe.org

Me to We, with Marc Kielburger, 2006

Take Action!: A guide to active citizenship, with Marc Kielburger, 2002

Free the Children, with Kevin Major, Harper Perennial, 1999

Satish Kumar

The root of war is fear and the route to peace is trust.

Satish Kumar has lived his life according to Gandhi's principle of being the change you wish to see in the world. At the age of 25, inspired by Bertrand Russell's campaign against the atomic bomb, he and a friend set off from India on a peace pilgrimage, walking to the four nuclear capitals of the world — Moscow, Paris, London and Washington. Settling in England in 1973, he has become a guiding light in spiritual, ecological and educational endeavours. He created the Small School in Devon, a secondary school which includes ecological and spiritual values in its curriculum, and is the Director of Programmes at Schumacher College, which runs courses for adults covering ecological and spiritual issues and holistic science. For 35 years, he has been the editor of *Resurgence* magazine, which focuses on similar topics.

I was inspired by Mahatma Gandhi. I was an 18-year-old monk when I read his autobiography, in which he said that some people leave the world, thinking that it is a bondage, a bad place where you cannot practise spirituality, non-violence, or truth. They retire from the world and think that they have liberated themselves. Then the people who are left behind in the world think that spirituality is only for the saints, that we cannot practise it in the world, so we do what we like. This kind of split and dualism has to be healed, so the best way is to be the change in the world — practise spirituality, truth and non-violence in everyday life.

So I left the monastic order, joined the Gandhian movement, and lived in an ashram. There, my greatest learning was to transform every activity, to see it not as a chore, but as a spiritual practice. For example, gardening. You can do gardening to produce vegetables to feed yourself, or you can do gardening as a spiritual practice, to serve the earth, to serve people and you get food as a by-product. Or cooking — as a spiritual practice, you are cooking to serve your family, your guests and friends, and through them, God. You transform, through your higher motivation. What you do is not so important as how you do it and why you do it. Sweeping the floor, doing the dishes, cleaning the toilets, whatever it is, everything can be transformed into spiritual practice if you do it with the right motivation — the motivation of service.

Walk for peace

At age 25, I was sitting in a restaurant, and while waiting for coffee, I picked up the newspaper. My eyes were drawn to a piece of news which said Bertrand Russell had been arrested and sentenced to imprisonment because he had committed civil disobedience to demand that the British government ban the bomb immediately. That was an example, for me, of being the change. Here was a man of 90, a Nobel laureate. He could be comfortable in his house, making speeches and writing articles about peace, but he did not do that. He went to Whitehall, sat in the street, and said, 'I'm not going to move from here until the British government bans the bomb.'

That became an inspiration. My friend and I said, 'Let's do something, let's be like Bertrand Russell.' So we decided then and there that we'd walk to Moscow, Paris, London and Washington DC, the four nuclear capitals of that time. And

You find the meaning of life in a relationship and whatever I do offers me an opportunity for relationship.

walk, not go by train or car or plane, because if you go like that, then it's like lecturing, it's not being the change. When you witness with your body, step by step, day by day, you are walking and touching the earth, meeting the people, being peace, not demonstrating for peace but demonstrating peace. Then your action and your thoughts become one.

So we started from the grave of Gandhi in New Delhi, and we walked to Moscow, to Paris, to London. Of course we crossed the English Channel by boat, and then we crossed the Atlantic by boat from Southampton to New York and walked to Washington DC and to the grave of John F Kennedy. We walked from the grave of Gandhi to the grave of Kennedy for peace, for 8,000 miles, without a penny in our pockets. The reason that we took no money was because our guru, Vinoba, who was also a Gandhian, said, 'I bless you for your journey but I want to give you advice: go without any money in your pockets.' I said, 'Any money? You mean nothing? Sometimes we might need a cup of tea. Sometimes we might need to make a telephone call.' He said no to any money because the root of war is fear and the route to peace is trust. If you have no money you have to trust yourself, you have to trust people, you have to trust God, you have to trust the universe. So we accepted Vinoba's advice and decided to take no money.

You find the meaning of life in a relationship and whatever I do offers me an opportunity for relationship. For example, going without money around the world, walking for peace, that gave me a chance to relate to the earth and to the people. If I'd gone by aeroplane or by car, and if I'd stayed in a hotel, I'd just have met politicians or media people. Not on a basis of relationship, but just on an intellectual level. But when you have no money and you are walking, you arrive in a village and you have to look for somebody who can offer you hospitality, who can offer you a bed for the night and food for the evening. Sometimes I did not get any food or shelter. I said to myself, 'This is my opportunity to fast, to sleep under the stars.' But 98 per cent of the time I did receive hospitality, and that way you are able to relate to people at the heart level. They are strangers, and yet you trust them and they trust you. They are giving you their utmost — their home, their bed, their food, celebration, friendship, friendly hands. So it's through relationship that I find the meaning of my life. When I serve others, when I relate to others, I find joy, a sense of happiness. When I'm kind to others, I'm happy.

Peace tea

It took two and a half years. We were walking through stormy weathers, deserts, mountains, snow, rain, and one day I was feeling in a very low spirit. I was wondering whether we were achieving anything. Was it worth doing? In despondence, I gave our flyer, which we carried in different languages, to two women outside a tea factory by the Black Sea in Georgia. They read it and said, 'Wait, wait! Have you really walked from India? All the way? Come and tell us your story. Would you like to have a cup of tea?' Any time is tea-time when you have no money! So we went into this tea factory.

One of the two women went out of the room, while we were drinking tea, and she came back with four packets of tea. She said, 'These are not for you.' 'For whom are they?' I asked. She said, 'I want you to deliver one packet of tea to our capital, Moscow, to our premier; the second packet to Paris, to the president of France; the third packet to London, to the prime minister of England; and the fourth packet to Washington DC to the president of the United States of America. And please give them a message from me.' So I said, 'What's your message?' She said, 'My message to them is, "If ever you get a mad thought of pressing the nuclear button, please stop for a moment and have a fresh cup of tea from these packets. That will remind you that a woman from Georgia has sent you these packets, and these weapons you are going to use are not only going to destroy your enemies, Russian, American, or some other enemy, but they will destroy everybody. Nuclear weapons are no weapons. They will destroy men, women, children, peasants, workers, factories, farms, forests, rivers, lakes, mountains, oceans — everything will be destroyed or contaminated. So think again, and don't push the button."

That was so inspiring. My low spirit was lifted. I said, 'Now we have to be the messenger of this woman. We have to carry these packets of peace tea and deliver them to Moscow, to Paris, to London and to Washington.' And so that's what

What's the good of learning all about science and technology and maths and Newton and Galileo and Shakespeare, if you don't know how to live?

we did in these capitals. But President de Gaulle would not accept them. He would not see us. We were refused any meeting and so we went to demonstrate. We said, 'We want to see President de Gaulle.' We were arrested and put in jail. In a way we were happy, because Bertrand Russell had inspired us by going to jail, so we were following in his footsteps. After three days we were released and then we carried on. This way, we did four capitals and then we ended our journey at the grave of Kennedy. It was a journey from the grave of Gandhi to the grave of Kennedy, to make the point that if you trust in the gun, if you trust in violence, then this is what happens; the gun does not kill only the bad guys, the gun can also kill the good people, like Gandhi and Kennedy. So you have to remove your faith from the gun and you have to eliminate the existence of the gun from your society if you want a peaceful society. From the grave of Gandhi to the grave of Kennedy was 8,000 miles and it took two and a half years.

And if that journey did nothing else, it transformed me. After two and a half years, I was a very different person. I realised that peace is not only the absence of war, the absence of nuclear weapons — peace is in your heart. And unless you make peace with yourself, you cannot make peace in the world. Quite often we are at war against ourselves. We think, 'I'm not good enough, I can't do this, I can't do that, I'm too weak, I'm too powerless.' We harbour an inferiority complex in our hearts. We underrate our own capacity. Walking around the world for 8,000 miles, for two and a half years, without money, gave me a kind of self-confidence and trust in myself, and that was a way of making peace with myself. I realised that every human being is given all the capacity, all the facility and all the skills that one needs to survive and to live, and to solve any problems that we face.

People are afraid of hardship, of difficulty, that, 'If I live my ideal it will not be comfortable, it will not be easy.' They are insecure in their heart. Being the change requires courage, and we are not taught to be courageous, we are not taught, 'Have no fear,' we are taught to be careful, be cautious, be aware that something may go wrong. From childhood, our parents, our teachers, our media, our politicians, our whole society injects fear in our heart, and so we are afraid to practise what we believe in, because of fear.

The antidote to fear is courage and trust. I say to myself that I was born without any security, without any money, without any job, without any education, without any anything, but something happened and I'm here. So how am I here? The process of the universe is helping me to be self-realised, to fulfil my potential, to meet my destiny. The universe is there cooperating, the universe is there supporting, and that gives me trust. If you trust the universe your fear disappears; if you love the universe your fear disappears. My life is driven by this trust in the process of the universe, and trust as well as love of the earth, love of people, love of nature, love of communities, love of living, love of life. That's when you are able to trust.

Gandhi's inspiration

Gandhi inspired me because not only did he say, 'Be the change you want to see in the world', he actually lived it. Once there was a very famous politician in India called Dr Lohiya. He was very educated — a very good orator, thinker and writer. He always wondered why Gandhi had so much power and influence, and a hold on people's minds. What was so special about him? One day he went to Gandhi and asked, 'What are the secrets of your power? Why is it, that when you give a call, thousands of people follow? You are not a great orator, you are not that handsome, you have no teeth, you're just wearing an ordinary loin cloth.' And Gandhi said, 'I don't know why people follow me. The only thing I can say to you is that I have never asked anyone to do anything which I have not done myself.'

Once, some people asked him, 'Please send us a message for our conference.' Gandhi said, 'I have no message. My life is my message.' He said, 'I have nothing new to teach. All the philosophy I'm talking about, non-violence, truth, love, compassion, freedom, self-reliance, all these virtues and all these philosophies are as old as the hills. They were taught by the Buddha, by Krishna, by Mohammed, by Jesus Christ; they were taught by hundreds and hundreds of teachers — nothing new. What is new is we practise it, we live it, we experiment with truth every day.' He experimented with truth in his life. That's why he called his autobiography *My Experiments with Truth*.

The problems we face today are not given by God, they are man-made, only in the last 200 years. What's 200 years in the history of evolution, billions of years of history?

Resurgence

In 1973, I was here in England giving a few lectures about non-violence. I was going to go back to India, but I met EF Schumacher. He said, 'Why do you want to go back to India? Why don't you edit *Resurgence*?' I said, 'I want to go and work with the Gandhian movement.' He said, 'Satish, there are many Gandhians in India. We need one in England. Stay here.' He persuaded me to stay in England, and I became editor of *Resurgence*. The vision of the magazine is not to dwell in the negative and the blame game — 'The government is bad, industry is bad, business is bad, the corporations are bad, globalisation is bad. Bad, bad, bad.'

Yes, we do say that they are all causing problems but our main concern is solution-based. What can we do? How can we create new, positive, constructive, visionary projects, through art, through craft, through imagination, through organic farming, through renewable energy, through new philosophy, new science? Our approach is more constructive, positive, visionary and creative, rather than doom and gloom and disaster and blame. Yes, there is a place for resistance, but resistance should emerge out of practice and constructive action. Non-violence is a way of life first and only then is it a way of resistance.

I have been editing *Resurgence* for 35 years, so I am one of the longest-surviving editors of any magazine in England, and I enjoy it. It's another way of relationship. You relate to your authors, photographers, illustrators, printers, staff, so it's a kind of family, a relationship. It's a way to serve, and it's a kind of spiritual activity.

Gandhian education

Twenty-five years ago, I established the Small School, very much based on Gandhian principles. I was also taken by the ideas of EF Shumacher, who wrote *Small is Beautiful*. I live in Devon, and I like to live in a rural community, in a village, where people know and care for each other. But when my own children came to the age of secondary school, they had to go to the town. If I wanted to live in the town and send my children to the town, I would have lived in the town. So I said, 'I want to have a school in the village.' When children go to the town school they take a bus, and that bus takes them from village to village collecting children, which takes one hour in the morning, one hour in the evening — a commuter's life from age 11. Then once they go to the school, what do they learn there? All this book education, intellectual, academic knowledge. I wanted to make it a Gandhian school where you can learn by doing, learn by being, learn by making. So I said, 'Let us start a school in the village.'

We started with nine children. How is the school different? I said, 'The first thing is, the kitchen will also be the classroom, and every day children will learn to cook.' What's the good of learning all about science and technology and maths and Newton and Galileo and Shakespeare and all the great academic knowledge if you don't know how to cook and how to live? The kitchen became the classroom. For the last 25 years the Small School has been going, the children prepare and serve the meal to their teachers, parents and fellow students. We started a garden, so children learn about biology and ecology by putting their hands in the soil. The printed books are fine, but nature is the greatest book. We take the children also to the sea, the valleys, the forest. They learn from nature as much as they learn about nature. Learning about nature encourages a kind of dualism — object and subject. When you are learning from nature, you learn ecological humility. Nature becomes your mentor. That is the special quality of the Small School.

Schumacher College is a similar project, for adults. At the time we were discussing the format of the college, I said it should be the same as the Small School. So every day, students who come from all over the world practise what they are studying. They learn to live an ecological lifestyle. There's no good sitting in the classroom talking about how to save the world, when somebody else is cleaning your toilet, making your bed, sweeping your floor, cooking your meal and doing your dishes. Every day the students do all of those things, and then they come to the classroom and learn about ideas and theories and so on. Practice leads and theory follows. And as with the Small School, students also go out in nature. They experience the wild sea and the wilderness of Dartmoor.

*If you sow the right seeds,
the right fruit will appear.*

Every week, they go on a field trip. Education is not just about academic and intellectual learning but also about more embodied, practical, experiential learning.

Optimism

I know pessimism is very fashionable. Hundreds of books, newspaper articles and magazine articles are full of it, and people are driven by doom and gloom and disaster. I feel pessimism is disempowering. I want to be an optimist because that is empowering. When you are an optimist, you can do something about the bad situation. If we are poisoning the soil, we can transform that through organic farming and local food and fresh food. If we are destroying our rivers and oceans, we can redesign our economic system so that we don't.

Because this industrial system is designed by humans, it can be changed by humans. This is what gives me hope. The problems we face today are not given by God, they are man-made, only in the last 200 years. What's 200 years in the history of evolution, billion of years of history? What was designed by humans has gone wrong; we can redesign it. So we bring new consciousness, new ideas, through *Resurgence,* through Schumacher College, through the Small School. If we can bring new consciousness and love of the earth into the equation, then we can bring a new design. We can create new systems with our imagination and our creativity, with human ingenuity and spirit. I have the faith and trust in the human spirit that it will rise to the occasion and stand up for Gaia, and not be subsumed by this pessimistic scenario.

The most valuable lesson I have learned is to live in the present moment, in the here and now, and do what you feel is the right action this moment, without worrying about the outcome. We are quite often too concerned and uptight, and we get obsessed with the result; and so we lose our focus on our right action at this moment. If you sow the right seeds, the right fruit will appear, so sow the right seeds. If you do the right action, the result will be good; you don't have to worry about the result. Whether the results are there or not, they are not in your hands. The results are in the hands of God. If you are living well in this moment, the here and now, then the future will take care of itself. But if you are too worried about the future, too worried about the past, you don't live in the moment.

So the greatest lesson I've learned is, live every moment as fully, as creatively, as imaginatively, as lovingly, as compassionately, as generously as possible — because every moment is the real building block of life. You cannot just think of the destination. This is why I called my book *No Destination*, no reaching anywhere. Life is a journey; every step is a journey. If you take every step rightly, you will not fall down and you will reach wherever you are reaching. But there is nowhere to reach. You are already there; we are living our life now. The fullest moment, the most pregnant moment is this moment, and if we live this moment well and fully, everything else will be fine.

www.resurgence.org

www.schumachercollege.org.uk

Spiritual Compass, Green Books, 2007

The Buddha and the Terrorist, Green Books, 2005

You Are, Therefore I Am, Green Books, 2002

No Destination, Green Books, 2000

Wangari Maathai

You can make a lot of speeches, but the real thing is when you dig a hole, plant a tree, give it water, and make it survive. That's what makes the difference.

Professor Wangari Maathai has lived a life dedicated to action, to democracy, to serving her country, its landscape and its people. For decades she campaigned for democracy in Kenya, at great personal risk, and was finally rewarded in 2002 when she was elected to parliament in the country's first democratic elections, by a landslide vote of 98 per cent. This came after 25 years leading the Green Belt Movement, through which she worked with Kenya's rural women to restore their land. In 2004, she was awarded the Nobel Peace Prize 'for her contribution to sustainable development, democracy and peace'. The extraordinary change that Prof, as she is known, has achieved includes the empowerment of women, the provision of much-needed food and materials for rural people, and the restoration of Kenya's environment.

When I first started, I just wanted to see a countryside covered with green vegetation, where women would have firewood, where we would have building and fencing materials and fodder for the animals. A countryside that is green. I don't like to see the soil exposed unless it's absolutely necessary, because when you expose the soil, you expose it to soil loss, and especially in Africa where there is so much loss of the soil through wind and water, it's very pleasing to the eye for me to see that the soil is covered. The dress of the earth is the green vegetation.

I went about achieving that by organising women into groups and then into networks to form a strong and big organisation. They produced the seedlings from seeds and they planted them on their farms; they talked to their neighbours and encouraged them to plant them on their farms. Then we moved to public lands, like schools, school compounds, church compounds, along the road reserves, and now we are into forested mountains, which have been degraded, trying to rehabilitate them. Always trying to ensure that the green vegetation is returned, and using the people, using the hands of thousands of people to do the work.

The first steps were really just to talk to the women and convince them that we could do something about some of the issues that they were raising: they didn't have firewood, they didn't have clean drinking water, they didn't have adequate food, they needed an income. I told them we could address these issues by planting trees. We have to start somewhere and I thought, planting a tree is a good thing. I don't know why I thought about the tree, but I know that the tree has become a very wonderful symbol of what is possible, of hope. A tree brings transformation within a very short time, especially in the tropics, and so this continues to be the dominant feature of our activities, and it always focuses us on informing, motivating and taking action.

The motivating you do by giving seminars, so that people understand why they should plant trees, so that people understand that the land is naked, that the land is being degraded, the land is being polluted. There are a lot of people who don't see pollution. Lots of people don't see the land is degrading. During some of these seminars, people tell me, 'For the first time, I can see empty spaces, bare hills, eroded landscapes. Before that, I didn't see.' Now, opening those eyes is extremely important, so that the people can see the damage around them.

*The dress of the earth
is the green vegetation.*

New frontiers

Many people wonder whether I had a vision, and whether I saw when I first started that the tree-planting project would eventually become the Green Belt Movement International, and I have to say, no I didn't. I did not have that vision. I started what became a walk, and as I walked I was constantly led to new frontiers of the problem. When I first started, I was looking for firewood, for fodder for the animals, for fencing materials, for building materials, for fruits. As I got into that, I realised I needed to organise. So I started organising into groups, and then I saw that organising into groups was not enough, I organised into networks and I created an organisation. Initially it was just within the National Council of Women, then it became necessary to create a project. Initially I did not see the need for money and then eventually I saw the need for money, so I started fundraising. So, as I continued, new frontiers presented themselves, and new opportunities presented themselves. And as I tried to deal with that, the programme just expanded.

I also must say that I was very lucky that I picked the tree, because a tree is a living thing. It comes out of a small seed and it grows; sometimes within five, ten years it is bigger than yourself. So it almost talks to you, it almost challenges you, but it also encourages you and it gives you a sense of what is possible. Within a short time, I started seeing the change in the landscape. Seeing the landscapes change into green where there was nothing before, barren ground completely being covered; seeing the change of women not having to go far to collect firewood, because now they have firewood on their farms; seeing them feed their animals and especially when there is drought, and hearing that in that region where they have been successful planting trees, the animals are not dying, because they have fodder — these things give much satisfaction. So these changes, these transformations that were happening in the communities, were almost like the oil that fed the enthusiasm. You wanted to repeat what you had done here somewhere else, you wanted to see that change, that transformation that you have seen here, you wanted to see somewhere else. And that in many ways encouraged me to keep going. And I was led by the success. What succeeded, I followed. What didn't work, I didn't follow. That was one of my big lessons, that if something doesn't work, you don't repeat it. And in governments, and in many institutions, people do the wrong thing for a long time before the boss says change. Here in the Green Belt Movement, we encourage people not to wait, because you can be the agent of change. So if you get inspired, and everybody gets inspired, and you see things better than I can see, don't wait for me, I'm not seeing the same thing you're seeing. That's how the movement really continued and gave women a lot of freedom to do what they felt was the right thing for them.

Challenges

Some of the challenges that we have faced along the way have been tough, some not so tough. One of the tough challenges was persuading women to believe in themselves, to believe that they can actually plant trees, even though they are not foresters. That is why I call them foresters without diplomas, because they initially believed that unless you have gone to school and have a diploma in forestry, you can't plant trees. They had to overcome that. And the second thing was the organising was difficult, because people were not used to working together in groups to plant trees. Also, the whole idea of planting trees was not very well accepted in the beginning because people were thinking that by making people plant trees, and by giving them trees free of charge, we would claim their land. So there was fear, and we had to overcome that.

We initially started without any money and that became a big challenge, because as the process progressed it became necessary to have money to be able to buy tools, to buy containers, to facilitate seminars, to move about, to supervise what was happening. That was a major problem because for some reason, people did not want to invest in us. For that reason I am very grateful to one of the organisations that really supported us on a serious note, and that was the United Nations Fund for Women, now known as UNIFEM, which was at that time led by a lady called Margaret Snyder. She had been in Africa for many years, she believed in the African women, and she was very instrumental. And another lady, Helvi Sipira of Finland. Helvi Sipira came to Nairobi in 1985, during the women's conference in Nairobi, and I took her round to show her what our work was like. I

We are always trying to ensure that the green vegetation is returned, using the hands of thousands of people to do the work.

did not know that she was looking around because she was wondering whether she should give us any money! But she went back and reported very positively about our work and we got $100,000. Which was at that time a lot of money, and that was really a turning point in our work.

I like to give credit to UNIFEM and to these women partly because it's so easy for people now to look at the Green Belt Movement and think it was easy to bring it to where it is. There is need to appreciate that it is partly because somebody believed, 'Here is a person who is bringing about positive change, and needs financial resources and we want to support them.' They gave us that money and gave it to the local United Nations Development Programme and said, 'Give it to them as they need it.' That was so important because sometimes donors can restrict you. They give you money, and they tell you, 'I will give you $100,000. But first of all I will give you $5,000 — when you are through with that, let me know.' It restricts you and you don't have the freedom to plan, and to have the confidence to tell people, 'I know we can do this.' Sometimes in creating change, you need that confidence that you can do it and not feel like you are too constrained.

Positive influence

One of the most wonderful things about this work is just observing the landscape change. That to me has really been wonderful. To demonstrate that, let me give you a little story that I like to give because it demonstrates that when change comes, it's not so much what you say as the agent of change, that 'I have changed…'. It's what people say has happened to them that is much more important. We had received some money from Denmark, and so we were planting trees. Some women came from Denmark, and I was taking them around to show them where we had planted these trees. They were beautiful trees. The whole area was looking so green with all these trees. There was a man who was herding his animals along the road. We approached him and we said, 'How are you?' I said, 'We are admiring these trees, these are very beautiful trees. Who planted them?' And the man said, 'Oh, we are very happy about these trees. These trees have been planted by our women, and they have completely changed the land-scape. Even the birds and the small animals have come back.' His wife was one of the women who were planting trees, and he was very proud of what his wife and the other women were doing. Now, that, for me, for women, for all the work we do to try to change men's attitude towards women, that in itself indicated to me how the women, by their work, by their very influential work of changing the land-scape had made the man be positive towards them and appreciate their work. I asked him, 'How do they support themselves in planting these trees?' And he said, 'They work very closely with a woman called Wangari Maathai.' And I said, 'Have you ever met her?' He said, 'No, I don't know her.' I was the one talking to him, but I didn't reveal to him that!

That was very pleasing, because here this man had become positively influ-enced by the change that was taking place in his community. He had assumed a very positive attitude towards women, who were doing this work, and he also was having a very positive response to us women, who were educated women who were working in Nairobi. He didn't know me, he didn't recognise me, but that was exactly the point. He knew that there was this network of women, including in the urban centres, who were working together to change the landscape for the better. I never forgot that story, because for me, it taught me so many things. We left the man, we bid him goodbye, and he never knew who he was talking to so proudly about women in his community.

Taking action

It's difficult to say why some people move and take action, and some don't. For me, I think that education, moving from one place to another, for example mov-ing from my country to the United States of America, and spending some time in Germany, seeing the possibilities of a country that is green, seeing the possibil-ity of a people who are not hungry, seeing the possibility of a people who are drinking clean drinking water, that's what motivated me. The truth of the matter is that when you are young, you have the energy and that energy has to be used. Unfortunately, if you are not careful, that energy is misused. But if your energy is not being misused, you will be driven to doing something positive. We should be directing our energies towards making change in our communities, improving the quality of life in our communities, rather than perhaps spending that energy in being destructive, even self-destructive.

I was led by the success.
What succeeded, I followed.
What didn't work, I didn't follow.

Working directly with the people whose lives you are trying to change is very satisfactory: it feeds you, it makes you feel like your time, your efforts, your energy are being spent for something worthwhile. So going to the rural areas and really working with the women helps me. Being a Member of Parliament at the moment is one of the experiences that I really enjoy. I know many of us Members of Parliament feel very stretched: you are trying to be an effective Member of Parliament, you are also trying to promote the message globally, and so it really taxes you. But that contact with the ground, with the soil, that possibility of planting a tree yourself, these are moments that you feel like, 'Whatever I can do, it's worth it. Because that's what makes the difference.' I tell people, 'You can talk a lot, you can go to the United Nations and give excellent speeches, you can go on the radio and television and make a lot of speeches, but the real thing is when you dig a hole, plant a tree and give it water, and make it survive.' That's what makes the difference, and that's what feeds and sustains you.

Being the change

You can't do something that you don't like. You have to like what you do. And if you really want to be a change agent, you will see what you want to change. It's not as if you can change everything. There are certain things you may feel you can't change, but it's also true that you can start with something very small. You can start with your own lifestyle. You can change in your own lifestyle and you will influence other people. So many of us watch what other people do and we follow if we think that it is correct. But I think it is very important for us first of all to identify what it is we think we want to change, and then love doing it, so that you can commit yourself to it. Because if you don't love it, you'll get tired and you'll hate it.

You need to love it so that you can stay with it, because you don't change things overnight. Very few of us can start something today and within a year see change. Especially if you want to make a big change. It takes time. So you have to be very patient, very persistent. But I would say most of all you have to enjoy it.

189

Because as you are doing it, you even are living your own life. That's your life, so you want to be able to say, 'I have lived my life well.' It's very, very important not to do something you don't like. And also, don't punish yourself and say, 'If it's not changing, I'm going to abandon it.' I like to use that word 'persistent', because I know, I've been trying to plant trees for 30 years plus. Not everybody will win a Nobel Peace Prize because you are trying to make a change. What is much more important is that you yourself will feel happy about what you have done with your own life.

You have to believe in yourself. You have to listen to yourself. I say that there is a voice inside all of us, I sometimes call it the God in me, the voice that doesn't cheat you, the voice that knows you best. It's very important to listen to that voice, believe in yourself. That doesn't mean that you don't listen to your critics and your friends. You do, but it is very important for you to believe in what you do, believe in yourself, because challenges will come. Nobody succeeds without challenge, because challenge is about overcoming obstacles and raising the bar. So every time you raise that bar and you have to jump it, it's a challenge. Sometimes you may break your bones as you try to do it, but if you believe, even if you break your bones, you still wake up and walk, you still rise up, you still pull yourself up by the strings. I always tell people, it's not a crime to fail. The tragedy is when you give up. So don't give up. Every time, try again and rise up!

I hope that many more people will appreciate the need for us to protect this planet. That we will understand that we need to manage the limited resources we have in a responsible way, and that we need to share them in a responsible way, and not be selfish and greedy. So that we can reduce the conflicts that we have in the world, and survive and enjoy this planet. Such a beautiful planet. We haven't found another one like it, so we want to enjoy it and we want those who come after us to be able to enjoy it. They can only enjoy it if they find the same resources that have helped us, to help them live and enjoy life on this planet.

Inspirations

Sometimes I don't know what inspires me, apart from the work. Other people. Moments! You encounter those moments all the time. Sometimes you're just looking at the moon and you get inspired. We don't know where thoughts come from. We don't know how we get those thoughts, how we get inspired by those thoughts, but I believe that through our senses, we get inspired. What we see, what we hear, what we smell, the environment we are in. These are all stimulations that sometimes will bring ideas. However, what is important in my opinion is that we are ready for the inspiration. We get many stimulations, but only certain stimulations stay with us and help us with thoughts that can develop into ideas and actually translate into action.

It's always very good to come across people, especially young people, who are inspired to do something about improving the quality of life on this planet, improving our understanding of the planet, committing themselves to changing the way we deal with the planet. It's very, very inspiring. Because you know then that the struggle continues. And that one day, we'll get there. One day.

www.greenbeltmovement.org

Unbowed: My autobiography, William Heinemann, 2007

The Green Belt Movement: Sharing the approach and the experience,
Lantern Books, 2006

Safia Minney

*We need to start paying the real costs of what we buy,
where we bank, and how we treat others — all have
an impact and all are political acts.*

Safia Minney is a social entrepreneur and a true pioneer, creating her fashion company People Tree with Fair Trade principles long before they hit mainstream consciousness. As Fair Trade means paying producers in developing countries a fair price, this enables them to meet social and environmental needs that otherwise would go unmet, for example access to education, health care, clean water and food security. Workers can remain in their rural communities and work in amenable conditions, rather than be forced to move away from their family to a city, to work in a factory or sweatshop. To promote Fair Trade, Minney initiated World Fair Trade Day, which is celebrated in May each year in 70 countries around the world.

The change we're seeking to create is threefold — social, environmental and structural. The first is the social change that we bring to the farmers' and artisans' lives and their communities through Fair Trade. This change enables them to meet their basic needs — to eat not only once a day but three times a day, and to be able to get basic health care and send their children to school. They go on to rebuild their houses, start a kitchen garden or rear chickens or goats that provide further income. This is the change that a livelihood, training and a good income brings.

The second change comes through pioneering environmental initiatives that strengthen the economic and environmental situation of a family or a community. For example, we started an organic cotton project in India 12 years ago, and now we are introducing it to Bangladesh; we promote natural fibres and hand production methods that have the lowest carbon footprint; and we work with groups to promote environmental awareness and education locally. With farmers' groups we look at ways, through a fair price, to initiate, support and strengthen natural and organic agriculture. Fair Trade is the only environmentally sustainable way of trading — benefiting the people with both the lowest income and the smallest environmental footprint. We need to push the values of Fair Trade into mainstream business.

Thirdly, the Fair Trade product itself is a tool for change. Not only does it empower producers in the developing world, but consumers are empowered too. While globalisation has meant that people know little about how and where things they buy are made, or about the exploitation of people and natural resources that happen in their name, Fair Trade has opened up a new chapter of transparency. It will become increasingly hard to find a skirt for the price of a sandwich, and eventually the directors of companies will be liable when labour rights and environmental laws are violated. We need to start paying the real cost of what we buy, where we bank, and how we treat others — all have an impact and all are political acts. It's also fun to learn about the world and your place in it.

We're all catalysts for change — good or bad. Before I started Global Village, I lobbied as an individual; today I lobby as an organisation — we are more powerful because we are many, but in principle it's the same. We lobby industry for change. I spend a lot of time working with the fashion industry, social innovation networks and at the World Economic Forum, to promote new ways of doing business that incorporate the triple bottom line — not just profiting financially, but also socially and environmentally — and we look at how those models for change can be scaled-up and put into fast-forward.

Beginnings

When I was 25, I moved to Japan, and I couldn't find very much in the way of Fair Trade products or organic products, or much opportunity to support or be involved with human rights groups, environmental groups, citizens' groups or alternative media. There was little awareness of social issues and Fair Trade, and little you could buy to support them. There was a huge lack of information to help people volunteer their time or use their shopping or their savings for change, and that frustrated me enormously. So I used my publishing skills to publish listings on how to recycle, by cataloguing 3,000 individuals and what they were doing to recycle in different areas of Tokyo and Yokohama. I used this to go into local authorities and lobby them to set up recycling departments.

In the same way, we published guides on where organic food was available, and where you could get organic or vegetarian food in restaurants or hotels, with the idea of promoting them and building a movement. Information is power. When people had access to that information, they could show that they cared. They could go out and effectively build a market for alternative products, products that were produced in an environmentally and socially responsible way.

It began with me in Tokyo, with two Japanese university students who went to college for half the day and then spent the other half day doing research work, putting together the listings and, because my Japanese was pretty rubbish at that point, doing stuff that I couldn't possibly do myself. The three of us set up a campaigning organisation, Global Village, and then after two years, in 1993 we initiated the Fair Trade programme working with Bangladeshi, Indian and Zimbabwean producers. Those were the first three countries where we started to develop partnerships and products.

When I was in Britain before that, working in publishing, I was quite experienced, having started work at 17 years old and run my own alternative communications company. I worked with Friends of the Earth, and I knew of Traidcraft. Designers from other Fair Trade companies would ring up and say, 'There's a

*It will become increasingly difficult to find a skirt
for the price of a sandwich.*

---

fantastic group in Bangladesh but they need orders desperately. Maybe you could work with them and build markets for their products in Japan?' We didn't have full-time designers then, but I've always had a good eye, and asked friends to help out with design when I got out of my depth. When we could afford to, we started to employ professional designers, but I still head up design — product development and technical support to producer partners is central to the success and sustainability of Fair Trade. When we needed specialists, we would bring in people to work on a voluntary basis, and that's very much how we started, marketing through events and through a little mail-order catalogue. Within three years we had 50 outlets — concessions in shops where people were really excited about the concept and the products, and who very much wanted to sell Fair Trade products.

Benefits of Fair Trade

We're working in 18 countries now, with 58 groups. They're Fair Trade organisations, so underneath those organisations would be about 120 independent producer groups. More than 70 per cent of them would be either running their own schools, which are supported through the Fair Trade premium, or would be giving scholarships to producers' children and children within the community so that they can access education.

By using traditional and hand skills, and training people in how to make products of a quality that will sell, we can pay them a price that would enable them, on average, to roughly double their income. For example, a woman who otherwise could only work as a maid, in a very rural area of Bangladesh, would be unable to look after her family on a day-to-day basis. She would leave her children with an elderly relative or a sister and would earn not very much at all. Through working with People Tree, she'd be able to live with her family, to educate her children and to afford access to good housing, medical and often legal support. She would also get access to loans, which would enable her to start other small businesses if she wanted to. And she'd have access to a network of people who care. For a woman, I think that's critical.

We support a producer group in Bangladesh called Swallows. At the same time as being our partner in Fair Trade, they run schools in their rural area for more than 600 poor children, as well as programmes to supply safe drinking water. There are huge problems with cyanide poisoning affecting over 50 per cent of the homes in the area, so they've checked all the wells, marked those that are poisonous and set up alternative water supplies, including harvesting rain water from the village huts. At the same time, Swallows runs a land rights programme, campaigning for landless farmers to get access to land. So that kind of legal work goes on as part of a comprehensive programme of social development. Fair Trade gives stability and ongoing income, whereas donor grants are often finished after three years.

Another social development programme operates through Kumbeshwar Technical School (KTS) set up in the 1970s in the Kathmandu Valley in Nepal, to help the most underprivileged caste, called the *Pode*, meaning the street sweepers. These families had to clean the human waste and sewage, were paid only with scraps of unwanted food, and lived very poorly in shacks along the street side. The discrimination they suffered amplified their poverty and gave them virtually no chance of bettering their lives. KTS changed this by creating a school for their children and offering vocational training that has allowed many to escape poverty and negotiate a decent wage for their street-sweeping. The school is financed through the profits and premiums paid by Fair Trade, with People Tree as the biggest customer. Their hand-knit clothing has been sold as a special collection into over 20 Topshop stores. This shows the strength of Fair Trade partnerships and the potential of scaling-up these relationships. KTS now educates 320 children, as well as running vocational training courses in carpet-making, carpentry and hand-knitting, and a new orphanage and handicraft centre is being built.

It's very lovely seeing the social and community impact we have. If you're a low-income family in a developing country, it can be an incredibly vulnerable position. But when you have a community, an organisation that works to bring people together to support each other, that brings a huge strength and stability.

It's very lovely seeing the social and
community impact we have.

Fair Trade promotes livelihoods and social development, but it's really challeng-ing, doing this breadth of work and still having to compete with products that are not Fair Trade. Fast fashion, after all, rarely covers the real social and environmental costs.

Consumer conscience

A lot of consumers sense that something's wrong, though. They know that the social costs and the environmental costs are not there in the price of a product. They feel uneasy when they see a pair of jeans or a top for three quid or five quid, and are increasingly reading stories of sweatshop labour and child labour. We know that the economic system doesn't really add up when we see the kind of sit-uation that farmers are in, especially in the developing world where the odds are stacked so highly against them, and thousands are facing starvation. In India, hundreds of cotton farmers commit suicide because they're stuck in a debt trap — unable to cover the costs of production or to repay loans for the chemical inputs and seeds. The US cotton subsidies — over $3 billion that benefit US large agribusiness — deflate the international cotton price by 25 per cent. Developing world cotton farmers need a price that enables them to cover their costs and to diversify into organic production, and into crops that give them food security. For me, the reason for starting People Tree was to try and create a system, an eco-nomic model, which puts people and the environment at the centre of a trading process.

Wider awareness and consumer pressure have helped build markets for Fair Trade and made meeting minimum ethical standards the least that large compa-nies can do. Last year we had a flurry of media coverage of sweatshop and labour issues around fast fashion — inhumane sweatshops and factory conditions for garment factory workers paid too little even to eat adequately. However, we still have a long way to go before fashion editors stop singing the joys of buying cheap, chic stuff.

Success against the odds

I think we've been successful partly because our partners in Bangladesh, India and Nepal trust us and see that we are in a long-term partnership. We're very much in contact with each other and give each other regular feedback. We'll go and visit them and we stay in each others' homes. The fact that the People Tree team is committed to Fair Trade helps to find ways to solve problems and make the impossible possible. But clearly, unlike the fashion industry, we can't chop and change supplier, and can't decide who to work with from one collection to the next. We're constantly using our creativity to develop new fabrics, using the local traditional skills, so that we can make a product that's as marketable as possible while we continue ordering and strengthening each group.

The biggest barriers to Fair Trade are advance payments, price and lead time — partly because the price is that much higher, but also because things are often hand-produced. We're looking at organic cotton that's Fair Trade, and we may be giving a commitment to the farmers as much as a year or 18 months in advance of using it, so we can't have lead times of four to six weeks as is quite typical of the fashion industry. We would be working as much as three to nine months ahead of any large company on product development, which is tough when it comes to reading trends. So we develop our own originality and commit early.

We're also an environmental organisation, so we're not going to want to bring orders in by air freight, which gives us a considerable handicap in terms of trading. There are obviously huge business costs attached to working in remote villages, rather than in a centrally-located factory. We also have to develop the infrastructure for small groups to be able to secure good quality zippers, safe dyes, etc, which is costly. In the villages, our designers and technicians work with the producers on training, quality assurance and environmental production, which is great fun but again, very costly. But this is the point of Fair Trade — to provide an income in rural areas, so that families can stay together.

As we're working with the most marginalised people in developing countries, clearly they don't have finances to fall back on. When we give an order, six to eight months before we're going to get the products, we have to make a 50 per cent advance payment on that order, so we have huge cash flow challenges. If you're placing an order for $100,000, you're putting up $50,000 before you're seeing

Fast fashion rarely covers the real social and environmental costs.

---

any of that come back. Trust is very important. That's one of the big issues with the high street. They would tend not to pay until products have been received or, if there's any difference in terms of expectation for quality or delivery, they would tend to penalise the supplier. People Tree would try and find a way of solving it, whether it's re-stitching it in Britain or in Japan, or trying to meet halfway and finding a solution that works and won't undermine the supplier and the relationship. I think that's the critical difference.

In the developed world, it's difficult to understand what it means not to have a livelihood available to you. In the rural areas of India or Bangladesh, only 30 per cent of people have access to work, and machines actually take away people's work. Fair Trade approaches economics in a Gandhian way, so that by using traditional and hand skills like hand-spinning, hand-weaving, hand-embroidery and organic farming, people can become self-reliant and develop their communities and make their voice heard. There are still 10 million hand-weavers in India and Bangladesh because it is robust as an 'industry', but we are caught in the age of the machine and value hand skills little. Our economic policy undermines it too — in favour of big solutions. But these skills supply an income, put food on the table and, with good policies and market access, there is no reason why these economies could not be scaled-up. I look forward to each high street fashion company adopting a community or region of weavers or farmers.

What empowers me and gives me confidence to push the Fair Trade fashion agenda is my great closeness to the producers themselves, because I know what the agenda is from the grassroots. We have a big debate in Britain between ethical fashion, which is meeting the minimums in terms of factory standards, and Fair Trade fashion, which is a tool for development. So I find myself being very boring about what Fair Trade fashion is! But I know that weaving communities and artisan communities in rural areas actually need something that is not a factory. I call it a workshop.

They would very often start working from home, and then maybe ten people would gather and work in a community hall or under a tree. And then gradually they build in their strength and numbers. For example, Assisi Garments started at the back of a convent. There were eight deaf and mute women who were picking up small jobs from the surrounding factories, stitching T-shirts and towels. We worked in partnership to develop products with that group, so they're now producing organic cotton T-shirts and fashion garments, with 150 other low-income women and men, and selling to Topshop and 400 other stores around the world. I have no problems with small — small is beautiful. Like People Tree itself, which started in our bedroom, small things can grow into something spectacular if they're loved properly.

Being the change

Does it not start at different levels, with different steps? We all have different values. We start by becoming vegetarian, or we start by recycling, or we start by joining Amnesty International or buying Fair Trade coffee. It's this gradual engagement and journey into social issues, human rights and environmental issues that excites me.

In terms of my own involvement, I suppose I had the luxury of being able to experiment with an idea — I felt that other people felt the same way as I did and I was right. But I worked from when I was 17 years old, so I never had a summer holiday as a student to explore different ideas, or a gap year. When I was 25, I moved to Tokyo because of my boyfriend's job and spent a year learning Japanese, and I was able to try different things, talk to friends, get active; I started being practical and political. For the first time in my life, as I wasn't working, I had the luxury of time to start something I believed in. It is a question of time to some extent, but as a green consumer you do engage, whether it's through your shopping — buying Fair Trade, organic or natural products — or within civil society.

There are so many different ways to be the change. I think it's very important to have experience in a certain field and apply that. You can always learn new skills. We're doing fashion, if you boil it down, and only one in a hundred businesses survives in fashion. Then if you add the Fair Trade component, OK, you've got the great story, but then you add the extra costs, the long lead time — how long are you likely to succeed in Fair Trade fashion? It's incredibly difficult. I think

*Small things can grow into something
spectacular if they're loved properly.*

you need to have relevant business experience, whether in fashion, in finance or in business, and then you need to bring in like-minded, incredible people to help your social business succeed. We're very lucky at People Tree, we have specialists in every field, whether it's a patterning professional, a marketing professional, or in catalogue development or finance — but, it has not been easy. It's really important to understand that you don't just need people who care — you need people with the right and the relevant business background.

A changing world

I had a sense of social issues when I was quite young. I think I came at it more from the human rights side, from the social perspective. Later I became an ecologist. I believe that we should be looking after the planet for future generations, but for me it's the undermining of people's human rights, their communities and livelihoods that makes me angry — the whole environmental and social injustice of what's happening with natural resource use, and who wins. We talk about global warming and we look at the number of environmental refugees that will be flooding out of Bangladesh in 20 or 30 years' time — these are the people with the tiniest environmental footprint. There has to be a model that would work for all of us. We've set ourselves standards, we've talked about the Millennium Development Goals, but no one has actually found or is able to scale up models that are working, that are having terrific social and environmental impact, and yet that's the model. It's the brokering and scaling up of social entrepreneurship that excites me.

The paradigm is shifting. Consumers are becoming more savvy. Business is having to change. Just before the 2007 World Economic Forum in Davos, at the social entrepreneurs' summit, insurance companies came together with financial institutions and business, talking about this need for an economic shift. And global warming has been a huge wake-up call, to look at something that adds up both socially and environmentally. Fair Trade does that — Fair Trade ticks all the boxes, and is the most fantastic tool to educate consumers. I think that's very, very exciting. True sustainability has to come through meeting the needs of the most marginalised people in the world. It's not just producing it in a nice factory where people aren't abused; it's a much, much bigger remit than that. I see a lot of signs of hope, signs of change.

www.wftday.org

www.peopletree.co.uk

Claire Morsman

__I'm really enthusiastic about people liberating their__
__sewing machines and dusting them off for the revolution.__

When Claire Morsman realised that marine animals were dying after ingesting plastic bags, she turned her horror into action. She decided that to stop this happening, we must find alternatives to plastic bags, and overnight, she devised the strategy of 'sociable guerrilla bagging'. Across the country and beyond, people are getting together to make beautiful bags out of recycled material, and then distributing them for free to friends, family and unsuspecting members of the general public during coordinated mass handouts. Since the campaign began in January 2007, hundreds have joined in, making thousands of bags, which replace more than 2.5 million plastic ones.

I would like people to stop using plastic bags, or to become aware of the problems — that when they accept one in a shop, there are consequences. Plastic bags are ingested by marine animals and then they die. Obviously there are other issues that are important, but my main concern is to stop them going into the ocean and to stop wildlife dying.

I grew up in Devon, and I did quite a lot of sailing when I was younger. I'd see all the bags in the sea, and that was frustrating. Now I live on a barge on a canal and watch all the plastic bags go by, and wonder where they end up. They end up in the sea if they're not disposed of properly, and sometimes even if they are. There's an expanse of plastic and debris in the North Pacific Gyre that is now the size of Texas. If plastic bags didn't exist, or at least didn't exist in such vast quantities as we see in supermarkets worldwide, fewer animals would die.

I looked on the internet to see if there were any problems with wildlife, and then I found a picture of a minke whale that was washed up in Normandy, and its entire stomach was absolutely stuffed full of plastic bags. It hadn't got any food in it at all and it had died of starvation. Lots of animals die like this. That was the key moment. It's frustration, really. There's a feeling of helplessness with the environment — you hear, day after day, all these different problems and I thought, 'Where does a person start? What can we do, on a practical basis?' This is a direct action that everyone can take in their own home. It's the simplest thing. My great aunt left me a sewing machine. I didn't even like sewing, I was useless at it at school, but I suddenly thought, 'I can do this! Let's spread the word and make these bags.' A simple action was needed, and it would make me feel better, at the very most selfish basic level, if I could make a couple of bags and give them to people. And I asked myself, 'Why can't everyone join in and do this? If they reuse a cloth bag, they're not going to accept a plastic bag.'

It happened overnight, literally. I'd just had enough. I thought, 'I've got to do something,' and I had the idea. I was walking along with my fiancé Joseph, so I told him. I asked him if he could make a website about it, because he's learning in his free time, and I phoned my mum up, asked her to create a bag design and that was it. It was as quick as that. I went to bed that night really excited. You know when you just know something's right? I wanted to start, so I made a bag.

When our first pods were set up,
we were jubilant.

Spreading the word

The website is an ongoing project. Joseph's adding things all the time, because he's learning as he goes. He's just added a Morsmap, so you can see all the pods and where they are. But to get the flash page up was overnight — he's a bit of a hero. That was in January 2007. We were a little bit shy about it at first. We sent a couple of emails out just to our friends. We were really excited because we've got a counter on the site so we could see who'd been there. I remember it getting to ten people, obviously a tiny amount in comparison to what it is now. The Gumtree website was where we first advertised it and we got lots of hits from there, and the word just spread. It was the most exciting thing watching people — strangers — come to the site, and when our first pods were set up, we were jubilant. Pods are groups of people who get together, drink wine, and have a wonderful time making Morsbags. They download the pattern from the site, and they find old curtains, or old duvet covers — they can get them from charity shops or people can donate them — and then they get together, chat and make bags.

This may be slightly ambitious: I'd love everyone to have a Morsbag, in the whole of the UK at least. That would be wonderful. My ultimate aim is to get rid of plastic bags in the shops. Globally over a million plastic bags are used per minute, which is mind-boggling. It would be great if a law was passed, although we're not particularly politically pushing that at all. Other people are doing that. I think it's our job to make bags and to raise awareness. Some people haven't even thought about where plastic bags go, understandably. That's fine, I'm not judging them for that. If the only thing we did was to make everyone aware of the issue, to make people think, that would be a huge result. I'd love it to be all over the world and for everyone to be frantically making bags. I think there's a big backlash at the moment as well, a sense of coming back to the community. People want an excuse to get together and be sociable, and if you're making something, so much the better. That's what I'd really like, that everyone was enjoying themselves making them and making a real difference.

We've got over 200 pods now and they're all over the UK. We've got some, very excitingly, in America, New Zealand, Spain, Japan, Morocco and France. And it's growing. Every day now when we switch on the computer when we get back from work, the most exciting thing is to see that there's at least another five pods who've signed up. And quite often, even more excitingly, they've already made maybe 12 bags, and then we go 'Ooh!' and we can add them onto the map. Together, we've made over 5,000 Morsbags. We worked out that each Morsbag is roughly equivalent to 500 plastic bags over its lifetime, so we've saved well over 2.5 million plastic bags. It's very satisfying to make one bag and to think that it really does make a difference.

Everyone does it in different ways, it's a most fantastic thing that they're all taking responsibility to make Morsbags in their own way. This has just been the springboard for everybody to do it. Some people are solo poddists, or tod pods — they do it by themselves. There are quite a few women who are happy to have a sewing machine set up in their living room, and while they're doing other things, they come and make bags. One of my friends, for example, occasionally works nights. She's a doctor, and she'll cut out material all night while she's manning the phones. People do it in all sorts of different ways. Some have set up fortnightly workshops. I want it to be really locally based, so it's all springing up by itself. I don't want to be in charge of it. People can put it in their local halls or villages and set it up. Others invite their friends around; it's an excuse to get together and chat. There's even a couple who go into a pub with their sewing machine.

People can't seem to help themselves, it's great, they just run away with this. Some have been saying, 'Watch out for your curtains if I come to your house!' Suddenly they're looking at the soft furnishings as if they want to make Morsbags out of them. Some people have been making them out of skirts, shirts, tea towels, anything that's cloth. It's been really imaginative. That adds to the enjoyment as well because if you can be creative, it's not a drudge.

Guerrilla bagging

People really enjoy giving them away as well. That's the whole other aspect, the guerrilla bagging part. We have organised mass public handouts, and at the same time other people like posting them through neighbours' letterboxes and giving them as presents. There are a couple of people who run B&Bs or guesthouses,

*People are putting their own energy
into it and it's flying.*

and they're leaving bags as little gifts for their visitors. Lots of teachers have been given end-of-term Morsbags. People were frantically bagging for the end of term, which was really sweet. There've been lots of really imaginative ideas that I couldn't have come up with. People are putting their own energy into it and it's flying.

You can get really bogged down in how many problems there are. Giving the bags out to people is amazing, and seeing their faces change. When we give them out, we've got armfuls of bags and they say, 'Oh, can I have the pink one?' Or, 'Can I have the green one?' I love that. You can give them to people who really care about their bag, and then hopefully they'll think about it. A penny drops about what's happening with plastic bags; that's really extraordinary. A bit like when I realised they were so bad — people say, 'That's really what happens to them? That needs to stop.' And then they ask, 'Oh, this is for me?' That's very nice, because they've been shocked, in a good way, so they will actually use them. If you touch people's feelings, I think the message is likely to stay in more. That's the guerrilla aspect of it.

Lots and lots of people want to talk more about it; hardly anyone just walks off with the bag. They want to find out how they can be involved. They'll say, 'I can give you material.' Or, 'My grandmother/son/daughter would be interested in that.' They immediately think about how they can do something practical. Many do promise to go to the website, have a look and dig out their sewing machine. I'm really enthusiastic about the thought of people liberating their sewing machines and dusting them off for the revolution.

The phenomenon spreads

Wandsworth prison are making bags, and other prisons are going to start in September, which is thrilling. Lots of the prisoners work with textiles, and the staff contacted me and said it would be wonderful to get them to work on something worthwhile, that they feel is doing something for the community. What makes me smile is the colours. Everything I see piled up in there is prison green and prison blue. It's quite monotonous. I walk in there and I'm giving them dinosaur duvet covers. I take charity shop stuff there and see them working away on all these lovely colours, and the wardens did say they enjoy the variety. That must be quite a nice break, I imagine.

A lot of those bags went to the Virgin Trains challenge, which was very last minute. It was quite soon after we'd set the website up, and not many bags had been made. I went to see the Virgin Trains people who'd asked me if I could provide bags for the Manchester Festival. I said I'd love to, and they said we had about two weeks to provide 1,000 bags. I ever-optimistically said, 'Yes, of course we can do that, no problem.' I came home and panicked slightly. I put a message out on the forum and said, 'Can we rally the troops? Would anyone fancy sending me their Morsbags?' I couldn't believe the response. We don't have very reliable post here, so I got everyone to send them to my mum. She said it was like Christmas. Every day packages of 20 bags would turn up and they all had notes inside, saying 'Keep it up!' The whole thing restored my entire faith in mankind. It was so sweet, and never a question asked; it was so trusting. They were all different and beautiful. I gave them to Virgin and they handed them out, and that was when I knew that people were really behind us, that they supported us and we could make it work. By this point, people were taking it on board to spread the word themselves and were involving local radio, and it started to get legs and wings.

That came about after we made bags on *BBC Breakfast*. After that, the hit counter on the site went sky high, and people wrote in and said, 'How can we help? Can we give you fabric? Can we give you machines?' Brother, the sewing machine company, got in contact as well, and they've given us machines to distribute to keen pods. They're going to support us to distribute a schools pack as well. In January, we're going to launch a pack for every single school. We're going to do a senior school one, a junior school one and there's a business studies one as well. Lots of schools are already making bags. If all the kids get involved, it should get much bigger.

The people at Brother have been so supportive and they don't even want to advertise on our site. They want to help. It was a huge surprise that anyone would

*It's so home-grown. There's us at our little table on a boat,
chattering about an idea together.*

take us that seriously, someone that big, and it was the same with Virgin. Save the Children are interested in doing something with us. Big companies want to talk to us and I find that a surprise, because it's so home-grown. There's us at our little table on a boat chattering about an idea together and the next thing you know, people are contacting us. Actually, whenever I send out press releases or chase publicity, it doesn't happen. All our publicity has come to us.

I think the naivety of the project is appealing — you can see it's not a slick operation. People have treated us so beautifully and wanted to help and genuinely trusted us, and given us anything they can and that's amazing. Sometimes I want it all to speed up, and then I realise it's going bloody fast anyway. I feel impatient; I just want to help out more, do more, set up more workshops, set up pod meetings. I want to chivvy. Thrilled is the general feeling. I'll get back to the computer, turn it on and there are always more things written on the forum, hundreds of emails. There are always loads of private messages and phone calls for me now, and I want to harness it, get it in. I feel guilty if I can't get back to people quickly to say thank you so much for seeing the same vision as I've got, and for not just paying lip service to it, but doing something about it. People have literally gone to their sheds and got out their sewing machines, or they've gone to their charity shop or they've asked all their friends. People have got up and done something and that motivates me, because I want to show that I'm doing the same amount.

I feel a bit guilty that I don't make enough bags sometimes because I want to show that I can do the same. I've made 180 or so. It's easy to become obsessive about it, it's so much fun. You do get addicted and once you've started a load, you're always mid-way, so you want to finish that batch and by the time you've finished you think, 'I'll just do a couple more.' There's no end to it. Also, it's so much fun coming up with new ideas, like when we came up with the idea of a 24-hour sewathon. We were going to try and get into the *Guinness Book of Records* because hopefully a gimmick like that would be such great fun to get everyone sewing for 24 hours and drinking wine, and hopefully we'll get people from different pods to meet each other.

Challenges

The only challenging thing is lack of time. I would love to throw myself much more wholeheartedly at the project. I find it quite frustrating that obviously I've got to go to work and have a real life. I get frustrated when I've got other things going on in my life. I have to snatch a moment to make a bag, because we have to keep up with the admin and reply to loads of emails. We've been asked, 'Why don't you just have standard responses to emails?' But you get out what you put in, don't you?

I'm asked to go to talk to schools and speak about Morsbags, and I'd like to do that more, because some people are a little bit afraid of making their first bag, which is understandable. But when they see it, they realise how easy it is and then they can't help themselves and they get addicted to doing it. Before we know it, they're churning out 70 bags. We're frequently asked if we want to sell them, which we can't do, we wouldn't do, because that's not our ethic at all. When we do handouts, some people look at us and say, 'What's the catch?' They're quite defensive. And that's quite challenging having to talk people round, but a good thing. I think the word 'free' has to come into it quite loudly sometimes. That's a bit frustrating because you think it should be more obvious than that. But the message gets out.

We want Morsbags to self-perpetuate, so that if you're given a bag, you'll know where it's from. So we put labels on. We've had quite a few difficulties because we bought those iron-on labels, but they're not the easiest things to use, everyone has to go out and buy them, they're quite expensive, and they will eventually come off. We wanted something much more durable so now we are much happier with the sew-on ones we have now. But we are asking people to dip into their own pockets. I'm amazed by the response I get — people order them by the hundred. They cost 7p each. I feel a little bit guilty about having to charge people for the labels, obviously just what I pay for them to make all the costs equal up. Sometimes I think these people are amazing: they're trusting me to send these labels out. Why should they pay for this? That's so lovely.

Joining in

I've learned there are a lot of people out there who want to do something and don't necessarily know how to start, and they're dying to be harnessed into something like this. Not in a sheep-like way, but there's so much energy and emotion and intelligence and pent-up activity ready to be unleashed. Everyone wants to join in and help. I've always thought there are many more good people than bad people, but I've learned how brilliant people are. I can't stress that enough. They're joining in and getting down to it and not giving in to desperation. If we all listened to the media and decided there's no hope, that would be very sad. It was especially touching when people started sending bags to us. We thought, 'Wow, it's real! They really are there. It's not just in the ether somewhere.'

At the end of the day we're just giving out presents to everyone. It's an excuse to be creative, and do something with an evening or an afternoon, to get together as friends and make new ones as well. People can find others in their local area on the forum to meet up with or they can just drag along a group of mates. Everyone inspires each other. It's a win-win situation. Anyone can do it, it's completely universal, and you're making a bag. How fab is that? You either get to keep it or you give it away. You can't go wrong.

www.morsbags.com

Jessie Nunes

Having been homeless, and then getting a flat and not knowing where to start, I can say Kids Company has been quite fundamental in my growth as a young person.
So it's only fair that I share that gift with someone else.

When Jessie Nunes was a troubled teenager in foster care, and then homeless, the only place she could turn to was Kids Company, a charity founded by Camila Batmanghelidjh in 1996 to help vulnerable children in inner-city London. She has remained with Kids Company ever since, moving from using their services to providing them. She is the co-director of Colour a Child's Life, a scheme where a team of volunteers provides a makeover to the homes of some of the Kids Company children and their families. These are often transformed from conditions of squalor, danger and lacking bare necessities, to clean, safe, beautifully decorated and furnished homes.

The change I wish to see is for people to be living better. Our work is trying to offer them a way out, a way out of the ghetto. That's how most of our clients refer to their living conditions. There's wallpaper stripped off and holes in the walls. Then there's furniture that's broken — some houses have no flooring, or carpets with holes in. There are broken windows, broken window frames. Some of them have no storage place for clothes — no wardrobes or chests of drawers. Things are just stored in a black bag on the floor or sometimes they pile their clothes up on chairs. I just don't feel anyone should have to live in environments like this.

Sometimes people blame them, saying they're lazy. But in Kids Company, we believe that lots of these people live like this maybe because of their upbringing, and also what they're going through; a lot of the parents have mental health issues. So I believe in not judging people. I believe it's good that they're crying out for help — you can offer them that help.

Tatty, the project coordinator, links us up with families who need our help. We get in there and totally gut the place. We throw out furniture, we pack up all the stuff that they don't need, we declutter. A lot of the time, it's lots of cleaning as well, even cleaning human faeces off the walls, cat poop, taking out rats — sometimes they have rats and mice — the list just goes on. We have to do all that before we can even get down to doing the decorating. Once all the hard part's done, it's painting, laying the flooring, getting the curtains up, making it look like a home that they can be proud of — a home that they can invite their friends to. A lot of the children get bullied about how they live — they feel like they're not able to engage or interact with other kids at home, so they're somewhat isolated. When you're five and six, this is quite fundamental in your growth, so I'd like to give them more confidence about it.

Beginnings

A lot of the young people at Kids Company got their flats, and when councils give you flats, they're sometimes in a very bad condition. And a lot of these people have never lived independently or they've come from a broken home. They don't know where to begin. Staff members from Kids Company were going in and helping them, and then realising that these kids didn't even know one thing about how to paint a wall, how to make a place a home. So that's how it initially started, just a very small project. Every once in a blue moon, a young person would be offered a permanent flat, and we'd go in there and redecorate and teach them about electricity and bills and stuff like that. And then because we work in lots of schools around London, we saw that a lot of families were living in bad conditions. After that, we realised that all this work was coming in and that there just weren't enough of us to do it.

We started to get involved with lots of companies, asking if they wanted to help us out. A lot of them had volunteer days, so on these days some of the employees would volunteer to come and work with Kids Company. Sometimes it could be up to 15 or 20 volunteers over the course of one or two days, helping us with the cleaning or the decorating. So that's what they do, they volunteer their time and the company would also give us money to buy the materials before-hand. Even though Annie and I do a lot of the work, if the volunteers aren't there, then these projects can't go ahead financially and physically, because really, who can turn a house around in one day? Not two people.

And some of the individuals from the companies while on the project days even contribute money to buy new bedding and other things for the house. We work off donations, so sometimes we have to wait for the money to come in, or for someone to donate things like bedding, kettles, curtains. A lot of these peo-ple are quite generous and on the day they do give us money to buy things for these families, and sometimes they actually go and buy them themselves. They'd buy the kids a beautiful lampshade and matching curtains, and cushions and beanbags and stuff like that. I think the volunteers get a lot out of the day as well. The families do and the kids do, and the volunteers do as well because they can actually see what they're doing. It's better than just giving us money and saying, 'OK, go and paint a house.' They're actually involved; they get to see it from the beginning to the end. So that's how it started out and it's just got bigger. Now we do up to three or four projects a week.

We work hard. We don't just go into a house and say, 'I'm going to stay here from nine to five.' We'll go there and we might not leave till 11 at night, because we do have deadlines on these projects. Sometimes the families are in bed and breakfasts for the time that we're in their house, so sometimes we work for 13 hours, sometimes 16 hours. We might start at eight and be there till one o'clock the next morning. It's just a question of rising to the occasion and meeting the challenge.

I believe in not judging people.
It's good that they're crying out for help –
you can offer them that help.

Challenges

One challenge we face sometimes is that some of the families are stuck in their ways and so used to living in that condition that they feel uncomfortable to start with; some of them feel embarrassed, or they get angry. A lot of people don't like change, and they agree to it one minute and then they're unhappy because it's all moving too fast for them. For a few days you might have to leave it alone for them to adjust to the situation. Sometimes they don't know if they're coming or going, everything's upside down, there are different people in their house. We're used to it now, so really it's just assuring them, 'No one's judging you, and when it's finished, you're going to be happy, your kids will be happy and it's worth going through all of this. It doesn't seem like it at the moment but we will get there.' No one's been unhappy at the end of the projects, so I guess it works. We just persevere. Like I say, we do understand. I don't know if I'd want someone in my house half the time; it's private, it's mine. So I totally understand where they're coming from.

I can't say that I've had major challenges, other than I'd never thought I'd see the day that I'd be cleaning human faeces off the wall. At first, I must say that I honestly thought, 'Oh my God, this is disgusting, how can I do this?' Then when I saw the kids, how could I not do it? They've got to live in this environment every day; how can I not get a sponge and wipe these walls off? This kid runs her hands across the walls every day. If we don't clean it, who else is going to? I have to do it. You see those little faces and you just know that you have to and it's all worthwhile. I think that's the worst — human faeces, dog poop, and cat poop. These kids are used to seeing that. They shouldn't be used to seeing it and we don't want them to see it any more. Hence why you just brush yourself off and say, 'You know what? I've got to do it.' When you go back though, the houses are not like that any more.

We see happy faces. It's like a new lease of life for a family, and we see changes in how they conduct their family life as well. It's not that we just decorate the houses; we tell them about the cleaning and things like that, so they make a lot of healthy improvements in their homes. The kids are so much happier. Really, that's what we aim for. For Kids Company, that's the most important thing — to give the child a slice of happiness. That's what these projects bring, a slice of happiness, like a slice of sweet cake. We have quite a few social workers who work for Kids Company, so they check on the families on a fortnightly or weekly basis to see if they need any help doing anything else. They give us feedback. Most families are living quite happily. They've got ongoing support from Kids Company, as they might have other needs, which might not be to do with the house. A lot of these families have emotional needs, so some of the kids will go and see a psychotherapist from Kids Company. After cleaning the house out, it's dealing with emotional needs.

Making a difference

I'm happy to make a difference. Some people are happy doing things like admin, but I'm happy getting my hands dirty and knowing I'm getting my hands dirty for a purpose, knowing that it's going to make a difference. When I leave that house I find it really rewarding. That makes my day. I'm an action woman, I can't see myself doing anything plain and simple. There's never a dull day. The kids inspire me, and the families, especially when you see how they're so grateful for the changes that you've made in their lives. In particular, when we did one of these houses, the girl came in and she said, 'I can have my friends over now, they can play in my bedroom.' I hold onto that. Every time I do a house, I remember seeing this little girl's face and what she said.

What else? I like it because it's challenging. I like the fact that I meet all these people from different companies who are from very different backgrounds, that's nice as well. We get to spread the word through the projects as well. A lot of the volunteers end up donating money to Kids Company when they see the work that we do. And the families tell their friends, so word gets around and we get to help other families. There must be 101 things that are really good about doing the projects. But most of all, for me, I just find it rewarding. Giving something back to the community, making somebody happy. If we can do that, that's a gift within itself really; you're giving something but also receiving something for yourself.

*That's what these projects bring —
a slice of happiness, like a slice of sweet cake.*

In a way, I find it quite calming. It helps me in my own life as well. Because sometimes you go through things, and then you see some of these families and realise that some of them are going through a lot worse than what you and I sometimes go through. So it makes me feel better about myself; I really have nothing to moan about in my life because some people are much worse off and I see it every day. So it gives me the courage to move forward and get on with my life.

I kind of fell into it by accident. It wasn't something that I had planned. I'd been in foster care for a few years and I've been at Kids Company for a long time so I've met a lot of people that have been through similar things to myself. When these young people started to get their flats, they just didn't know where to start with them. Kids Company wasn't so established when I was there years ago, so we really didn't have the funds to do certain stuff, or the staff resources to help young people out as much as we can do now.

It started with a place we were doing in Clapham with a young gentleman who'd just got his flat. He'd been in care just like myself. He had a very rough background, and when I got there and saw how he felt — he was suffering, he just didn't know what to do with himself or where to start — I could relate to where he was coming from because I remember what it felt like thinking, 'How do I gloss a skirting board? How do I paint a ceiling?' I could really relate to being thrown in at the deep end. The other girl from Kids Company, Annie, came into the room and she taught me how to paint. It's because of her that I'm so skilled now. Working alongside Annie, I started to use my skills in other places. That's more or less how it started off. We were both tired of seeing these kids going through that kind of experience of feeling, 'I'm here and I'm abandoned and I don't know what to do.'

This is what Social Services does to a lot of these young people. 'Here you go. Here's the flat, here's the key. Bye.' They did it to me, and it hurt me to see that so many of these young people at Kids Company were going through exactly the same thing. So I was in a position where I could help. I could say, 'All right, you don't know what to do, but I do. I've been there and I've done it, so I can help you.' That's more or less how it started for me.

Coming to Kids Company

I was at home up until I was 14. I wasn't getting along with family and my mother placed me in foster care in 1994. Then I went back to the family home in 1997. We got a bigger house and I finally got my own room. I thought maybe with the space, we would start actually being a family. It didn't work out like that, unfortunately, and my mum kicked me out in October 1997. I slept rough, in different people's houses, on sofas if I was lucky, boys' houses, just wherever I could because Social Services at the time, even though I was under 18, weren't willing to house me. I wasn't 16, so I wasn't quite young enough to meet certain criteria, and I wasn't 18, so I wasn't old enough to meet other criteria. I was slap bang in the middle. It took me two months to even get a place in a hostel. I was 17 and still under Social Services care to a certain degree. When I got to 18, that was it. Not even a birthday card or, 'If you need help, contact us.' It was, 'You're 18, see you later.' Even before I got to 18, I didn't have an income. I'd maybe get £20 from Social Services a week, and I was living rough, so £20 hardly went anywhere. Once I got to 18, they just washed their hands of me and that was it.

When I did get my flat, I had to try and find a way of working around the system and trying to get money to decorate. I had to get my head down and find out this information. Kids Company was quite helpful in that respect. They didn't have the finances to do most of the stuff that we do now, but they were still helpful, pointing me in the right direction, and we did get donations of duvets. It was actually Camila who bought me my first cutlery and crockery set. No one else was going to say, 'I'm going to take you to Argos and buy you cutlery and crockery and a kettle.' She doesn't have the time to do all those things now, but she took me herself to Argos, went through the catalogue and picked out the items that she knew I needed. I feel like she gave me a start, even though they couldn't afford to buy furniture; it was just the basics like pots and pans and an alarm clock. I was at college at the time, and she said, 'I know you're going through all of this emotional stress right now, but I really want you to continue your education.' So she bought me this alarm clock that went cock-a-doodle-doo about 10 times. It was so loud!

So I've had it hard like a lot of other kids, and a lot of them have been through a lot more than I have. But having been homeless, and then getting a flat and not

> *I was in a position where I could help.*
> *I could say, 'All right, you don't know what to do, but I do.*
> *I've been there and I've done it, so I can help you.'*

knowing where to start, I can say Kids Company has been quite fundamental in my growth as a young person. So it's only fair that I share that gift with somebody else. I do feel quite blessed by being part of Kids Company, growing up. I feel like I'm a product of Kids Company.

I first heard of Kids Company when I was 16. A neighbour told me about it. They were putting on a musical about what young people go through living in the 'ghetto' parts of London, as people like to call them. It was about being on the dole, getting a giro, parents being on benefits, alcoholic parents, abuse and everything else. The project was working towards getting this musical done, which we put on in a little theatre in Holborn. Camila invited some important people to come and watch. Basically, it was our story and how we viewed life. That's how I got involved. At the time I was a performing-arts student, so I was well up for it. Then I realised that they offered counselling and other support services. I was still in foster care at the time, and I'd go there for one-to-one counselling sessions. Some sessions I had with Camila herself, some I would have with other people.

It was the kind of place where I fitted in. I'd just started college then, but even throughout school, I'd never quite felt like I fitted in anywhere. And at Kids Company, I actually felt like I belonged there. I found people that I could really relate to, so actually I did fit in. I'm not just a misfit in society. There are lots of misfits like me and we all make one big jigsaw puzzle. That's how I saw it; we all made up part of the puzzle. At the start it was good, and right now it's still good. For me, it just gets better. I've been there for ten whole years, all the way through. And like I say, I'm really happy to be part of Kids Company; I'm really happy that they've given me the opportunity to help other young people as well.

That's most probably one of the biggest gifts they've given me — the gift of being able to help somebody else. With the staff and the other young people, even the kids, if you see how they are with each other, it's like we've all learned how to help each other. We're all a family. I do have living family, but it's the one place where everyone feels like they belong. I feel so much love here as well, and I guess that's why I'm still here. Lots of the time I tell myself, I really should do something new, there could be something else out there, but these projects and these young people, they're really what keep me here. But I won't be here for much longer, I'm going to university in September. I decided as I had so many crap social workers in my life, that that's what I was going to study. Camila's encouraged me to go to university to study social work. Colour A Child's Life will still go on. Annie will definitely keep it going. There's nothing she can't do.

Being the change

Go for it. You can help make changes in someone else's life, but the changes that you'll get in your life will be plentiful, that's how I see it. If you work to make a change with no expectations, not wanting anything out of it, you will see that you'll always get a lot more out of it than you've put in. And it doesn't always have to be costly. Sometimes it can just be your time. So if you can help someone, whatever it is, then it's always good to be a giver. I always find it better to give than to receive.

Sometimes you feel like your life is empty. You might work, you might have all the money. But if you're not doing the right things in your life, sometimes it could just be giving someone your time or donating £10 — that can actually make a world of difference because you feel like you're doing something. You're not just living every day for yourself. You've got to live for yourself to a certain degree, but life always tastes better and feels better when you can give to somebody else as well. There are other people who could do with your help and it's not always major things. It's not always like the adverts, where it says, 'Donate £3.' At Kids Company, we need money too, but you know what? A lot of people just volunteer their time. That could just be sitting down as a counsellor and saying, 'I'm going to counsel this child for an hour a week for free.' That's just giving their time. Wherever you can help, just help out; it doesn't always have to cost. As a nation I think we think too much about money. You can help someone for free.

www.kidsco.org.uk

Jonathon Porritt

I'm not just interested in the environment;
I'm interested in the relationships between people,
the environment and an economy.

Jonathon Porritt began his lengthy career in the environmental movement as an activist in what was then one of the world's first green parties, the Ecology Party, which later became the Green Party. He went on to become a director of Friends of the Earth, before leaving to found the sustainable development charity Forum for the Future with Sara Parkin and Paul Ekins. Other contributions include chairing the UK Sustainable Development Commission and developing the Prince of Wales' Business and Environment Programme. As the wider world begins to catch up with his way of thinking, he now enjoys a rare position as both a pillar of the movement and an advisor to governments and businesses.

The change that I want to see is people acknowledging the need to co-create a future with the natural world, to renounce completely this old paradigm of progress through subjugation of nature, and to start living out in practice a paradigm which is based on cohabitation with nature. This is a huge philosophical shift that I'm talking about on one level, a meta-transformation of the human mind and spirit. I start at that level because I've become convinced that unless we change mindsets fundamentally in that sort of way, then a lot of the behaviour change which is going on at the individual and community level will wither, will simply perish. If it's not properly embedded in a philosophical, metaphysical shift of that kind, it's very ephemeral; often it's very vulnerable to the old world order, the old mindsets crushing energy on the part of new pioneers. So that's the high-level place where I would want to start, and then one can translate that down through into all sorts of more practical, applied ways of being a change agent.

Forum for the Future is undoubtedly the biggest part of the transformative work that I'm involved in now. When we set that up, the whole idea was to work with people's positive energy regarding their own lives and their relationship with other people and the natural world, to work with that positive energy to accelerate change processes that are already going on in the world. Now, the reason why I put it in those terms, 'working with positive energy', is that much of my time before that as a green activist had been spent working with people's negative energy: with people's *guilt* about the terrible things that they were doing to the world, advertently or inadvertently; with *fear* at the prospects for themselves or their children if the environment were to go on disintegrating; and *anger* at the fact that the planet was being trashed on our behalf by incompetent and procrastinating politicians.

Positivity

If I look back on the Green Party and Friends of the Earth, where I spent my first 20 years, that's the energy that we worked with. I don't think those organisations had any choice in those days; nobody wanted to work with any positive energy — there wasn't any sense of a transformation available to us at that stage, so it had to be confrontational, it had to be negative, stopping people doing things, because there wasn't any sense of a licence to create new things. The opportunity didn't really exist in those days to do it differently, but a young activist coming

This is a huge philosophical shift,
a meta-transformation of the human mind and spirit.

---

into the scene today has a choice: they can either go into campaigning organisations that will still take on the wrongdoers and those that are out to advance their own self-interest at the expense of other people and the planet, or they can go into a whole host of organisations that have emerged in the last 15 years which are about bridge-building, about working with positive energy, creating solutions. They've got a choice that wasn't there before. But when I got back from the Earth Summit in 1992, which was a complete turning point for me, I realised that I couldn't go on working any longer simply by criticising other people, it was kind of wearing me down. I needed to find a different kind of energy to release my own energy.

What the Forum does very simply is to work with many different partners in the private and public sector, and in education and the professions. We work alongside sustainability champions to challenge them, empower them, make them more effective change agents in their own organisations, and through that engagement process, accelerate this critical change going on. Now, that's the high level thing that we do, and the combination of advice, support and challenge is obviously a very important part of how we do it. It'll be different for different partners and different contexts as you can imagine. But in essence, the Forum's work is precisely the same at that high level. It then cascades through into completely different projects, initiatives and ideas with different partners depending on what their priority is. We tend not to go in there and tell them, 'You must do this,' as we've found that that isn't always very helpful! What we try to do is support a process inside an organisation where they discover for themselves what the gaps are in what they are doing, what the priorities are, what they need to be doing next and how to do it. Once they've discovered what that is, then we work with them to make it happen.

When we set up the Forum in 1996, we did it with an intuitive sense that working with the business community would be challenging and rewarding and could still be done with integrity. This sounds a bit obvious now in 2007; everybody works with the business community and there's not a particularly big deal about it. When we were talking about this back in the mid-1990s with our colleagues in the green movement, there was a ton of stuff about being 'co-opted' by the enemy. 'No spoon is long enough to sup with that bunch of devils, Jonathon, you'll be betraying your radical beliefs. They will corrupt you. By definition, working with business will corrupt you.' And this was quite tricky to deal with, especially the personal bit; that I would be letting down the movement, letting down my colleagues, particularly in organisations like the Green Party and Friends of the Earth, by creating a mechanism to work closely and intimately and in trust-based circumstances with business.

So we had to take a punt at that stage. Either you believe that all these people working for companies are inherently wicked and out to destroy the world and they're getting a real buzz out of it; or you accept that actually they're not particularly happy about what they're doing, but they're part of an economy which reduces choice for many individuals working for companies and indeed, what people don't really recognise, that reduces choice for the companies themselves in terms of their imperatives to meet the mandate of profit-at-all-costs capitalism.

So we took that punt, we took that decision very consciously, and I must say the surprise in all of this is that, in all of the 12 years since then, we haven't met a single company that has tried to abuse the Forum's trust. We haven't been manipulated for PR purposes, for greenwash purposes. And almost without exception, the individuals we've worked with have proved to be as passionate about finding answers to these problems as people in the NGO world. And that's a really interesting insight for me, as there is an assumption that anyone who goes and works for a company isn't going to be open to that kind of passion and commitment, because if they were, they would have gone to work for an NGO. Discovering that isn't really the case, and that given half a chance and an opportunity to free that sense of passion about sustainability, they're not that different in their soul from people working in the green movement — that was surprising!

A different approach

I've noticed over the years that my environmentalism is a tiny bit different from many of the people with whom I work. I spent seven years at Friends of the Earth

Sustainable development is the only big idea that can really sustain the weight of political response that we now need.

and I was a trustee of the Worldwide Fund for Nature for 14 years, so I've done a lot of completely conventional environmental things at the same time as pursuing sustainable development as my real interest. I think it's fair to say these days I'm reluctant to be described as an 'environmentalist' and I call myself a 'sustainable development activist'. It sounds a small difference, but to me it's a critical difference because I'm not just interested in the environment; I'm interested in the relationships between people, the environment and an economy — hence my obvious belief that sustainable development is the only big idea that can really sustain the weight of political response that we now need.

When I was I was a boy I did fairly conventional green things, like bird-watching. I used to watch wildlife programmes on the television as much as I possibly could. I was always interested in that stuff, and then I took a gap year and worked on farms, planting trees. So I was always interested in the natural world, but not from the normal perspective about protecting it, I just wanted to be part of it. What then got me into joining the Green Party in the mid-1970s was that I was teaching in a school in London in Shepherd's Bush, in a very interesting comprehensive school just opposite the White City estates, and our catchment was those estate areas. I taught there for nine years, and became absolutely obsessed with finding ways of giving these kids access to a rather better environment than anything they had available to them in White City. So we set up a lot of new initiatives for them, some of which were, looking back on it now, very environmental. We'd take groups of these kids to a farm in Wales every year to teach them about farming, the land, nature and so on. I can't honestly say that I launched that scheme in Burlington Danes with a view to setting up an environmental scheme; I launched it because it was a way of filling a gap in their lives.

So I came into the Green Party world and the world of sustainable development more from the perspective of social justice than from the perspective of conventional environmentalism. There's an absolutely inseparable connected-

225

ness between social justice and environmentalism, and if you don't hold that at the centre of your mind all the way through, you're never likely to change anything in life. If you're an environmentalist, you're certainly not going to change anything unless you pay attention to the structures of society, to issues about equality and wealth in that society; and if you're a social justice campaigner, I can assure you whatever you achieve in the short term will be worth absolutely nothing in the long term if you don't pay attention to our life support system. So for me, these two things cannot be boxed out separately into different zones of activism.

I wasn't really thinking about it from the perspective of building a long-term career. It just seemed to be the right thing to do. I have tended to trust instinct about the right thing to do. (It doesn't always work — there've been lots of failures, which are important because they help shape one's own growth and development as a change agent just as much as the successes.) Then I got to be good at being a spokesperson for causes and things. Because I was a teacher, I was dealing with some very stroppy kids. Those kids taught me as much about communications as I ever needed to know, so I became fearless about standing up in front of groups of people and prattling on. Doing an interview didn't worry me at all, so I lost all my nervousness about that, knew that I could handle media stuff. Once that happened, it just built and built. But when I went to Friends of the Earth in 1984, I do remember saying to the Chairman at the time, Des Wilson, 'OK, I'm going to come and do this for three years and then I'm going back into teaching. My real life is as a teacher.' Well, I'm still in teaching but it's of a slightly different kind!

Patterns of challenge

It's gone through different stages. Early on, the main impediment to achieving any change was ridicule, basically. People who professed to the kind of ideas that I did in the 1970s — lots of people like me, but tiny as a proportion — were subject to large amounts of ridicule! When I wrote the Ecology Party Manifesto in 1979, we did some interviews on TV, and the basic line of questioning from the journalists was, 'Well, this is all a bit of a laugh isn't it? How nice to have someone out there to protect the bees and the birds and all that, fantastic stuff!' Even my friends thought that this was completely dotty, bonkers, that this couldn't be

*I was always interested in the natural world,
but not from the normal perspective about protecting it;
I just wanted to be part of it.*

turned into a political party. That was difficult and I had to get used to that constant level of good-humoured invective about the fact that I'd seemed to have lost
my mind. I suppose I developed defences against that and gradually ignored it
after a while. Ignoring things sometimes works.

The next phase was nothing really to do with ridicule, it was more to do with
indifference and inertia, and that lasted for a very long time. I overcame that by
getting cross. I would find this stimulated lots of new energy in me, and it would
be a challenge to see how one could shatter the complacency that allowed people to be so inert in their response to what was even then emerging as an
absolutely enormous challenge in our midst. That was easier to deal with,
because I have a relatively easy route to ratcheting up my emotional energy to
take people on at that level. I'm a bit more moderate about that these days.

But then underpinning all of that, and the most complicated bit in terms of
coping with this, is dealing with the constant flow of totally depressing information about people's lives — particularly the lives of people in the developing
world — and the state of our planet, of our physical environment. This is a non-
stop flow of negative information and stories and data that passes in front of people like me, day in, day out. I've had to develop ways of managing that, of not
being crushed by the weight of that extremely depressing backdrop to what I do.
I suppose that's part of the reason why I set up Forum for the Future and other
things like the Prince Of Wales' Business and the Environment Programme,
which again is all about solutions and not about the problems. I needed to be
more in contact with people making things change, with solutions emerging from
people's energy of that sort. Otherwise I think my spirits would have been on a
permanently declining trajectory, and I'm not sure then I could have sustained
myself as an activist for that length of time.

So I have developed all sorts of ways of doing that, and tried to keep a sense
of humour about this; I'm a great believer that the green movement could do with

a lot more humour than it is normally exposed to. People get very gloomy very quickly, so I try and puncture the inherent gloominess. If I'm feeling really depressed, I'll often just remind myself what this is all about and go for a walk and get back into contact with the natural world. That's what provides me with a lot of energy in this respect; and I have a vague and rather loose spiritual practice which also helps me to come through some of the gloomier bits of being a sustainable development activist.

Job satisfaction

There are lots of joys, it's absolutely fantastic! One is the joy — I don't mean this in any patronising way — of the sinner converted, as it were. There's a real sense of fun and uplift in seeing how people are coming to this agenda now, as if they're discovering something completely new. Which I still find slightly baffling, but it doesn't really matter! They're just there, suddenly, and it's wonderful to see how this liberates energy and determination in them. There's a lot of that around at the moment, lots and lots of people.

I was listening to the radio yesterday and there was a story about a 16-year-old boy who had decided that climate change was really awful. He lived on a farm in Yorkshire, so he worked with his dad to make the whole farm completely self-sufficient in energy, by developing a biogas plant. It was an amazing story, this 16-year-old kid who from when he was 14 onwards had said, 'OK, we can do this. This is easy!' There was his dad on the radio commenting with a mixture of horror — remembering what it was like when his son had first got this bug — and now this sense of real pride and satisfaction, since his son was saving him thousands of pounds a year, by virtue of running the farm so much more efficiently.

Now I listen to that and my soul leaps a bit. We need stories like that day in, day out on the radio, on the telly and in our newspapers, because what we normally get about all this stuff in the media is, understandably, just another great stream of all the things that are going wrong and destroying the world. We have to take joy from the success stories of those who are creating a better world right now.

I sometimes get a bit embarrassed about how much fun I have. In the green movement, you don't really own up to that, because how can you have fun with the world falling to pieces around you? I keep my spirits up, by and large, because

*Enthusiasm is infectious, and you will never change
people unless you yourself are full of enthusiasm
for what you are trying to do.*

it's always been enjoyable, even in the early days when I joined the Green Party
and there was not much going on. It was still fascinating. It was enormous fun
putting together an ideological infrastructure in my mind so that I could cope
with all of these odd things happening in the world. And my feeling is that enthusiasm is infectious, and you will never change people unless you yourself are full
of enthusiasm for what it is that you are trying to do. In a way, that's always been
the success model for social entrepreneurs and activists in any progressive
movement. You have to share that enthusiasm and allow people to take a little bit
of it, as a reinforcement of their own passion, and help to grow that and nurture
that.

Keeping going

The core motivation is still what's happening in the world, and the speed with
which we are undermining our prospects for a better future. That's just a constant refrain every single day. One's surrounded by the evidence of unsustainable
behaviour and very foolish economic policies that constantly re-affirm the need
for commitment of this kind. So I don't have any difficulty about motivation.
Getting up in the morning is not a problem!

The things that keep me going include a peer group that I use a lot. I take a lot
of strength and ideas from people inside the Forum, and from colleagues on the
Sustainable Development Commission. That's becoming an extremely inspiring
place to be. There are 18 other commissioners and they're amazing, they're fantastic people. So I have this wonderful resource network of inspiring people, and
not many of them are conventional environmentalists either, they're all from different walks of life. That's been hugely empowering for me. So it's mostly people.
Otherwise it's books — I read as much as I can, usually over the summer holidays
and at Christmas. I read very fast. When I was writing *Capitalism as if the World
Matters*, I read 40 books in research, and suddenly came away full of new ideas
and insights and thinking, and I have this massive ongoing debt of gratitude to

people who fill that space intellectually. I'm particularly keen on looking at books about economics — Herman Daly, Paul Ekins. I read quite a lot about psychology and the shape of society. This is a constant source of nurturing for me and I do need that.

I feel I have a duty — any individual has only got so much energy in any one 24-hour block of time — and I want to know that my energy is being deployed as creatively as possible. And as soon as I come to a conclusion that something is not letting energy flow, that there are too many blockages in the system, then recently, in the last five or six years I've just come to the decision: fine, cut your losses, get out, move on. There are so many things to be doing. So I am actually a bit ruthless about that and that sometimes gets people a bit pissed off but, you know, I'm 57, getting old! I keep thinking there's so much to do, so those decisions come more quickly now than they used to do.

It's huge fun to be in a place where you can help other people make changes in their life. It's immensely rewarding. It's also something that can be done at so many different levels — very ambitiously or very modestly — and it doesn't really matter actually what level it's at, and nobody need have great grandiose thoughts about not making much of a contribution if their change processes are quite modest and quite small. That's immaterial.

But on the other hand, it's bloody hard work. It is demanding. It's pretty tough stuff. You've got to constrain your passion and commitment at certain times, and get a sense of perspective. I think the best thing for that is having children. That certainly did me a power of good. When our two girls arrived, I stopped doing a lot of the things I was doing before that. I was working every weekend, I was an absolutely mad workaholic, a 'willing workaholic' as we call them in the Forum! We have to control our willing workaholics, we have to stop them, sometimes intervene and say, 'You're not to come in this weekend. We don't want to see any emails from 10 o'clock on Sunday night, just stop!' That's important. I've learned a bit how to do that. I don't do much work at weekends. So that's important: watch the willing workaholics.

In the change agents' toolkit

In my neck of the woods, I've needed a lot of obstinacy. And a lot of self-confidence that the basic analysis, which was developed not by me but by the key

I'm a great believer that the green movement could do with a lot more humour than it is normally exposed to.

thinkers in this movement back in the late 1960s and early 1970s, was correct. Throughout my life, I've met people who've accused us of being neo-Malthusians, Cassandras who know nothing about how the real world works, misreading the laws of thermodynamics, blah blah blah. Paradoxically I kept listening to them and reading that stuff, and trying to work out whether they were right, so that I wasn't off on some intellectual fantasy about a collapsing world. So I've had to be very obstinate about that analysis and trying to get to grips with that and not giving ground on some of those things, even though some of the horrors haven't materialised until later than people thought that they might. So persistence is critical, patience, and a sense of humour. I just have to have a laugh at all this stuff, and at myself and our movement, which is full of pretentious moments. We're all much too pious — I tend to not do any of the preachy stuff, I don't do personal lifestyle guilt-tripping. Proportionality is important, non-preachy proportionality.

We are sort of 'winning'. And I don't mean that in any mad, over-ambitious way, but the arguments are being won and the intellectual hinterland that we've developed over 30 years is now widely accepted by a lot of people. All of these things which were dismissed as mad green fantasies 25 years ago are suddenly established views in the *Economist*, and I think OK, we're making progress here. So we're winning arguments; we're not winning the battle against stupid policies, there's still massive amounts of stuff to be done there, but at least people know the gap now between what we are doing and what we need to do.

Earth Summit

Rio was a complete turning point for me in 1992. I wasn't going to go, but by chance the *Daily Telegraph* said, 'We haven't got enough journalists out there, we need you to go to Rio and act as a commentator.' So I thought, 'Well, that's a laugh, me writing for the *Daily Telegraph*!' So I decided to do it pretty much on the spur of the moment and had the most astonishing three weeks of my life. I met people from every walk of life. I spent three days with the business community; I spent three days at an astonishing conference which brought together all the faith leaders around the world — the Dalai Lama and everybody else — talking about faith and the environment; there was a women's conference which was utterly inspiring; a youth conference. The Global Forum was a massive churn of NGOs from all over the world, thousands and thousands of NGOs. I went around with my brain just buzzing. There were parties every night until three or four in the morning, and then you'd get up again at nine the next day. It was just astonishing. And I came back from that saying, 'That's it, I know now there are thousands of organisations out there that want to make the solutions to these problems work, thousands and thousands, and I'm going to work with that now; I'm not going to revert back to my more pugilistic style of confrontation.' And that was a complete turning point.

www.forumforthefuture.org.uk

www.sd-commission.org.uk

www.jonathonporritt.com

Capitalism as if the World Matters, Earthscan, 2005

Richard Reynolds

*It's all about having a vision for public space
that's different to what the authorities have for it.*

By day, Richard Reynolds is an advertising executive. By night, a guerrilla gardener. Without a private garden of his own, he began gardening by stealth in publicly-owned spaces — first, the communal gardens of his London tower block, and then more widely in the local area. His neighbours are delighted. He discovered that guerrilla gardening goes on all over the world, for different reasons — to reclaim neglected land, to grow food, to beautify the environment, and sometimes to make political statements. Rather than remain stultified by monotonous and unloved landscapes, Reynolds is keen to encourage more people to reclaim and revive their public spaces.

I got into gardening as a hobby when I was a child. I grew up in a rural part of the country and my family had a big garden. My mother and my father are both enthusiastic gardeners, and we'd always be out there, me and my brothers and sister, doing a bit of mowing or digging, and getting mucky. So I was lucky, growing up, to have that kind of space to play around in, and it's always been something I've felt comfortable with.

Guerrilla gardening is about cultivating someone else's land without their permission, illicitly. In most cases it is public space. We take the land and say, 'I've got a great idea for this; I'm just going to go and do it.' Typically that would happen on roadside verges, roundabouts and abandoned lots where a building once stood and has been cleared away. The most obvious places to look after are abandoned flowerbeds, where there quite clearly once was a garden, but the person who was responsible for it has lost interest. There are plenty of these near me and I concentrate on four large areas and get help from other people locally to do that.

Beginnings

My first act of guerrilla gardening was at university. I was at Christ Church, Oxford. It was a beautiful college, but very boring from a horticultural point of view because in the main areas it was just grass, which we were not allowed to walk on. I left the grass alone, but I did put a window-box of busy lizzies outside my college window. That was against the rules but seemed to be tolerated. It was there for the whole of my last term. This box of flowers wasn't doing anyone any harm at all — it was just slightly upsetting the simplicity of the Georgian architecture. It looked great, and it cheered people up on the way to their exams as they passed by.

I came to London ten years ago, and always had at least a windowsill which I put boxes on. And then I moved here, to a flat in a ten-storey tower block. At the time I didn't think, 'I need a windowsill,' or, 'I need a garden.' But I missed the opportunity to get my hands dirty. I soon noticed that right outside were huge neglected flowerbeds and it seemed very obvious to me that I might as well look after these.

More specifically, I chose to do it as a guerrilla gardener because I saw no other way to get this done sooner rather than later. The tenants' management

I set the alarm for
two o'clock in the morning.

---

organisation had recently been shut down by Southwark Council after some financial irregularities. I felt that in this environment, me writing a letter saying 'Can I look after the gardens?' wouldn't get anywhere because they had more important things to be dealing with. So I thought I was doing everyone a favour, as well as myself — I was much more interested in gardening than dealing with red tape. I'd just go ahead and do it, in a way that should cause no trouble at all. That's what I did.

I set the alarm for two o'clock in the morning, and to start with I worked on the large, square raised flowerbed next to the main entrance. I was really nervous. I didn't want anyone to ask any questions and I didn't want any trouble from it. I felt in my heart that if I could get it done and they could see the finished result, then it would be fine. Then I could begin to be less secretive about it. The first two or three times I worked at night like that. My confidence rapidly built. And now the area there, which I've been looking after for three years without permission, I now do any time of the day. On a summer weekend, like any gardener, it's nice to be out there in the sunshine, and you can see the weeds better.

In fact, it's thanks to my neighbours and the guerrilla gardening that I've just bought my flat, in this same tower block. People knew that I wanted a flat and the gossip network was very effective. My neighbours were very keen to help — they know I'm good for the building. And when people have heard I've bought somewhere, they've said, 'Richard, that's great! What's the garden like then?' 'Garden? No, no, no! What's the point in me having a garden?' Years ago, I would have loved a house with a garden. I'm not in a hurry for that at all now. I don't see the point. I feel really privileged. I've got a huge area around me, beautiful locations, and I don't pay a penny for the land. I have to look after it and share it with other people, and that's not really a cost, it's actually a benefit.

More guerrilla gardening

I was blogging what I was doing, because I wanted to share it. Although I had been very nervous initially about sharing it with my neighbours, I wanted to share it with friends — 'Look, this is what I'm doing. This is the picture of it before, and this is the picture of it after.' Also by putting it online, there was the chance that some like-minded person somewhere else would come across it. The web's really good for joining up people with unusual hobbies, and I'm a persistent web-builder. I've always got some little website project, so it seemed very obvious to me. I found the domain name. At this point, I actually was unaware that there was any other kind of guerrilla gardening. I thought I'd invented the term until a week or two later I was Googling to see how the website was performing in the search engines, and discovered it was all over the place.

So I emailed a few people and found out a bit more what they were doing and over the subsequent year, I took on a couple more areas local to me. You begin to notice things in the landscape when you do this, where you think, 'I could plant a Christmas tree there — that would look amazing.' After a year, a radio journalist got in touch with me. She'd found my website and she wanted to do a short piece on guerrilla gardening, which gave a huge boost of traffic to my website.

It flushed out lots of people who have been guerrilla gardening but, unlike the ones I'd found early on, who tended to be more politically motivated, these were people who'd done it very much like I had — they'd started looking after the public space in their area, feeling a little bit rebellious about it but not aligning themselves with any broader movement. They were really excited and delighted. I kept getting emails saying 'I've been doing this for years. I planted daffodils all down the M62. It's great to hear that there are other people out there doing it.' I then took on the role, through the website, to invite other people to share what they had done and put reports up. Then last summer I got some help in launching the community forum, which is used occasionally by people to find other people in their area if they want help or to share what they're doing.

I want to encourage people to take responsibility for the world around them outside, just beyond their doorstep, in a tangible and immediate way. By habit and by society we are very much encouraged to take responsibility for our private space, but public space, in most people's minds, is considered the responsibility

*I kept getting emails saying,
'I've been doing this for years.
I planted daffodils all down the M62.'*

of someone employed by a public body. That's wrong, to me. It's not only wrong, it seems a bit silly — it seems like a missed opportunity.

Motivations

It's all about having a vision for public space that's different to what the authorities have for it, and the motivations for doing that vary hugely from straightforward beautification to the really fundamental reason of being able to eat. Guerrilla gardeners include people in shanty towns and land occupiers all over the world. A lot of the land they use is just waste ground or roadside verges, which they use to grow vegetables. You generally have a bias towards beautification or food, but obviously you can do both at the same time through choosing colourful vegetables like Swiss chard and fennel, or by mixing your garden.

I've met people who will do guerrilla gardening in public areas because they really want to drive the point home that we need to be growing our food locally and in a sustainable way. There's lots of different ways of getting that message across, but I think a good one is to grow those vegetables in a way that people are going to notice, which means doing it in public space, probably on land that you haven't got permission for.

Also, because most people are doing it in public space, there's definitely a motivation of community, to reach out to the community and get them working together. That's particularly relevant to those who take on sizeable abandoned lots where they need the help or the opportunity, and it becomes a gathering place. It works particularly well for them. But even for me, where I'm more or less doing it on my own around my tower block, I get help. I put out an email and get lots of help from other troops when I want to do something bigger elsewhere. Most of the time, it's just me on my own, and I enjoy this because it's a way of meeting my neighbours when they're passing by, now that I'm not doing it at night.

And then what I see as important is the sense of expression. It's communication, it's creating something that is yours but in a public way, which is really quite difficult to do these days. We live in quite a controlled environment, a particularly monotonous environment in terms of the richness on the public high street. Whereas in the past, local businessmen could bring a lot of personality to the high street, you don't see that so much any more. Even corporate bedding and public landscaping schemes increasingly all look the same, with their granite and limestone and delicate wispy tree and sophisticated grasses on the one hand, or their blowsy beds of busy lizzies on the other. I see guerrilla gardening as a great way of being able to bring more distinctiveness into the landscape. I like to do something a bit different.

We planted a huge patch of lavender on Westminster Bridge Road in Lambeth. Actually, it's on border territory. It's a large triangular bed split in the middle by a cycle path. One half is owned by Lambeth, the other half by Southwark, which in my mind explains why the area is totally neglected, because it's far too complicated for the two councils to coordinate their maintenance regimes, so they appear to have agreed a truce of neglect. As guerrilla gardeners, we don't see borders anywhere. So we have unified this with a huge bed of at least 250 lavender plants, which are under-planted with red tulips and foxgloves and bearded irises and some shrubs. It's one of my favourite projects. We're going to harvest the lavender, stuff it into linen printed pillows, and sell them to raise money for gardening.

The sunflower one is another favourite. We planted a great triangle of 50 or 60 of them on the junction of Stamford Street and Blackfriars Bridge Road, an incredibly fine location. We could see St Paul's Cathedral from where we were doing it. This is the first year I've grown sunflowers, and they are so incredible — the enormous flower, their height, and the speed with which they reach it. There's something slightly anthropomorphic about them. They really do feel like my frontline soldiers out there, standing up to potential attacks. We had a run-in there with a local resident. He came over and really tore into us, saying 'What's the point of doing this? No one's going to notice, it's a total waste of time.' I was determined to win him over and I did in the end, and he parted with a £30 donation. He felt quite sorry that he'd had a go at us. The sunflowers are still standing.

*We planted a huge patch of lavender
on Westminster Bridge Road.*

History of guerrilla gardening

The term 'guerrilla gardening' was invented in 1973 by an artist called Liz Christie, who was living in the Bowery Houston area of New York at the time when it was really in quite a state. People were leaving the city; landlords were abandoning buildings; things were falling down; parks couldn't be maintained. She and her artist and student friends noticed the potential in the landscape. Tomatoes were growing in the discarded litter and children were playing amongst it. They decided to sort it out and build a community garden. They found an abandoned lot on the corner of Bowery and Houston and began turning it into a garden, and called themselves the Green Guerrillas. That's how the term was coined, very much in a climate in the 1970s of guerrilla warfare. Che Guevara had just died, there were guerrilla struggles going on in Latin America. Guerrilla had become a word that had a bit of countercultural edge to it. It very much captured the spirit of what they were doing.

The earliest, most acclaimed act of guerrilla gardening as we know it was in 1649 when a chap called Gerard Winstanley dug up a hill in Surrey called St George Hill and planted vegetables with the poor folk of Cobham, who came to be called the Diggers. So he was a guerrilla gardener. Unfortunately Gerard Winstanley was as enthusiastic about writing polemic pamphlets of his visions for a better, more just and equitable society as he was about gardening. So whilst the authorities couldn't have cared less when they first heard what he was up to, it began to worry the landowners, who were very concerned that this was going to turn into some form of rebellion, even though the land he was looking after was waste ground, public space. They attacked it, ripped up his vegetables, locked him in a church and sent him to court. But he'd very much sown the seed — excuse the pun — by then. He's gone down in history as quite a character, considered as an early communist.

The biggest problem is if the landowner where you're gardening objects to what you're doing. Guerrilla gardeners do lose their gardens because they just get pulled up or they get evicted. But that's not happened to me and is actually quite unlikely. If you use your common sense, a landowner usually doesn't mind and may even give you permission. Guerrilla gardening is an efficient strategy to enable that gardening to be done. My council have told me I would not have got permission had I asked before I started gardening, but now three years on are poised to allow me in one area. It seems they say no, because they wouldn't trust that volunteer to actually maintain an area and stick at it without it becoming a very formalised community project, which does not always suit the small casual locations a guerrilla gardener can transform. They can't go handing out permission and then risking the thing becoming worse than it is already. Also, there's the issue of health and safety. Many authorities, much as they would like more volunteers to help look after their land, are not prepared to deal with the implications.

The scrapes that guerrilla gardeners get into are generally caused by a bit of confusion. I've had police patrols stop, concerned that I'm stealing plants, and I've been able to point out that they are dandelions that I am 'stealing', and that I planted all the other stuff around them. I've been taken for a terrorist, because my car was considered suspicious. It was heavily laden with sacks of wood chippings, which the police thought were fertiliser bombs. There is that incongruity that causes people concern. It's easy to deal with. You just explain, 'Oh, no, nothing of the sort, Officer. I'm just doing a spot of gardening.'

Passers-by inevitably take an interest in what we're doing too. That's part of the fun. Once they've worked out we're gardening, the usual comment is, 'Hey mate, can you come and do my garden too?' Cabbies seem particularly keen on asking us that. A few cheers from drivers waiting at the traffic lights rally us on during an evening, and sometimes strangers will even join in for a bit. I bring spare tools with me and encourage newcomers to linger and get involved in what we're doing. In some ways, perhaps, we're a form of street theatre; the only things missing are the costumes.

Beginner's guide

A beginner's guide to guerrilla gardening would be: find some neglected public

I've had police patrols stop, concerned that I'm stealing plants, and I've been able to point out that they are dandelions that I'm 'stealing'.

___

space, start small and build up your confidence. You hear stories of people starting with huge areas and them falling into disrepair. So you start small. Plant some snowdrop bulbs round the bottom of a tree in autumn, or sunflower seeds in a neglected bed in springtime. Start on your own or do it with a friend. Don't feel the need to have a huge army of people helping you. Just get out there and start scattering a few seeds. There's a woman called Lucy who lives in south London, who always carries wildflower seeds with her and scatters them at railway stations along her way. She knows some of them won't grow, and some of them do and that couldn't be simpler.

Do something very local to you, so it's easy to maintain. It's important to keep the weeds and the litter clear from it. It's critical because if you don't, neglect attracts neglect. More litter will be dumped. And worse, an eagle-eyed gardener will spot a beautiful plant growing amongst a neglected landscape and liberate it. I've seen this to my own cost, where I've done areas away from home, which other people are then meant to look after. I've gone back to a scene of devastation. You do need to keep on top of it, that's why I say start small. A garden, particularly in spring/summer, needs regular looking after. An ideal spot is the tree-pit outside your house or the little corner bed at the end of the road that you're walking past every day, and gardening then becomes habitual. It's not a case of, 'Let's put on the overalls and get the tools and go down to the garden centre.'

Sunflowers, daffodils, tulips, lavender and Mediterranean-style plants are quite good in this environment, because they don't require too much watering and are evergreen. Then there's typical council stuff, like spindle trees. I've planted pittosporums, rhododendrons, rosemary, photinea. You need plants that are self-sufficient and hardy. And the key thing is they've got to be able to survive without too much water, that is unless they're right on your doorstep, because watering in these locations is difficult — you've got to carry it. You never need to water daffodils, because they grow at the time of year when it's generally wetter anyway. Lavender doesn't need any help after you've planted it; plant it in March and it shouldn't ever need watering.

Revolution

I see guerrilla gardening as an everyday revolution. It's about realising the land is ours to take care of, not just in a big, global, eco-friendly way but also in a very local and tangible way. Red tape, laws and protocol need not get in the way of a common sense vision for putting wasted land to better use. In this war, everyone's a winner.

www.guerrillagardening.org

On Guerrilla Gardening, Richard Reynolds, Bloomsbury, 2008

Vandana Shiva

We are not shoppers in a global supermarket;
we are citizens of the earth.

Dr Shiva is a renowned activist, with a background in quantum physics, who has written many books and led many campaigns on a broad range of issues, including globalisation, biotechnology, agriculture and biodiversity. She founded the Research Foundation for Science, Technology and Ecology, and Navdanya, an organisation that protects biodiversity conservation and farmers' rights. Working locally with farmers in India, and campaigning internationally, she has led three successful challenges against transnational biotechnology companies, preventing the patenting of seeds. Dr Shiva strives tirelessly to defend the rights of both nature and people, combining the two in a philosophy she calls 'earth democracy' — the democracy of all life on earth.

The change I wish to see in the world is to make sure this beautiful planet is not devastated by human action, and that ordinary, hard-working people in communities are not robbed of their lives and livelihoods.

When I found out that the life on this planet, the seeds and plants, were sought to be owned as private property by corporations, through patent regimes, it was totally unacceptable to me. I decided to start saving seeds, so that there would be seeds in farmers' hands that would not be patented, different crops and crop varieties would not be pushed to extinction, and our farms would flourish. That's the change I've tried to be over the last 20 years. I founded Navdanya, the movement that defends the alternative that works for nature and people.

The Chipko movement

My quantum leap out of quantum physics into the kind of work I do today happened after I became involved in the Chipko movement, this amazing movement of peasant women to protect the forest of the Himalaya. I was a physics student at that time. I continued to do my PhD while being engaged with Chipko in my holidays. My holidays I would give for Chipko and the rest of the time I would do my quantum theory.

In 1962 we had had the war with China. As a result of that war, India wanted to increase its defence in the Himalaya. The increase in defence meant building lots of roads, which meant pulling out every standing tree, and the deforestation was so rapid from the mid-1960s to the early 1970s, that entire forests would be cut down. There would be landsides and floods, and women were having to walk further and further for firewood and fodder. And one fine day the women just decided they wouldn't let the trees be cut down and they started to blockade the logging. This movement then spread from village to village and part of my work as a student volunteer was to do these walks from village to village to spread the message. I also started to do the early documentation of the movement, and by the end of it, 1981, the women had managed to get a logging ban in the high Himalaya. Chipko means to embrace and basically the movement was, 'We will hug the trees, we won't let you cut them', with the declaration that people would give their lives. Basically it meant that women got organised and came and sat in the forest to protect it. People were prepared to give their lives. The issues might have changed, but I think people still have that.

Today, progress is literally riding on a bulldozer; you have progress when you can bulldoze the earth, tear down a tree, build a highway or a runway — that is 'progress'.

It was in 1982, on the basis of this holiday work — I did a lot of ecological studies in holiday time — that the Ministry of the Environment asked me to do a major study on mining in Dehradun, which is the valley I come from. I did the study, and it led to a Supreme Court case and the closure of the mines. And I said to myself, 'If my holiday work can lead to this and save the valley where I was born from being totally devastated, I must spend more time doing this kind of work, no matter how much excitement intellectually I get from doing quantum theory and solving the puzzles of quantum mechanics.' The permanent perennial puzzles never disappear and I felt it was too indulgent. At that point I thought it would be for ten years. Well, those ten years have extended — that was 1982 and I'm still doing this.

My ultimate passion is biodiversity, seeds. From Chipko, I learned the value of diversity, because what the Chipko women were fighting was not just logging, they were fighting monoculture, commercial monoculture plantations. The value of a biodiverse natural forest was something I learned on my walks into the forests with them, and I've often said that I went to the University of Western Ontario for my quantum theory, but I went to the Chipko University for my ecology. That's where I really learned the value and the richness of biodiversity.

If it hadn't been for my years with Chipko, my eyes would not have been trained to recognise the farms of Punjab and the farms in the mid-west of the United States as green deserts, where biodiversity had been devastated and there were just monocultures — miles and miles and miles of wheat or miles and miles and miles of corn, miles and miles and miles of rice. For someone who has not learned to train their mind to biodiversity, a monoculture field is still a prosperous field. For me it was an impoverished field, and that helped me do my early studies on the green revolution. If I hadn't been in Chipko, I couldn't have assessed the green revolution in terms of the lost production of the disappeared biodiversity, and therefore question the claims of higher yields and higher output.

Quantum theory

Quantum theory has helped me tremendously. It has helped first and foremost in developing a worldview that recognises there aren't essential qualities in things; the world is made of multitudes of forces in interaction, and out of this, things are some expression of it. The most important point about quantum theory is it tells you there's nothing like a fixed quantity; what you have is potential. A particle can have a spin up or a spin down and it has both potentials, and which potential will get expressed depends on the context you create, which is why in quantum theory it's also said that the observer makes a difference to what is observed. But the reality of it is, there are no determinate quantities. As in classical mechanics, they are potential, and that is why I can totally question the absurdity of genetic engineering and the absurdity of genetic determinism that says, 'We have found a gene that is going to do this that and the other.'

The expressions of genes are results of multiple interactions between multiple genes. The behaviour of a particular seed is a result of the water you give to it, the soil fertility you give to it, the care you give to it. In and of itself you can put any seed into a totally impoverished soil and give it no water, and you are not going to get a yield. That's why these claims of miracle varieties, high-yielding varieties — these are all false claims. I couldn't have seen that falsehood if my mind had not been trained through quantum theory to recognise that properties are created through interactions between systems, they don't inhere in individual parts and fragments of systems.

Quantum theory informs me a lot in thinking about progress. Any stable atom has a nucleus, around which an electron moves. The fact that the electron moves does not mean that the electron goes out of its stationary level. It moves in the same orbit and it keeps moving. The earth is also moving in an orbit. In quantum theory you can see the mobility of that electron, as you can see the movement of the earth in astrophysics, but you do not imagine that the earth should have the freedom to break out of its orbit, just as you do not imagine that the electron should break out of its stationary state. A crude classical mechanical thinking sees stationary and thinks static; it does not think stability, and that is the core problem with our thinking of progress.

Every society has constantly moved; every human being has to evolve; every seed we plant must grow into a mature plant and give us seed. But in the fact that

I'm among those who believe that you live the right idea long enough, without any sense of ego or power attached to it, because it is the right idea. Sooner or later there will be a larger acceptance.

---

we replenish a cycle, people who have a linear mechanical concept of progress think, 'Oh, static.' What they would like to see is the kind of movement that we see when an electron collapses into the nucleus and unleashes uncontrollable energy. For them, devastation has become movement, and that is why constantly there is an assault on sustainable societies which do progress, change and evolve, but in a pace that can be sustained over time. Today, progress is literally riding on a bulldozer; you have progress when you can bulldoze the earth, tear down a tree, build a highway or a runway — that is 'progress'. The bulldozer has become the symbol of progress, not the electron.

I was invited to a conference in 1987 on biotechnology. The conference was called Laws of Life, and the participants included United Nations officials, scientists and corporate representatives. The corporations laid out their plan about the future of the world, based on genetic engineering, patenting of all life forms, and free trade as their rights to invest and market what they wanted to, without any interference from government, or any kind of social regulation. For me this sounded like a dictatorship, that a handful of corporations would own life on the planet. When you hear something that big, obviously you get overwhelmed. How do you deal with something as big as this, at your small scale?

I thought of Gandhi and his pulling out the spinning wheel to deal with an empire that controlled 85 per cent of the territories of the world, and I thought, 'What would be today's spinning wheel, in the face of these biotechnology giants wanting to have patents on everything?' It was a seed that came to my mind. So I went back and started to collect, save and distribute seeds. I'm still doing it today. I was just recently in the areas where farmers are committing suicide because of corporate seed monopolies, and I was distributing seeds in these villages, because I think these suicides are wrong and I think they can be stopped. 150,000 farmers have taken their lives in the last 10 years of the so-called trade liberalisation that has meant liberalisation for Monsanto and slavery for our farmers.

Persistence

In a way, I would say the external world as structured in power has been a world that would like to have made sure that someone like me did not exist, that someone like me didn't do the things I do; that Monsanto could freely sell its seeds with never a question; that patent laws would just get implemented, because the WTO had enshrined them in the Trade-Related Intellectual Property Rights agreement. Having decided to go against that current, equipped just with my own personal emotional, ecological, intellectual integrity, and the connection with ordinary people, I've just been there, obstinate and persistent, even when the external environment has basically said, 'Shut up, don't keep going on about seed patents.'

I'm glad I didn't shut up. If I'd shut up, the suicides of Indian farmers would never ever have made their way into policy discussions. If I hadn't kept going on about the illegitimacy of patents on life, there wouldn't be the kind of questioning that is there today. It needed that kind of persistence even when the external environment was not supportive. I'm among those who believe that you live the right idea long enough, without any sense of ego or power attached to it, because it is the right idea. Sooner or later there will be a larger acceptance.

As I mentioned, I started Navdanya really to save seeds, to deal with patent monopolies, and it very naturally grew into an organic movement. I did not want a conservation movement based on paying farmers to conserve, because I knew sooner or later the money would run out and would they then start to destroy? The only way we could conserve that biodiversity and those amazing seeds would be bringing them into production. And so we brought them into organic production and then helped the farmers build markets, so that the millets that were going out of use or the unique dhals that were no longer produced, all of this we could build up as an economic self-reliance for small producers, while connected to the conservation of the biodiversity of their farms. Today, Navdanya connects biodiversity conservation, sustainable production and fair trade, and closes the loop from seed to table. We have 300,000 farmers associated with us in the production side.

Within the mobilisation side, like when we fight patenting and defend our seed rights and farmers' rights, those movements work with 10 million, 15 mil-

*We need a deeper democracy. We need a deeper
way to make a difference to the state of affairs
of our societies, and that must grow from the
earth upwards, from the grassroots upwards.*

lion farmers because I work across the country on creating awareness and getting campaigns organised. So Navdanya works at both levels, the actual production and conservation work, and also advocacy and the political mobilisation part.

There are three different patents we have fought. We have called these patents 'biopiracy', which is patenting the traditional knowledge and biodiversity of third world countries. The first case we fought was the *neem*, a wonderful Indian tree patented by the US government and WR Grace. The legal process was first to build a movement in India, called the Neem Campaign. 100,000 people joined and we took this issue to friends in Europe, because the patent had to be fought in the European Patent Office. Magda Aelvoet, the President of the Greens in Europe, and Linda Buller, the President of the International Federation of Organic Agriculture Movements joined. The three of us, as women, took this on. Ten years we fought and won it twice over, because the US government and Grace appealed.

The second case was of *basmati*, the very famous aromatic rice from Dehradun, being patented by a company called Rice Tech in Texas. And in that case, the legal process was somewhat different. I went to the Supreme Court of India, to instruct the government of India that it should challenge the patent. It's the government's duty to protect our national heritage. Eventually, the government did not go far enough, so we still had to build a movement. I also built a movement in the United States and the combination of the movement and legal action led to the striking down of most of the claims of Rice Tech.

The third time was when Monsanto had patented an old Indian wheat variety and we fought this in the European Patent Office along with Greenpeace. We didn't even have to argue for it. We didn't have to struggle 10 years. In four months, the patent was struck down on the basis of our challenge.

Earth democracy

Earth democracy is a very ancient concept in many, many cultures. If Indians worship the little *tulsi* in the backyard, or the people tree, the sacred ficus on the roadside, it's because in our cosmology all of this is part of an extended family. And we as humans are just one member in this extended family. But for me, earth democracy is not just this very ancient, timeless concept of living as one in the earth family, in the community of life. It is also a new way of living in the world today, to get out of the traps of globalisation.

What are the traps of globalisation? Trap one is to imagine that commerce cannot be regulated, that free markets have arrived and will go on and you can't change anything about this. Trap two is the belief that what matters most is to get the cheapest goods from China, and not how many people are laid waste in terms of not being able to produce. For me it is extremely important to recognise that we as humans first produce, then we consume. To have us destroy these producers and reduce us to consumers is a trap that more and more societies are being pushed into. Another trap is to believe that we can't make a difference, that all this is beyond us, that we are inconsequential.

For me, earth democracy is, in a way, a post-globalisation philosophy. First and foremost, it reminds us we are not shoppers in a global supermarket; we are citizens of the earth. That's our first identity. Secondly, as citizens of the earth, we have a double link with the earth. We have a link with the particular place of the earth where we are — for me it's Doon Valley. But while I am of Doon Valley, I'm also a child of the planet as a whole, and therefore the collective responsibility for the earth as a whole is as much part of being an earth citizen as being responsible for our particular place. The third part of earth democracy for me is that globalisation has left our representative democracy at best impotent, at worst destructive.

We need a deeper democracy. We need a deeper way to make a difference to the state of affairs of our societies, and that genuine democracy must grow from the earth upwards, from the grassroots upwards. It has to be a democracy that combines our responsibility to protect life on the planet, the economic issues of livelihoods for all, and the justice and equality issues of ensuring that the divides between people are not inhuman and huge.

*Economic issues and environmental issues
are not oppositional issues, they are the same.*

Earth democracy, in a way, becomes a convergence of what had been approached as totally different movements. There's an environment movement that protects the resources of the earth. There's a social justice movement that tries to address some of the questions of social injustice. But none of them are able to connect the roots of these problems. There's a peace movement that marches for Iraq. But Iraq is about oil, and oil is about fossil fuels, and fossil fuels are connected to climate change, and climate change is related to creating economies that destroy livelihoods; all this is connected. Those connections are made vivid and obvious through earth democracy. And so earth democracy gives us two amazing new openings, I believe, to be the change. The first is, it's so specific. It says you don't have to be a prime minister to make the change — you could start with making your food choices to make sure local farmers aren't destroyed. That's an element of earth democracy. But the other element of earth democracy is to recognise that the same processes that are devastating the life of the poor, are devastating the planet's life. And suddenly economic issues and environmental issues are not oppositional issues, they are the same.

Gandhi

Gandhi is a huge, huge inspiration for me. I wasn't a political scientist; I'm not a sociologist; I have not read political thinkers as my first choice in life. But this I know: that every time I have felt totally stuck, in terms of defending and enlarging freedom, both my personal freedom as well as my society's freedom, and I have exercised my mind in terms of what to do, it is always Gandhi's thoughts and actions that come as lights in the darkness. I'll give two simple examples. One, as I mentioned, the very starting of Navdanya was a Gandhian inspiration. For me, the seed became the spinning wheel. If he hadn't had the spinning wheel, I wouldn't even have been able to imagine what do you do with a Monsanto which wants to own all life, genetically engineer every seed and have the freedom to sell them without regulation in any society. I'd have just sat there, and started to either write more papers on patents, or just said, 'Forget it. Physics is what I'm going to do. It's so much more peaceful, wonderful, satisfying.'

Second, the laws on patenting started to be changed. Again, it was Gandhi's inspiration that enabled us to defend our rights. When the British tried to monopolise salt, Gandhi walked to the beach and said, 'Nature gives this for free. We need it for our survival. We will continue to make our salt and we will disobey your salt laws.' He gave us the name *satyagraha*, the fight for truth. His salt *satyagraha* became the inspiration for our seed *satyagraha*.

The commitment and declaration, 'We will not obey laws that monopolise seed; we will not obey laws that give Monsanto the freedom to release genetically engineered seeds on our farms and in our ecosystem' — that satyagraha started with hundreds and thousands of farmers taking pledges in India. It is now a practice in at least 6,000 villages, where farmers have made a commitment that they will never allow those seeds to enter. More recently I've signed an agreement with 45 regional governments of Europe, which have taken a pledge never to allow GMO seeds to enter their regions. This is the Network of GMO-Free Regions of Europe. *Satyagraha*, the idea of the duty to not cooperate, the duty to disobey bad, immoral, unjust, brutal law — that's a duty we have as human beings, who have to live according to higher laws of the universe, of ethics and of ecological sustainability. Again, Gandhi is my inspiration for all of this.

Being the change

As a young girl, when I chose to do physics, and then as a growing teenager and a woman, my preferred life was a quiet life, sitting with my own pieces of paper, in my own little head — really a life of reflection about the way the world works. I did not choose to be an activist in the beginning of my life. Many people know that's what they'll do. I did not want to be a public person; it was something I did not like. I've given up many of those initial choices, to be the change, for a number of reasons. First, on the issues on which I work, I realise the costs are too high for nature and people, and I cannot be a mute witness and watch destruction around me.

The second reason I have decided to be the change I want to see is because I realise that many of these issues have been made so complicated, so mystified, that ordinary people cannot see through the jargon, the mystification. If I were to sit back and do my physics, I know that the destructive mystification would continue to engulf more and more people's minds, and that's why I've kind of thrown myself into the public sphere — to tell the truth about agriculture, the truth about biotechnology, the truth about patenting. It's not an easy choice, because frankly, to live the quiet life is the easier way to be, especially for someone like me. I could have had a tenure track position in any university in any part of the world, and to opt instead to walk the villages where farmers are committing suicide at 45 degrees centigrade, is a tough choice in every sense — physically, psychologically, monetarily, politically. But at this point of my life, I can't see myself doing anything else.

Individually, I have my own leanings in terms of where you begin to be the change. I think we have to begin with matters of life and death, and those are about the food we eat or don't get to eat, the water we drink, the air we breathe. And collectively? What is collectively, but many people doing their small things, and turning it into a big symphony?

www.navdanya.org

Earth Democracy: Justice, sustainability and peace, Zed Books, 2005

Protect or Plunder?: Understanding intellectual property rights,
Zed Books, 2001

*Monocultures of the Mind: Biodiversity, biotechnology
and scientific agriculture*, Zed Books, 1998

Clive Stafford Smith

Everyone's better than their worst 15 minutes.

Clive Stafford Smith is a British civil rights lawyer who has spent his career defending prisoners on death row in the US and, more recently, detainees in Guantanamo Bay. He is the founder and Legal Director of Reprieve, a non-profit organisation that specialises in investigation and legal representation for American prisoners and British nationals worldwide facing the death penalty. Reprieve's remit also includes raising awareness of human rights abuses relating to the death penalty and the war on terror. Stafford Smith considers it a matter of bringing power to the powerless, and calls for a more constructive and compassionate judicial system.

I want to see a world where everyone's happier and treats each other more appropriately than they do now. One can begin by looking at and eliminating the negatives, such as the hateful way in which people approach their fellow human beings — most obviously in something like death row, but going on through all the rest of it. I disapprove, obviously, of the way we treat the people we call criminals in our society.

The reason I do death penalty work and Guantanamo work is because it's a matter of bringing power to the powerless. So for me, the immediacy is taking people that the world most hates, and getting between the people doing the hating and the people being hated. It strikes me that there are some things that are just simple, black and white. And everything is black and white when it comes to such issues as the death penalty. Killing is wrong under any circumstances, so that makes it very easy. You always know what to do, but that's the easy part of change. Stopping the negative is much easier than forcing the positive.

I was quite young when I became opposed to the death penalty. I was in school and we were studying the Hundred Years War. One was taught how the English were the good guys and the French were the evil perfidious ones, and I remember very clearly seeing a picture of Joan of Arc being burned at the stake. This really had a big impact on my view of the world because she looked a bit like my sister. The idea that we were burning this poor girl at the stake struck me as so barbaric that the English could no longer be uniformly the good guys. That gradually led me to an opposition to the death penalty. I didn't really know it was an issue. I thought it was a history issue actually, until I was writing something in school later when I was about 16, about the death penalty, and I discovered that America was still doing it. That came as a big surprise to me. By serendipity, along came an offer to go to university in America and I thought, 'Yes, I'll go there, I'll go straighten them out.' Typical patronising British attitude.

Death row

I wanted to be a journalist. I wrote a bit of juvenilia when I was 19, a book on a guy on death row, called *Life on Death Row*. It has never seen the light of day, I'm glad to say. Researching it, I spent six months visiting people on death row, and it was really something. Instead of this theoretical view about the death penalty, suddenly I saw the real world and the real human beings. And I discovered that all these people on death row had no constitutional right to a lawyer, that if you were sentenced to death in America — the most powerful, rich country on earth — you were meant to represent yourself. So I thought I'd go and be a lawyer and help them out. So I went to law school and that's that.

I'd much rather be a do-gooder than a do-badder, but people act as if that's somehow altruistic and difficult and tough every day. It's rubbish. It's an incredible privilege to get up every day and be able to go out there and help people; and yes, we win 98 per cent of capital cases, because at heart, however much politicians go around saying we want to kill people, we don't. People are terribly ambivalent about it. I've had six clients who've been executed over the years, and that's tough. But you have to always remember it's exponentially tougher on the poor guy who's getting executed. It's not me that's suffering, it's him. You have two choices at that point. You can spend your time wracked with guilt, which achieves nothing and prevents you from helping the next person, or you can just get on with it. That's what you have to do.

Guantanamo

I was so incensed when that came up. George Bush announces that his brilliant idea in the war to preserve democracy and the rule of law is to take all of these people to Cuba — where the Americans say they don't have any rule of law — and hold them there without any legal rights. It was so profoundly hypocritical, and it is hypocrisy that is the yeast that ferments hatred around the world. What's got us in the west in so much trouble is propounding all these grand human rights ideas and then doing the opposite. That's what makes people so angry at us, and when I read that, I was flabbergasted that Bush would do that. I immediately assumed all of my death penalty colleagues would want to sue him, so I started calling them up. It was December 2001, still quite soon after September 11th. I couldn't get anyone to agree to do it. Finally I found a couple of friends who did, and we sued him in February 2002, to stop Guantanamo. I got involved in it because it was so patently wrong, and it was so obvious to me that this was just an extension of death row.

What they do on death row is they take these prisoners, who have absolutely no power, off into the middle of nowhere, which is where death row always is. Then they try to inspire all the electorate to want to kill that person. There was a

It's a matter of bringing power
to the powerless.

documentary about one of my clients, where they killed him. Edward Johnson was his name. I'll never forget going up to his execution. We were able to prove pretty powerfully later that he was innocent, but at the time of his execution it was all a great crisis. As I was driving up they were having a radio call-in show. People were calling in, talking about how Edward should die, and how they should make it painful and all these sick things. These are people who have no knowledge about the case, no idea that the guy's probably innocent, and yet they're expressing the fact that we should torture him to death. That's what hatred is all about and it's the blind prejudice of ignorance. They have Edward there in the gas chamber, they do it at midnight, so no one's around. It's this whole process that's designed to allow society to do these hateful things.

Well, when you think about Guantanamo it's just that, plus. Every single person in Guantanamo faces the death penalty. All the charges that can be brought in their military kangaroo courts are capital offences, and yet instead of having them in the middle of the Mississippi delta, miles away from anywhere, they have them in Cuba, which is even further away from everywhere. And instead of having some talk-show shock jock on the radio say that Edward Johnson is a despicable person who should die, they have the President of the United States standing next to Tony Blair saying, 'The only thing I know about these people is that they are all bad people.' So it's all the same thing, it's just exponentially worse, because in America with the death penalty, the hatred is an internal thing, and it's bad enough — you've got millions of Americans wanting to kill this poor guy in prison. But when you move it Guantanamo you've made it international, and the hatred has been exponentially ratcheted up.

We sued George Bush in February 2002. It was three of us — me, Joe Margulies and the Center for Constitutional Rights. We were suing the most powerful person in the entire world and he lost. I think that's fantastic. We've beaten him. When we finally got up to the Supreme Court, he lost and we won, and that's because the US system gives you so much power to help people under those circumstances. In Rasul v. Bush, which was the case that we brought, the US Supreme Court said that George Bush could not hold these people beyond the rule of law. So that was when we got lawyers in to see them, that was June 2004. It took two and a half years but even so... Since then we've won again in Hamdan v. Rumsfeld and we're about to beat him again in Boumediene v. Bush. It's about a structure of society where the individual is given rights, given power to stop the government from doing wicked things.

It's wonderful. But in the broader scheme of things, George Bush has lost his battle to do away with these people's rights. Guantanamo's a nightmare for my clients but it's a nightmare for George Bush too, and that's because we've taken the battle to him, and gradually more people have come along to do it. It's amazing when you think about it, how easy it is to tell the most powerful person in the world he can't do it. I find that incredibly encouraging. So that's easy. Stopping people from doing injustice is easy, because basically human beings know what's right and they know what's wrong. Sometimes they get misled, but basically they know. What's much harder is to get people to see how to be happy. They can see how they should avoid being miserable, but it's much harder for them to see how they can be happy.

Job satisfaction

People spend so little time on trying to work out what they want to do, trying to make the job that they want to do, and so much time and energy working on something that they really hate. It's crazy. What I've always tried to do for myself is create my own job. It's not that hard. You just raise the funds and do what you want to do. It's not difficult, people can do that, or they can figure out a way to do it.

I'm lucky that I don't really have what I consider work. It's incredibly varied. For example, last month I went to Morocco for two days to see a client of mine who had been released. I stayed with him in his house. This poor guy had been in Guantanamo for five years. The US thought he was the general of al-Qaida, and we proved that in fact he was a chef from London, and that was really fascinating. I flew back that night to go to some book festival at Althorp where Diana Spencer was from and that was really interesting, to go and stay in some posh house. Then the next night I had to fly to Newark and sleep on the floor of the airport on

Instead of this theoretical view about the death penalty, suddenly I saw the real world and the real human beings.

the way to Guantanamo. It was the only way I could get a flight. I spent two weeks in Guantanamo visiting my clients, and then I came back here. It's fascinating. I view myself as incredibly privileged.

I would rather live in a society of my clients from death row than any other group. These are people who are much more attuned to the real world. I'm talking in generalisations here, and there are different people in every society, but someone who has sat on death row with the world wanting to kill him or her is much more likely to have thought about what life is about, than someone who's running around and not pausing to think why they're here. You see so much inspiration. Sami Al Haj, an Al Jazeera journalist, is in Guantanamo. As we speak he's on the 250th day of his hunger strike, and he's still able to smile, he's still able to see the positive side of what he's going through. That's incredibly inspirational. There's very little despair involved in this. Having to get up every morning and go to a job that you know is pointless, where you're just waiting till five o'clock, that's despair. I did that once in my life, when I was 17. I had to get up every morning and do something that I hated. If I'd had to do that for the rest of my life, I just couldn't have. Despair is having no purpose to your life.

There are some very easy and key lessons. It should be said first that I think it's much easier to say these things if you are as privileged as I've always been. That makes life much easier and I accept that. But what holds most people back is fear. It's fear of starving, it's fear of failure, fear of this, fear of that. You talk to people and they say, 'Well, I'd really like to be such and such.' 'Well, why don't you do it?' 'Oh, well, I've got to pay my mortgage, I've got to do this, I've got to do that.' Well, don't do that. You don't need to live in a big house; you don't need to have a posh car. Why do you need all that stuff? There's so much societal pressure on people to conform to this ridiculous materialistic world, and all it does is steal from them the opportunity to do what they'd really love to do. You've only got one life. Unless you believe in reincarnation, you've got to get it right this time. We've got to help people see how they don't need all that stuff. We're in the luxurious situation in our society where we're not going to starve to death. It doesn't matter how hard you try, you're not going to starve to death. So there's no point in being afraid of it, and the moment you throw that fear aside, doing what you'd love to do becomes much easier.

I know without a pause for doubt that if anything catastrophic happened to me, I don't have to worry about it, that I've got people who are going to come and make sure everything's OK. That's not going to happen, but merely being confident that you've got people who love you that much, that you don't have to worry — that then frees you up to do whatever else you want to do. I think most people are in that situation, it's just they don't realise it.

Compassionate justice

I would like to see a justice system where we treat each other the way we treat people we love. Who do you love most in life? If they were accused of something, what would your natural reaction be? Exactly. And if we all approached the world that way, the world would be a much better place. I would like to see the kind of justice system where we treat people the way we would like to be treated. It's not a brilliantly original idea, that you should do as you would be done by. But what's interesting to me when you look around the world, is not to try to identify how we were uncivilised in the past — that's easy — it's to identify how we're being uncivilised now. And that involves questioning what authority's constantly telling you. That's much more interesting than history.

I don't think a criminal justice system is a terribly useful concept. The word 'criminal' is offensive. If you look at the past, there are all sorts of offensive words that we used to describe categories of people who we liked to hate, and criminal is the same thing. Except the only problem is it's still accepted by our society. I think our society is sick in that regard, I think it's just totally wrong.

When someone is saying how despicable my clients are, 'How can you represent people who do that?' and all that nonsense, I always ask them this — I say, 'Tell me right now what is the single most reprehensible thing you've ever done. And I guarantee you it's not a crime; it's not going to be something like stealing sweets from the candy store. It's going to be something where you did something really mean and nasty to someone you love, and you're horribly

There's so much societal pressure on people to conform to this ridiculous materialistic world, and all it does is steal from them the opportunity to do what they'd really love to do.

embarrassed about it, and the last thing you want me to know about you, is that. The thing is, if you did tell me the answer to that question, you would be sitting there thinking, "Oh gosh, he's going to hate me for this. He's going to judge me based on the single worst thing I've done in my life.'" And yet that's what everyone's doing when they're talking about my clients — they're judging them based on the worst 15 minutes of their lives, something they may or may not have done even. It's actually much more interesting trying to understand *why* people do horrendous things than it is whether they did.

Before you start talking about a criminal justice system — and I use the word Justice loosely — you have to consider what the whole process is in the first place. We're creating a system that is designed to make us feel better about ourselves, by looking down on other people. That's the root of the whole process. The attitude that creates and accepts our judicial system is the attitude that accepted race discrimination and all sorts of other discriminations. And the moment you accept that you should treat people under those circumstances the same way that you would treat the person you love, then you begin to see how we can deal with this process. You would come up with a great defence, no matter what the crime, and that's admirable, but we need to apply that to people who are not your friends or family as well. Once we start doing that, everything will be fine. We're not going to get to Utopia this month; we'll just have to start moving gradually in that direction.

Towards Utopia

Most of us agree basically on what Utopia is. It's where people are nice to each other, it's where there's equality, it's where there's justice, it's where there's all these different things. It's pretty obvious how to move towards Utopia too; we could give examples. It doesn't include the death penalty, so clearly if we want to move towards Utopia we get rid of the death penalty. It doesn't include huge disparities of wealth, so if we want to move towards our Utopia, we reduce disparities of wealth. And when it comes down to any action that society takes, for example any law that society may pass, it's not hard to assess whether it's a good idea. You simply think, 'I know what my dream is, my Utopia. Does this law move us towards it or away from it?' If it moves us away from Utopia, then it's almost certainly something you don't want to do. It's a simple rule, and people might argue that there are exceptions. I think there probably aren't, but I can see how they'd argue. It's just a very, very simple way of moving towards happiness.

So in terms of improving the judicial process, you would never take the position that we want to encourage people to be vengeful, because obviously we want to encourage people to be compassionate. You would never take the position that we want to be locking more people up for more crimes, because that's obviously going in the wrong direction. I think that most sane people would agree that if what we call a crime is not a huge threat to the physical safety of others, then locking the so-called criminal up doesn't achieve a lot. I don't see the necessity; you would never do that to someone you care for. Every different decision that's made needs to be made through the lens of moving toward our dream, our ideal.

There's obvious movement in the right direction. Take New Zealand, and the concept of restorative justice. Instead of just flagellating people, the New Zealanders have programmes where they bring the perpetrator in contact with the victim, so that the perpetrator learns what he or she has inflicted on the victim, and the victim learns why it happened. That's obviously good for both parties and it moves us away from this notion of retribution and towards the notion of understanding. There are lots of examples of those sorts of small steps.

We're never going to achieve Utopia, but the thing about most folk is they don't have a dream. If they know what their dream is, it's easy to move towards it — it's very simple to see how to get there. So I guess my advice to people is to know what their dream is. 'Our reach should exceed our grasp, or what's a heaven for?'

www.reprieve.org.uk

Bad Men, Weidenfeld & Nicolson, 2007

Lynne Twist

To confront our dysfunction around money,
own it and transform it is one of the most
powerful things we can do to make the world work.

Lynne Twist has long been a global activist, in many arenas. A particular field of interest is finance. She been a fundraiser for many organisations, raising hundreds of millions of dollars, and she founded the Soul of Money Institute to help individuals find peace and sufficiency in their relationship with money. As a director of the Hunger Project, with the mission to end world hunger, she travelled to some of the poorest places on earth. More recently, she co-founded the Pachamama Alliance, a non-profit organisation that seeks to empower indigenous people to protect the Amazon rainforest, and to bring their wisdom to the rest of the world.

It's my joy and delight to work with people and money. I started the Soul of Money Institute in San Francisco, and it's designed to shift us from an economy of fear, domination and control to an economy of love, generosity and sufficiency. And I think work with money can be a very critical lynchpin in having us shift the way we're being, and really be the change we all wish to see.

Money is a construct of the human family; it's not real. It's very real in our lives but it's not part of the natural world — it's actually something we made up. We become at the effect of our own creation. One of the things I teach and love to do myself, is to realise that we're not at the mercy of money — money is our invention. We have given it way more importance than it deserves. It does have some importance, but we've given it more meaning than human life and that's just not true. We have a dysfunctional relationship with money and we often resent it, especially a lot of activists, and that's very debilitating, it ends up not working.

I think we need to own money, we need to own our responsibility for it, we need to see it like water, that it's moving through life. It moves through every family, every institution, every life. It goes in and it goes out, just like water moves through the world. And when it's hoarded, or held or stuck, just like water it becomes stagnant and toxic and makes us sick. If we allow it to flow — not just anywhere, where it will leak and flood — but toward the things we're committed to, then it starts to become a nourishing part of the human condition.

So for me, money is a huge area of growth and development for everybody, and to confront our dysfunction around money, own it and transform it is one of the most powerful things we can do to make the world work. Particularly for activists, who've given each other permission to resent money or to say, 'Money is the reason why we didn't... We had the commitment, we had the relationship, we had the vision but we couldn't pull it off because we didn't have the money.' You know I say, nonsense. I say we activists need to get our act together with money, so that we can play a powerful role in a world that respects and listens to where money is moving. Not to overcommit ourselves to the monetary system but to actually know that we have got to deal with it effectively to be effective in our work. That's a big area for me; I do a lot of work with fundraising, and to me it's an important lynchpin to have the world work.

We're not at the mercy of money —
money is our invention.

_____

Wealth vs. abundance

I work with a lot of really wealthy people on their relationship with money, and they for the most part aren't happy. For the most part, they're dysfunctional, they're confused; no one relates to them authentically because they have so much money; they think everybody is trying to get something from them. They become fearful, there's a lot of drug addiction, a lot of alcoholism, a lot of problems in some of our wealthiest corridors and families. I'm from the United States, the wealthiest country in the world. Our wealth has blinded us, we've lost our soul. Not permanently, hopefully, but we're confused by our wealth. That kind of wealth or that kind of abundance, in a mindset of scarcity, actually turns into excess, which is what's filling up our landfill.

The kind of abundance that I think is healthy is that which flows from the appreciation and recognition of the exquisite experience of having enough, and that is so fulfilling that it turns into a sense of true authentic abundance, true wealth — the word wealth comes from well-being. That's true abundance; the abundance that often we talk about when we use that word is more stuff, more money, more treasures. That actually isn't that satisfying, and people who are already in that position, to the person, can tell you that it's not what life's about.

I tell them to give as much as they can away. I tell them that they've been entrusted with resources that aren't really theirs, that they are the trustees of it for the moment and they're privileged to make a choice for all of us to send it where it will do the most good for the most people. So I do a lot of fundraising, inviting them to engage in philanthropy, which heals a lot of that dysfunction and can be miraculous for people who are swimming in excess and flooded with more than they need. And that's true for all of us; it's true for you, it's true for me, it's true for anybody reading these words. We all have more than we need, and to express that abundance or that overflow in a way that makes the world a better place is such a fulfilling part of life and such a great privilege. You start seeing yourself as a flow-through; money comes through us like water. For some people it's a little trickle, for other people it's a rushing river, but it doesn't belong to us. It belongs to everyone or no one; it's meant for the universe. And if it's a little trickle, you get the opportunity to send it to where it can do the most good, and if it's a huge flood the same applies. Either way, it will nourish your life in the world to do that.

It's from the world's poorest people that I've learned these ways of looking at things. If you're lucky enough to travel in places like Mozambique or Ghana or Senegal or Botswana and you are invited into a family's home, they may have what you and I would call almost nothing, but it turns into a meal, it turns into a banquet, it turns into dancing and singing and music. It turns into the most bountiful situation you've ever seen, and it's their way of seeing it that you're inside of, not the material amount of a chicken or some beans or a banana. People who have fewer resources are not confused about sufficiency. Those of us who have massive excess are confused about sufficiency.

Gratitude

One of the things that one of my teachers, Brother David Steindl-Rast — the great Benedictine monk who studies the distinctions of gratefulness — has said to me, is that there are two branches of gratitude. One is gratefulness and the other is thanksgiving. Gratefulness is when the bowl of life is completely full but not yet overflowing. In fact it's almost bowed at the top, it's so full. That's the experience of the great fullness of life. When you're in touch with the great fullness of life, you're one with the universe, you're one with God and you're one with everything, all creatures. When the bowl starts to overflow, you move into the other branch of gratitude, which is thanksgiving. When you're in thanksgiving you're thrilled that there's an other, because all you want to do is give and share and contribute and serve.

And when the container of life is just about full to overflowing, often in the consumer society we go out and we get a bigger container, so that it never actually ends up overflowing. We never have that experience of overflowing abundance because we just keep getting a bigger container to fill things up in, like a bigger car, a bigger house, a bigger closet. The joy comes from the overflowing,

People who have fewer resources are not confused about sufficiency. Those of us who have massive excess are confused about sufficiency.

from that moment of enough and then overflowing. People in situations of poverty and oppression often have their container a more adequate size, and so it overflows more frequently, and that gives a sense of joy and appreciation and abundance. Also they're not as confused as we in the affluent world are by the consumer culture, which is filled with messages that tell us that we don't have enough, we aren't enough, and we've got to have more. They're not as confused by that, they're not exposed to that as much as we are. So they're saved a little bit from that, although it's coming their way. Indigenous people, in particular, appreciate what's actually there, and in appreciating what's actually there, there is this sense of absolute overflowing abundance.

I think that abundance is miscast in today's culture. Some of the messages that are in popular culture can be misunderstood and can sometimes be spun in a way that it makes it look that all we all want is more stuff, more money, more wealth. I don't think we really want that. I believe what we're really looking for is sufficiency. Sufficiency is really, profoundly satisfying. And that's when the universe meets your needs or you meet the needs of the universe. It has no excess in it, no fat, no overflow; it's actually the perfection of the universe and that's what people really, really want, in my experience.

Sufficiency

Rather than an amount of anything, sufficiency is a domain of distinction. It's not halfway between scarcity and excess, it's different than that. It's letting go of all of that and looking at what's already there, and honouring it, and loving it, and making a difference with it. Because when you honour, love and appreciate what's already there in front of you, it grows in the nourishment of your appreciation. Another way I say this is, 'What you appreciate appreciates.' As I say, sufficiency isn't an amount of anything, it's a way of being, it's a state of being. It's a state of being that allows you to access your gratitude for even the simplest thing. And when you're grateful for even the simplest thing, that simple thing grows in the nourishment of your gratitude. That simple thing appreciates in the appreciation that you give it.

So sufficiency is a way of being in the world. It's recognising that the world is actually a friendly place, that it's constantly providing to us — nourishment, oxygen, relationships, beauty — and paying attention to how deeply enough our lives already are, our organisations already are, and appreciating that. And taking our attention away from scarcity or away from trying to get more, and paying attention to the present. So the principle of sufficiency is this: if you let go of trying to get more of what you don't really need, which is what most of us are scrambling to get more of, it frees up oceans of energy that was tied up in that insane chase, to turn and make a difference with what you already have. When you make a difference with what you already have, it expands.

It's a mind-shift, a mind transformation. It's a sea change to move from scarcity and trying to get more all the time, to actually recognising that what's there is precious, beautiful and enough. Out of recognising that it's enough, it begins to grow. My view is that you cannot reach abundance through the doorway of more. You can only reach abundance through the doorway of enough. The recognition of enough is actually the source of overflowing abundance. It sounds theoretical and abstract, but it's very real, what I'm talking about.

If you just think about the relationships that you have; the people that love you; the joy of your work, the number of souls who are putting their heart and soul into what you're doing; the beautiful environment in which you live, the incredible trees and grass and the air you get to breathe; the access you have to water and to food; and you start appreciating that, your cup overflows with gratitude. From there you begin to see the bounty of the universe and you stop thinking about and seeing scarcity. What you see starts to be the power, beauty, fullness, gratefulness and — as Brother David Steindl-Rast would say — the great fullness of the universe for which you are nothing but grateful.

So sufficiency or enough is a state of being, a state of mind, rather than an amount of anything. When you apply it to any setting, what you see is the bounty. And that's really an important thing for the environmental movement, I think, because our activism is often based in some sort of scarcity experience. I think the opposite will get us where we want to go — recognising the deep and pro-

When the container of life is full to overflowing, often in the consumer society, we go out and we get a bigger container.

found enoughness of the world in which we live. That there is enough for everyone.

Taking a stand

I owe a great debt to the EST training, a training that is now called the Landmark education forum, and I took that in January 1974. It totally opened my eyes to the experience of knowing I could make a difference with my life. Shortly after I took the EST training, the Hunger Project began and that is the organisation I have worked for for most of my adult life, and was very lucky to be part of as a leader from the very beginning. I was in the right place at the right time when it was born. I helped facilitate the meeting of Buckminster Fuller, who was a great teacher of mine, and Werner Erhardt, who was the founder of EST. When these two great souls came together, what got born out of that was the Hunger Project.

Bucky had always taught that the real job was to find a way to make a difference with your life. It was in that crucible of the transformational work of EST, the amazing opportunity to know and work directly with Buckminster Fuller, the great architect, engineer and futurist, and the birth of the Hunger Project Itself through Werner Erhardt's vision that I saw, my God, I can make a difference with my life, I can have a life that's meaningful, I can actually make a contribution beyond 'my life, starring me'. I took a stand for the end of world hunger and the transformation of the condition of life on earth. And from that stand, everything has unfolded for me in ways that I couldn't have possibly imagined or planned. From that moment on, my life has been completely transformed and I've given my life over to the stand that I've taken. That's ended up giving me a kind of nourishment that I never could have had from my work, from my family, from the world itself. As Albert Schweitzer said so eloquently, many years ago, 'The only ones of us who will truly be happy are those of us who've sought and found how to serve.' I can say that in my life that's truly been the case and a great blessing.

I feel that I'm guided by something much larger than myself — some would call it God, and I often do, or you might call it the spirit of the universe. The indigenous people call it *pachamama* or the *arutum*. I sometimes call it the soul. But I'm clear that when I'm in the zone, when I'm telling the truth, I'm guided by something way larger than myself. My identity moves to the background, and what moves to the foreground are the commitments that I've made and using my life as an instrument for something larger than just whatever it is that I'm doing for myself.

Indigenous wisdom

The Pachamama Alliance is a gift in my life, giving me the opportunity and privilege to work with the indigenous peoples in the rainforest of the Amazon and to disseminate and honour their wisdom, to make it available to other people, and then to change the dream of the modern world which is really what being the change is. The work of our Awakening the Dreamer symposium programme is to create and bring forth an environmentally sustainable, spiritually fulfilling and socially just human presence on this planet. This symposium is now being delivered all over the world and is growing rapidly.

I think there's a real transformation taking place in all arenas of the human family. We have been in a 500-year period of dominance, the indigenous people say, and obviously they would say that because they have been dominated. And they say we are coming into a new 500-year period, a *pachacuti* they call it, of balance and light. And in the *pachacuti* of balance and light — and this is my view, they have not said this — I feel that what's becoming available is people's voices are being heard at every level. We're moving from a world organised by privilege to a world organised by community. And the word community means coming into unity. So I think we're coming into a world where community is the ethic, rather than hierarchy. I think we're moving into a world that has a completely different order and there's this wisdom that's coming from the collective rather than from our own individual voices. That's the new dawn of our times; that spirit is speaking through the human family now, and I think that's what we need to listen to.

Love

My core belief is that my life is an instrument; it doesn't belong to me, and I have the opportunity to use it for the highest good. Another core belief I have is that love is the most powerful energy in this world, there's nothing more powerful. Fear is not the opposite of love, it's the absence of it, and love will always overcome fear. I had the great privilege of working with Mother Teresa for some time in India, and she and Gandhi both talked about love in a particular way. There's a beautiful quote that says, 'The unadulterated love of one person can nullify the hatred of millions.' I totally believe that that's true. For me, love has an immense and profound power, and it is the central ethic of my life. I can give and receive love in every encounter: in the interaction I have at a stop-light with someone who cut me off; at the grocery store; in every meeting. And I don't mean to be sappy, I mean *love*, which is profound, it's tough, it's hard work. That to me is the way through; that's the path. That's the prayer of my life.

www.soulofmoney.org

www.thp.org

www.pachamama.org

The Soul of Money, WW Norton & Co, 2006

Jo Wilding

We put an email out saying, 'It'll be really dangerous,
you won't get paid, come and be a clown in Iraq.'

Jo Wilding's first trip to Iraq was in 2001, to break the sanctions imposed by the United Nations. She delivered much-needed medical supplies. When the second Gulf War was approaching, she went back to gather first-hand accounts from ordinary Iraqis of their experiences, both before the war and after it began. She returned again a few months later, this time inspired to bring some joy and delight to Iraqi children. She brought with her a small travelling circus. The group spent three months touring Iraq, performing for thousands of children in squatter camps, schools, orphan-ages and youth centres, while the war raged on around them. Returning to the UK, Wilding completed her legal training and now works as a barrister.

I first went to Iraq in August 2001 to break the sanctions. I thought they were wrong and I wanted personally not to just campaign but actually defy the government ban on taking things to Iraq and to Iraqi people.

Iraqi people were very isolated by the sanctions and by living under Saddam. They weren't able to speak freely, and the borders were literally being closed around them and they weren't able to communicate with the outside world. They weren't even allowed legally to have satellite TV, although a lot of people did. They had to hide it and risk a fine or imprisonment if they were caught. So the people were very trapped and isolated. Just going there was the first step, and I took things to break the sanctions, like vitamins for pregnant women, and medicines. Also I took medical training CD-ROMs, because the doctors were completely cut off from increasing medical knowledge. Their knowledge was stuck in 1990 and as their equipment broke down they couldn't repair it, and they were cannibalising life-support machines to keep things going. Bit by bit they were running out of everything and they weren't able to get things repaired and replaced.

And then having met and talked to people as much as was possible in those days, then when the war was obviously approaching I wanted to go back again, and speak to them and hear people's stories and their views. We were hearing what political figures were saying and what military people were saying, and nothing about ordinary Iraqis and how they felt. If you were in a public place, people would just say what they were meant to say — 'We love Saddam Hussein' — or they wouldn't say anything. But if you were in a taxi with someone or on a fairground ride or something, then they would feel they could speak to you, if they trusted you personally. So I went back in February 2003 and when the war started a few weeks later, I was going into hospitals, interviewing civilian casualties, and taking witness statements from them and from people at the place where the bombing had happened wherever possible. I wrote damage reports and medical reports and just tried to build up as full a picture as possible of what had happened in a particular case.

I knew that the mass media wasn't going to report people's stories; they were covering the military and the political aspects. If they printed a human interest story, it was tiny. Nobody was interviewing the civilian casualties and trying to take any detailed reports of what was actually happening, how a civilian house or market would come to be bombed, what happened, who to. All of that information was not getting out of Iraq.

So apart from the first couple of houses that were hit in Baghdad, there was no mainstream media coverage. When the first house was hit, loads and loads of journalists went out on a bus to where it had happened. With the second one, some of them went. But the third and the hundredth houses bombed didn't make the news. I thought that people in Britain and people in the States and other countries that had soldiers there in particular really should know about what was happening. So I was mostly talking to people, taking these statements and damage reports, and I was writing a blog. I started writing stuff down and emailing it out to a few people, but then some of them were passing it on. Someone was putting it up on the web for me and it was being posted on all these other websites, and it just grew and grew and spread and spread. It was put up on the *Guardian* website, so people all over the States were reading it as well and passing it on. The really good thing about it was that there were obviously all these people desperate for more human, more independent information, so they were looking to independent sources and web sources.

The idea

We met a family in the hospital, whose house had been bombed. There was a mother there cradling a little boy and he had shrapnel wounds all over his face and his sister was very badly hurt. She had a big open wound on her skull, a skull fracture and a huge gouge out of her leg. One of their sisters and their aunt had been killed. It was the most horrific scene of gore and terror and this little boy just wouldn't be put down. If he was put down he cried and he called for his mum, and then when he was in her lap, he was in a world of his own, terribly traumatised. The next day, we went back to see them again, and the little boy was just sitting there. Shane, one of the lads I was with, started drawing a picture, and he started to watch. Then Shane started blowing some bubbles, and he watched those as well and followed them with his eyes. He put out his hand and popped one. And he actually smiled. It was the first thing that had happened since that awful experience that had made him smile, and that had brought him out of his own trauma a little bit. That image stayed with me.

In the summer, back in the UK, I saw someone with a great big bubble blower at a festival, wafting it about and making huge bubbles. I was already planning to

*I knew the mass media wasn't going
to report people's stories.*

---

go back to Iraq, so I said, 'Right, I'm taking one of those with me.' We walked through to the circus field and I thought, 'I'm taking one of those with me!' I had these grand ideas of a travelling big top and trapeze rig and funfair. I had to slightly scale down my grand ambitions, but a friend of mine said, 'Yes, that's a great idea.' He set up a website the next week. We put an email out telling people to pass it on, saying, 'It'll be really dangerous, you won't get paid, come and be a clown in Iraq.' It had happened before. A circus had gone to the Balkans after the wars there, also East Timor and various other places. I'd heard stories about it and how effective it could be. Cirque de Soleil were working with street kids in Mongolia, and it's now also happening in Moscow. Peat, who was one of the clowns with us, went to Beslan a couple of times working with the kids. He hooked up with a group called Maria's Children, and they teach street children and orphans in Moscow circus skills. The kids from Moscow went to Beslan to teach the children there some circus skills and Peat went with them. It is a really powerful thing, where kids have got absolutely nothing.

I did have doubts, though. I went to Iraq two months before the rest of the circus people came out. A friend from Lebanon was asked by a Swedish aid agency to go and find out what the children needed, and I went with her. The thing that most children said that they wanted was blankets, and I started thinking, 'What on earth am I doing bringing them a bunch of clowns? They need medicine, they need food, they need blankets, they need heaters.' I emailed Peat saying, 'I'm really having doubts about this.' He emailed back and he said that he remembered being in Kosovo about 70 days after the conflict ended, and going into a village and the kids all ran and hid, because strangers were people who came to hurt you. And when the kids did come out to play, the only place to play that didn't have landmines all over it was the graveyard, and it had fresh graves from the conflict, children's graves. He said that they had about 80 kids around three different play parachutes, all laughing and shouting and having fun, and in the middle of it all there was an old man just beaming and crying and saying 'Thank you for bringing my grandchildren back. I never thought I'd see them laugh again.'

Also my friend Jenny sent me an email about teaching kids in Palestine to juggle with stones. She used to escort ambulances that were taking relief supplies to places. She'd be waiting while people did the distribution, and she'd play with the kids, and she was teaching them to juggle three stones. She said it was the first time they'd seen them as something other than a weapon, and seen them as a toy. It transforms everything around them. If it hadn't been for Jenny and Peat, there wouldn't have been a circus after all.

The circus

The circus toured for three months in 2004 and there were four of us going anywhere where there were children — schools, orphanages, youth centres and the squatter camps especially, where there were lots of kids that weren't in school and had next to nothing. We even held it in the street to begin with, when things were a bit safer. We would turn up, put on a bit of face paint, get into our costumes and then do a show and then play games with the kids and spend some time with people. We performed for about 10,000 children. Some of them we performed for and played with more than once, but we reckoned it was about 10,000 individual children, at least once. One day there were 500 kids in the morning and 500 in the afternoon, 1,000 in a day. At other times it was smaller groups of 20 or 30.

Not only were these children cut off from the outside world — they were almost cut off from their own childhood because they'd been through so much and they'd seen so much and were still suffering so much. A lot of them weren't going to school, particularly in the squatter camps. They didn't have proper housing, they didn't have proper anything, not even heating or blankets, and so it was about breaking through the isolation and also helping the children to feel like children again. I know that it sounds really trivial, but I wasn't in a position to bring in a shipment of blankets. That wasn't really the problem, it was the fact that the massive so-called civilian military infrastructure that was supposed to be running the country wasn't getting those things to the people who needed them. They were supplying hand grenades and weapons to the soldiers, and the ordinary people weren't getting the very basic things they needed. There were aid agencies to do that, but for me it was about communicating with ordinary people. Also, whenever I met someone, if there'd been a bombing, people would tell

*It is a really powerful thing,
where children have got absolutely nothing.*

---

me their story and say, 'Please tell everybody this, tell people in England, tell people in America.'

At the start of the circus, Peat used to go out and take a big, furry puppet round and let the kids stroke it. And then when we were all ready, I'd walk out on my stilts and we'd start shouting 'Hello!' at the kids and getting them shouting 'Hello!' back. And then we were shouting 'Wo-oh!' at them, and getting them all to yell it back. And then shouting 'Boomchucka!' at them and getting them to yell it back. The sound of hundreds, sometimes a thousand little voices yelling 'Boomchucka!' back at you... You could be as absolutely exhausted as you thought you'd ever be when you got out of bed, and just drag yourself to wherever you were going, and get your costume on, but you knew that the minute you got out there, all the kids would be yelling 'Boomchucka!' at you. When we turned up at one of the squatter camps for the second time, all the kids came running towards us yelling 'Boomchucka! Boomchucka!' It was brilliant, absolutely brilliant.

There was a sketch where I'd steal Luis's hat and tease him with it, and he'd get a kid up on his shoulders to try and get it off my head. Then Sam did magic tricks, and Peat and Luis would do a juggling act together, and then there was a sketch where I was a clown that was supposed to be sweeping. I had a magic cardboard box, and when you opened it, it made music, which was done by Pete playing a penny whistle every time I opened it. Luis was the boss, and he was a bully, and he would try and stop me from playing with my musical box and dancing. He'd get really cross, and he'd jump up and down on my box and shove it into a rubbish bin. I'd look sad and lift the lid of the bin to look at my box, and the music would start playing again, so I'd skip off happily with the bin. Then Sam would do another magic trick with a colouring book which looked like it had just plain pages. He'd get one of the kids to rub it with some coloured fabric from his coat, and then he would flick through the pages again, and it would have pictures but not coloured in. Then he'd get another kid to rub it with another part of his coat. He'd get three kids to rub it with the different primary colours and he'd flick through and all the pictures were magically coloured in, and they'd all go 'Aaaaahhhh!', which was brilliant.

The last thing was a custard pie saga where Peat would get three people up and one of them would always be an authority figure. If we were in a school, it was often a teacher, or sometimes we'd have a police officer. He would ask two people a very simple question and then the third person a question they couldn't possibly answer, and the first person to get three questions wrong was going to get the custard pie in their face. At the last minute, this person would be whisked out of the way and the pie would either go in Peat's own face or in Sam's or Luis's face, and then they would run around roaring and shouting and we'd run off and that was the end.

We'd play games with the children afterwards. We had a parachute, a big, big piece of bright red cloth. It was round and about five metres in diameter. We'd get all the kids around the edge of it to play different games. We'd start by shaking it and then they'd lift it up and run about underneath it. Then we'd sit them all down just inside and tuck it under, so we were all sitting in a big, bright red bubble. There were a few different games, like parachute football. The children were divided into two semi-circular teams. You'd throw the football onto the parachute and they had to shake it to try and make the football move, and they'd score a goal when the ball went off the parachute over the heads of the other team. They'd get really into it. Another game was cat and mouse. One child would be the mouse and would crawl about under the parachute, and then everybody around the outside of it would shake it to disguise where the mouse was. Another child would be the cat, and they had to get on their hands and knees on top of the parachute and try and catch the mouse.

Activism

I started getting involved with activism when I was 23. It was mostly environmental at first, and then got I involved with peace issues as well. To me, it's all about the same thing; it's about what kind of place you want to live in.

I wasn't the least bit radical. I used to go mountain biking a lot at Ashton Court in Bristol. I heard that they wanted to extend a quarry into the wildflower mead-

I came to understand that there was something that you could personally do about it by using your own body.

ow there, and that's one of the most beautiful places. It was quite wild, and people didn't go up there so much because it was at the far end of the park, so it was very peaceful, very tranquil. Bordering that was gorgeous woodland. I didn't think that it was right that they should just blow a hole in it, and do something that was very environmentally unsustainable. There were other things that could have been done, that would have created more jobs, and that also would have kept the wealth within the local community. It was an Australian multinational that owned the quarry at the time, and the money was all going to go to shareholders in another country. So I got involved with that campaign and started living on the protest site there. Because I was living there, I wanted to understand everything about what was going on, and so from quarries, I learned it was the same thing with roads and with nuclear power stations, and my understanding of the damage to the environment and the system that we were living in increased. It went from there. Also, I came to understand that there was something that you could personally do about it by using your own body.

I remember when we'd just started the camp up, Deirdre in *Coronation Street* was put in prison, and the story was that she wasn't guilty. A massive national campaign suddenly sprang up: Free Deirdre. There were posters up everywhere, and people were contacting the TV station and the advertisers, demanding that Deirdre be released, as if they hadn't realised she wasn't real. What I understood from that was that they knew they had power to change that. Because if they rang up the advertisers and said, 'We're not going to watch this programme unless they let Deirdre out of prison,' the advertisers were going to say, 'We're not going to advertise unless everybody's watching.' So the programme makers were more or less compelled to let Deirdre out of prison. People knew they had the power to change things, whereas with the quarry, people would always say, 'What's the point? You're not going to win this campaign.' But you can still change things without necessarily achieving your ultimate intention of preventing there being a quarry, which, in some cases at least, is beyond possibility anyway.

I don't see it as two poles of winning and losing and only those two possibilities; I think there's a whole array of achievements in between.

In activism and probably in most things — raising children, whatever it is — you can't add up what you've achieved in the way that you can with a day at work: 'I've written x number of things and I've done this, that and the other.' Within activism campaigns and projects, you can't always tell whether you're achieving anything and if you can, you can't add it up. So you've just got to stubbornly stick with it in the belief that it's the right thing to do. Blind faith and stubbornness. I think that's it. Each time that I've been to Iraq, and with the protests that I've been involved with, and with going into law as well, I've started out thinking, 'I'm not certain if this is going to work, or how this is going to work, but I'm going to give it a go.' And then just stuck with it. You're only powerless until you refuse to be powerless any more. Even if you can't add up what you've achieved, you have, because you've changed yourself, and that's one to add to all the other people who have changed.

Being the change

Just use what you've got. After being in Iraq I was invited to go on a speaking tour in the States, and there were a couple of other people there on the tour. One of them was saying, 'There are more cracks in the façade of the status quo than there have ever been. Things that once seemed insurmountable now have visible cracks in them.' I was thinking about that, and about chisels. Everyone's got a chisel — you've just got to work out what yours is, where it is, how you're going to use it. Your chisel could be a circus, it could be writing, it could be generating your own electricity, making your home environment more ecologically sound. It could be conflict resolution within your own community. It could be so many things.

I've spent a lot of time challenging big corporations, and that I guess is where co-ops come into it. If you're in a workers' co-op, you control your own labour. You don't work for someone else and you're not then going to be told you've got to make a cluster bomb that's going to be dropped on children in another country. If you're buying your food through a food co-op with other people, you're not dependent on a supermarket, which might be actively promoting things that are damaging to the environment or to farmers. If you're in a housing co-op, you're

You're only powerless until you refuse
to be powerless any more.

---

not contributing to the rental and housing market, which actively deprives a lot of people of a decent place to live. And so I think that in everything you do you can be the change. I'm not in a workers' co-op, but it's as close to one as it can be; everyone has a vote. In everything you do, you can think about ways of taking more control yourself, and that's where co-ops are so brilliant. They are definitely a brilliant way of being the change, because you're revolutionising not just your own life, but also the structure of what's around you.

I've done loads and loads of talks in this country and in the States, and the slightly depressing thing is always that it's people who are interested who are going to come. How can we reach beyond that? One of the things that I've really enjoyed is that I wrote the blog and then I turned the blog into the book. Someone learned a piece of it and performed it as a storyteller. Someone else made a graffiti stencil about Fallujah. Someone wrote a song, someone wrote a poem, someone's written a play using some of my stuff, and it gets transformed and passed along and spread that way. It is difficult. I think the main thing is that on the one hand, you've got to just stick with doing what you think needs doing, but at the same time you've got to engage with people on their own level as well, and relate what you're saying to something that has meaning for them. So rather than just saying, 'I don't want this quarry to be built because it's really bad for the environment,' being able to show that it's better for them to have more jobs in an aggregate recycling plant than to have a few jobs for a short time in a quarry. It takes creativity.

Childhood activism

I remember watching telly when I was a kid, and there was something on about the Vietnamese boat people. They were in detention camps, including children, locked up with nothing but a bunk, and no country that would take them. I was outraged and I wrote a letter to my MP saying, 'We've got to let them come here, it's not fair that they have to live like that.' I suppose what drives me is a mixture of empathy for what people are going through, and thinking, 'Someone's got to do it, otherwise nothing's going to change.' I also started a petition against people being allowed to keep tortoises in this country, because their stomach juices set like jelly and only melt when they get to a certain temperature. They can starve to death without realising they're hungry. That was when I was 12 — I suppose I've always been a pain in the arse!

www.jowilding.net

Don't Shoot the Clowns!, New Internationalist Publications, 2006

Mel Young

***If you say, 'Would you like to play football for your country?',
everybody turns up.***

Mel Young is a serial social entrepreneur. He has founded two magazines
dedicated to social change. The *Big Issue in Scotland* empowers homeless
people by allowing them to earn an income, and *New Consumer* champions
ethical shopping as a way for individuals to change the world. In 2001, he
and a colleague applied some creativity to the problem of homelessness,
and came up with a language to unite homeless people all over the world
— football. The first Homeless World Cup took place in Austria in 2003,
and has gone from strength to strength. It has been extremely successful
in helping the players turn their lives around, and in changing perceptions
of homeless people.

I want the world to have nobody living in poverty. That's it, full stop. I feel absolutely certain that we don't have to have any homelessness in the world. I'm a Scot. The DNA of Scots people is a mix of all sorts of things, which I think brings us out as strong believers in community with a sense of fair play. We don't like it when people don't get a fair kick at the ball, if you'll excuse the pun. I find it quite appalling that in this day and age, there's homelessness. We can put people on the moon, we can get rockets to go round corners, and we can create the internet. We're really, really smart, clever people. And it doesn't matter which way you do it — technologically, creatively or commercially — if we were able to create the internet, why can't we stop homelessness? We could, if we had the drive.

The idea

In 1993, I was the co-founder of the *Big Issue in Scotland*, which is a street paper sold by homeless people. The thing I really like about it is it gives empowerment to the people themselves to change their lives. Later, I was involved in the establishment of the International Network of Street Papers, which is a trade association, if you like, for the street papers. The INSP has an annual conference, which is always a passionate affair, because people are coming together from all over the world, and talking about what they've been doing. Everybody spins off each other and there's a lot of energy and passion and learning. You sit there working out how to change the world until two or three in the morning, and then the delegates go back to their country inspired for the 12 months until the next conference.

At the end of this conference in 2001, I was having a beer with a friend of mine, Harald Schmied. We were saying we'd been inspired and energised, but there were no homeless people there. There were editors and directors and founders, but no homeless people. How could we involve them? We thought that maybe we could do exchanges, but there were problems like visa laws and language. We were just playing around and we figured we could maybe make up a language for homeless people that only they could understand. We were in a relaxed creative box, if you like. Then we said well, there is an international language, it's football, and everybody can play. It doesn't matter what standard you are. So I told Harald, 'Well, we have a team in Scotland at the *Big Issue*, some of the sellers.' And he replied, 'I have the same in Austria.' So I said, 'OK, we'll be Scotland and you can be Austria and we'll play each other, and we'll win!' He said,

The teams were selected and they were representing their country, so they were playing in their national strips.

'No, Austria will win!' We were kind of playing around like this and we decided, 'OK, let's do that!' We had a couple more beers in this kind of atmosphere, and by the end of the evening we'd created the Homeless World Cup.

You can have these discussions in that type of atmosphere — nothing more than a good idea — but we made it happen. The next day we confirmed that we were going to do this, and we built it around the INSP, so we immediately had partners. We simply said to the other street papers there, 'Would you like to do the same? Why don't you be your country? Let's try and do this.' Sixteen other countries joined in. By the end of the night, we had all the other countries — Brazil, the USA, Russia and so on. And so in 2003 we had the first Homeless World Cup, which was held in Graz, in Austria. It was so successful in all sorts of different ways that we decided to have it every year.

Changes

In Graz, three changes were taking place. First of all, and our main objective, was that the players were changing out of all recognition. We'd set up training schemes for people who wanted to get involved, and lots of them did. Football's a really good way to include people who won't want to be involved in other things, particularly young guys, who are so marginalised. But invite them to play football — they'll be interested. In the training schemes, they'd have to tackle issues like drugs and alcohol, and health problems if they wanted to play football, and our projects were picking up on that. Then the teams were selected and they were representing their country, so they were playing in their national strips. It was amazing to watch because they were standing there singing the national anthem; they were really proud, better than the professionals, I think. They were standing up properly now. You could see the confidence coming into them and the self-respect. They were telling us that this was amazing for them, they were really going to change. You could actually see that change in front of your eyes; it was quite moving.

The second area that change was taking place was within the people who were watching. We play street soccer, and we built stands. We didn't know if anyone was going to come and watch, but slowly — it's a week-long event — the stands started to fill up to such a point that we were worried they were going to fall down. We had to hire screens so people could watch it in the square outside. The crowds were amazing. They were screaming and shouting for the players. The players were really reacting to this and behaving like football stars. Kids started going up to them and asking for their autographs. I always remember one day in the middle of the tournament, Harald and I were standing in the back of one of the stands and there was a noise out in the street behind. We wondered what it was, and it was the Dutch team walking down the road, and the people in the cafes and in the street were standing and applauding them. Also by this point, they had groupies following them around. Harald and I looked at each other and said, 'So that will be homeless people then.'

Of course the situation is that only the week before, these people had been vilified in their own city. The media stigmatise them, and the public spit at them, they abuse them, and often they attack them. Being homeless, you're much more likely to be the victim than the perpetrator of violence, in reality. A few days later, these same people are standing there applauding them. All we'd done was change the environment. We'd just built a couple of stages and been a little creative with something really simple like football, and created this transformation. We would say it was a kind of magic. Magic happened.

So the players were changing out of all recognition, and the audience. I would always say anybody that's been to watch a Homeless World Cup will never look at homeless people in the same way again. The third area of change was the media. They started to come, and rather than actually looking at these homeless people as problems, they began to look at them as heroes, to paint these players as some kind of football stars! The media came from all over the world, from countries that weren't even playing. It was incredible, there were banks of TV cameras!

Harald and I presented the Cup to the winning team. It was finished and it had been such a success and we felt really proud of everybody. It was a phenomenal atmosphere. 'The world shook for a moment and it's still reverberating.' One of

Rather than actually looking at these homeless people as problems, they began to look at them as heroes.

the homeless poets came up with that one. We were getting a bit romantic at that point. Homelessness is horrible, and you always get brought down to earth. You can have these moments and they're good, and we should all have them, but we need to not forget what this is all about.

Success

After this event, which had been successful beyond our wildest dreams, we decided it was important to find out what was happening to the players. We started doing research. We found an astonishing number of them — 77-80 per cent — had made a change in their lives. They'd been so motivated by this experience that they'd gone on to find jobs, they'd got into houses, a lot of them then stayed in sport and got coaching certificates, a huge percentage of them had come off hard drugs completely, and some were even signed by football teams. We couldn't believe these percentages, initially, when we got the results. I work with homeless people all the time, and I know it's very difficult to get this re-integration. So we checked them and checked them and checked them and they were correct. Because of that, we decided, 'Right, we're going to do that again.'

So we did. It was in 2003 we had it in Austria, 2004 in Gothenburg, 2005 in Edinburgh, 2006 in Cape Town, 2007 in Copenhagen and in 2008 it will be in Melbourne. In the first year, we had 18 teams participating in Graz, and last year in Copenhagen we had 48 countries. We had about 500 homeless players actually playing, and we would estimate that in terms of the training, 25,000 players are trying to get on the teams. So these projects don't just run during the Homeless World Cup. All these homeless people are playing football all the year round.

In some ways you could describe it as a health project, if you think about what it is, because they are having to address both psychological and physical issues as a result of getting into the training. And you can be really good at football or terrible at it, it doesn't matter, with the way we structure the tournament and the training and so on. This is the beauty of football. If we were to say, 'We've got a health project, why don't you come along?', nobody would come along, because there's no motivation. But if you say, 'Would you like to play football for your country?', everybody turns up. It's not a trick, it's just a different way of marketing what we're trying to do in terms of creating a change, just using our imagination a little. I think sometimes, particularly in the west, we get all het up about serious issues, and it's absolutely right that we do. But we remain sad and depressed and serious about them, whereas if you were just to inject a little bit of creativity and a little bit of off-the-wall thinking, you could create something which is good fun, and create the change at the same time.

That's what we've done. We've simply used football. It's very, very simple, anybody can play it. You can have two a side, or 20 a side, you can play it in the street or in a park, with any size of ball. Some of our African teams don't even have proper footballs; they play with rags that are all pulled together, and it's perfectly OK. And it's not expensive, so it's a great way of involving lots of people who wouldn't otherwise be included in anything.

The way we organised the first one, Harald and I had different roles. Luckily in Graz, it was the European Year of Culture. They were putting on opera and music and art, and so on. Harald went to the organisers and said, 'On the programme, why don't you include something for people who are disadvantaged? And by the way, football is culture! Why don't you support it, as the city of Graz?' They were a bit sceptical about this, as you might imagine. It's OK now because we have our track record and reputation, but then it was just an idea. Harald sat there and he had all these street papers with him. He said 'Look, Graz will get publicity in all these papers, all around the world,' and he started pulling them out of his bag. 'Here and here and here!' So they agreed, and the Homeless World Cup became an official event in the European Year of Culture in Graz, which gave it a certain amount of credibility and also infrastructure support. All of a sudden we didn't have to pay for things like a media centre. So he got all that end sorted out, and then my job was to organise it internationally. I was doing international fundraising and contacting the other countries, and so on. Between us, we made the event happen.

We took a huge risk to put this event on,
to get the whole thing back on track —
we worked like crazy and we pulled it off.

Challenges

We were going to hold the Homeless World Cup in New York in 2005. We'd got sponsorship deals set up, we'd been over there, and it looked like it was going to be really, really fabulous; there was a lot of political support. And then we came up against a real problem with visas. They couldn't guarantee visas into the country for the homeless players, because they didn't have addresses, or because they might have had some kind of misdemeanour in the past — drink, drugs or something like that. They were saying they couldn't guarantee the players would get in the country. You can imagine all these people working all the year round to get on the team — they'd get on the team, they'd get to the airport and they'd get refused. We had to make a decision, so we decided we couldn't proceed in New York. The next decision was, do we skip a year or do we put it on somewhere else? We decided that if we skipped a year, we'd lose all the momentum that we'd built up, and it would be a disaster. So we decided to put it on in my home city, because I know my way around here. We were only six months ahead. I wasn't getting paid; I had no income for six months. We took a huge risk to put this event on, to get the whole thing back on track — we worked like crazy and we pulled it off. One factor was sheer hard work and determination, and a refusal to take no for an answer. Secondly, it was a team of brilliant people. If you walked in the door, we'd give you something to do. I don't do this by myself. I have brilliant people working here, and we all support one another. The team atmosphere that we have is very important.

Again, we had a visa problem, this time in Britain. There are teams that are potentially at risk in terms of visas — African teams. We'd been speaking to the Home Office from the word go about this issue. We said, 'Look, it's the Homeless World Cup, so they're going to have some issues about their background, and they won't necessarily fit your criteria.' The Home Office and Foreign Office were very, very helpful. And then about a week before, five African countries were denied visas. It was just after the G8 summit, just after Blair and Brown had made these huge announcements about attacking poverty in Africa. It was outrageous. For me, it was a disgraceful episode. You have to remember, these players in these African countries have no shoes even. They'd gone to the embassy, they'd gone through an awful lot of trouble, they were so excited about coming, and we were able to vouch for the organisations that sent them. They were crying on the phone, it was just awful. It really made me feel embarrassed to be British — a lot.

What did we do? There was nothing we could do to get them there. So basically we did two things. One was to shout very loudly and angrily about it, so it was in all the front pages of the African papers. We gave messages of solidarity from all the other teams and ourselves to these countries and gave them some support. The second thing that we did for them is that we've made it a condition for any other tournaments that the government of the host country has to put it in writing for us that those teams will be allowed into the country. It was ludicrous and horrible. We're growing and many things are really good, but it's never, never straightforward. Everything goes up and down, and you just have to be ready to deal with whatever is being thrown at you.

Motivations

For me, it is about the change that takes place. It's coming across the players. I almost don't recognise them. They say, 'It's me, I used to be in the football team.' They've changed. They're not quite wearing a suit, but you know what I mean. They have a job, and a sparkle in their eye. That's a continual joy. That's what motivates me primarily — that's the thing. The actual event of the Homeless World Cup, that week is really intense. I don't want to romanticise it but it is a magic atmosphere. The way the teams mix together, the way the homeless players are so unbelievably generous with what little they have, in their relationship with the crowds and the way they're open, it's magical. To see some of the people that have come from really, really difficult backgrounds, to see them leaping around after scoring a goal and everybody standing applauding them — it's a brilliant, brilliant feeling. There are always what we call 'not a dry eye in the house' moments.

I remember in Edinburgh when the Irish football authority decided to give international caps to the homeless players. They did it on the pitch, and I don't

*The Irish football authority
decided to give international caps
to the homeless players.*

think you could have found a dry eye. It was very moving. These players didn't know what was hitting them, to be homeless and then to get recognised. The man from the Irish FA said, 'We'll always recognise sportspeople in Ireland for what they do and give them caps.' It was a tingling kind of moment. There's lots of those. I don't believe anybody does anything for nothing in life. I believe in partnerships and you create win-win scenarios. That's what I get out of it — a really good feeling.

Psychological shifts

The Danish manager told me what happened when their team were going down to Cape Town in 2006. He told the team, 'By the way, when you get down there you won't have seen poverty like it. The homeless people are much worse off than you.' The team disagreed. 'No way, we're homeless, you can't get lower than us, we're the bottom.' The manager kept saying to them, 'No, no, no.' And the players were insistent, 'No, no, no, it's not possible.' Within forty-eight hours they said, 'We've never seen anything like this.' They'd seen the townships and so on, and because of this, their whole view of themselves and everybody else was changing because now they weren't the bottom, as they perceived it. Psychologically, they were starting to change. Also, they made connections with the South African team and started to say, 'How can we support you and connect with you as players and as individuals?' So a major psychological shift was taking place in the Danish team.

But, the other way round, the South African team said, 'We can't believe that there are white people who are homeless.' They had never seen anybody white being homeless. In their country, only black people are homeless. So their whole perception started to change psychologically as well, because it was saying that it wasn't anything to do with the colour of their skin, that this was indeed a global issue affecting other countries, apparently rich countries. So you get all these other changes going on that are quite profound, that we're not even monitoring. There are lots of lovely stories about them exchanging things and some of these players go into internet cafes and keep in touch with one another by email, even though they can't speak the same language.

Creating change

Whatever the issue is, if you woke up in the morning and said, 'Right, I'm unsatisfied with this, I'm going to have to do something, I'm going to have to change,' that's great. Then the question is, what? And how? Sometimes you feel disempowered because you think nothing will change. Let me give you the example of the Iraq war. There were the biggest demonstrations in Britain ever, I think, against the Iraq war, which the government completely ignored and just went ahead. I'm not going to go into the whole history of it or the pros and cons, that's just what happened. For the people who were protesting, to be ignored like that is really disempowering. You think, 'If I want a change and I go on a demonstration, what's the point? Nobody listens any more, nobody's bothered.' That's what's really disempowering. That whole method of protest, demonstration, that's something of the past now, I believe. You could do it as long as it's part of something wider. A demonstration or campaign in itself, isn't going to create a change, I don't believe.

But positive action will, actually, and individuals can do that. For example, consumers can now buy Fair Trade coffee. If you wake up in the morning and you want to change the world, I would say, start off by changing what coffee you drink. And then you start to become aware of and get involved in other things and understanding what you can do. So that's what I'd encourage people to do — get involved somehow, because change is taking place. I believe this very strongly. I'm quite lucky, the past few years, I've been to the World Economic Forum in Davos. I was walking in past thousands of anti-global demonstrators, and naturally I'm from their side, if you like, if there were sides. But my issue with them was, 'OK, I get it, you're against all of these things. I agree, now what?' And what I could never get out of a lot of these people was the 'Now what?' I think there's a kind of general agreement that the world needs to be changed, so we don't have to run around demonstrating about it. Let's just get on and change it. That's what's really exciting.

I'm really optimistic about the future. I think there's a lot of big challenges, but I'm really optimistic because there's a lot of really positive things going on. And I think politicians that continually get heavy with young people are crazy, because in my experience, if I give a talk in a school or amongst students, they are absolutely engaged and understand the politics of what's going on. Media commentators say, 'Young people aren't voting, isn't this terrible? It's because they're non-political and disengaged.' My response to that is, maybe they're a damn sight smarter than those of us that are voting, because maybe they're saying, 'There's not much difference between the lot of you, and actually we're involved in a different sort of politics, like single issue politics and campaigning on the internet, or doing something that is making a real difference to the world rather than voting for you lot.' I'm just using that as an example. I'm optimistic because I think young people get it, actually, much more than older people.

www.homelessworldcup.org

www.bigissuescotland.com

www.newconsumer.com

Afterword

My favourite metaphor for the current world transition, first pointed out to me by Norie Huddle[1], is that of a butterfly in metamorphosis. It goes like this: a caterpillar crunches its way through its ecosystem, cutting a swath of destruction by eating as much as hundreds of times its weight in a day, until it is too bloated to continue and hangs itself up, its skin then hardening into a chrysalis. Inside this chrysalis, deep in the caterpillar's body, tiny things biologists call 'imaginal discs' begin to form. Not recognising the newcomers, the caterpillar's immune system snuffs them out as they arise. But they keep coming faster and faster, then linking up with each other. Eventually the caterpillar's immune system fails from the stress and the discs become imaginal cells that build the butterfly by feeding on the soupy meltdown of the caterpillar's body. It took a long time for biologists to understand the reason for the immune system attack on the incipient butterfly cells, but eventually they discovered that the butterfly has its own unique genome, carried by the caterpillar, inherited from long ago in evolution, yet not part of it as such[2]. If we see ourselves as imaginal discs working to build the butterfly of a better world, we will understand that we are launching a new 'genome' of values and practices to replace that of the current unsustainable system. We will also see how important it is to link with each other in the effort, to recognise how many different kinds of imaginal cells it will take to build a butterfly with all its capabilities and colours.

Elisabet Sahtouris, PhD

Evolution biologist, lecturer and author of *EarthDance: Living systems in evolution*, iUniverse.com, 2000

1 *Butterfly,* Norie Huddle, Huddle Books, 1990

2 *Acquiring Genomes*, Lynn Margulis & Dorion Sagan, Perseus Books, 2002

Thank you to the following people for their permission to use the photos:

hafsat abiola-costello	© *TY Bello*
Boo Armstrong	© *Christian de Sousa*
Katie Alcott	© *Tom Alcott*
Maude Barlow	*courtesy of the Council of Canadians*
Taddy Blecher	© *Robbie Tshabalala*
David Constantine	*courtesy of Motivation Charitable Trust*
James Dakin	© *Hugh l'Estrange*
Paul Dickinson	*courtesy of the Carbon Disclosure Project*
Scilla Elworthy	© *John Hamwee*
Jeremy Gilley	© *Fran Perry*
Gill Hicks	© *Tara Darby*
Rob Hopkins	© *Sean Derioz*
Chris Johnstone	© *Kirsty Reid*
Van Jones	*courtesy of the Ella Baker Center*
Craig Kielburger	*courtesy of Free The Children*
Satish Kumar	© *Nick Hart-Williams*
Wangari Maathai	© *Martin Rowe*
Safia Minney	*courtesy of People Tree*
Claire Morsman	© *Joseph Walters*
Richard Reynolds	© *Gavin Kingcombe*
Vandana Shiva	© *Nick Hart-Williams*
Clive Stafford Smith	© *Ian Robins*
Lynne Twist	*courtesy of the Soul of Money Institute*
Mel Young	© *Tom Finnie*

Many of the people included in this book have spoken at the Be The Change *conference that inspired it. Here's some more information about it from director, Nick Hart-Williams.*

In January 2004, business coach John Whitmore called together a group of friends to discuss how we might make a difference. John asked 'Can we afford to leave the fate of our world in the hands of our current leadership?' We decided to bring together as many good minds and hearts as we could muster, and by May some 400 of us gathered at London's Friends House for three days we called *Be The Change*. It was such a success that we decided to do it every year.

Our aims were, and are still:

To get the right people talking about the right issues.

To cross-fertilise ideas and experience.

To change the way we think about issues that are not being solved at the current level of thinking.

To explore the means of achieving effective systems change.

To inspire us all to make it happen!

Our community comes together to discuss, celebrate and share the latest thinking and experiences that are moving us forward to a brighter future. The inspiring speakers, the leading-edge information and the opportunity to meet like-minded souls provide sustenance and support for all the participants, empowering them to be the change in their own lives when they go back home.

In 2006, we added an important local component, *Change The Dream*, a day-long symposium, which takes place in meeting spaces, town halls and sitting-rooms up and down the country, and in fact across the world. With the help of some inspiring short films, new insights and dynamic group interactions, we explore the connected issues of social justice, environmental sustainability and spiritual fulfilment, asking 'Where are we?', 'How did we get here?' and 'Where do we go from here?'

For more information, please visit us at www.bethechange.org.uk

We'd be delighted to hear from you if you have any feedback about this book, stories to share or nominations of people to include in a new volume. Please email them to bethechange@lovebooks.co.uk

If you would like to buy extra copies, you can do this on the Love Books website at www.lovebooks.co.uk . Orders placed online are usually sent out the same day if received before 2 pm. Alternatively, to order by post, please fill in the form below and include a cheque for the appropriate amount. Please allow 28 days for delivery.

Please send your completed form to:

Orders, Love Books, 35 King Street, Bristol BS1 4DZ

Name _____

Address _____

_____

_____

_____ Postcode _____

Number of copies @ £12.99 each (P&P free) _____

If you would like to be kept informed of forthcoming publications from Love Books, please write your email address below. Your details will not be passed on to any other organisation.

_____